Redesigning English

Edited by Sharon Goodman, David Graddol and Theresa Lillis

The Open University

ROUTLEDGE

Routledge
Taylor & Francis Group

Published by

Routledge
2 Park Square
Milton Park
Abingdon OX14 4RN

in association with

The Open University
Walton Hall
Milton Keynes MK7 6AA

Simultaneously published in the USA and Canada by

Routledge
270 Madison Avenue
New York NY 10016

Routledge is an imprint of the Taylor & Francis
Group

First published 2007

Edited and designed by The Open University.

Typeset in India by Alden Prepress Services,
Chennai.

Printed and bound in the United Kingdom by CPI,
Glasgow.

This book forms part of an Open University course
U211 *Exploring the English language*. Details of this
and other Open University courses can be obtained
from the Student Registration and Enquiry Service,
The Open University, PO Box 197, Milton Keynes,
MK7 6BJ, United Kingdom: tel. +44 (0)870 333 4340,
email general-enquiries@open.ac.uk

http://www.open.ac.uk

A catalogue record for this book is available from
the British Library.

Library of Congress Cataloging in Publication Data
A catalog record for this book has been requested.

ISBN 978 0 415 37688 4 (hardback)
ISBN 978 0 415 37689 1 (paperback)

1.1

Contents

Preface to the series

The books in this series provide an introduction to the study of English, both for students of the English language and the general reader. As Open University course books, they constitute texts for the course U211 *Exploring the English language*. The series aims to provide students with:

- an understanding of the history of English and its development as a global language
- an appreciation of variation in the English language across different speakers and writers, and different regional and social contexts
- conceptual frameworks for the study of language in use
- illustrations of the diversity of English language practices in different parts of the world
- an understanding of how English is learnt as a first or additional language, and of its role as a language of formal education
- introductions to many key controversies about the English language, such as those relating to its position as a global language, attitudes to 'good' and 'bad' English, and debates about the teaching of English
- explorations of the use of English for new purposes and in new contexts, including multimodal texts.

Parts of these books were published previously as:

Graddol, D., Leith, D. and Swann, J. (eds) (1996) *English: History, Diversity and Change*, London, Routledge/Milton Keynes, The Open University.

Maybin, J. and Mercer, N. (eds) (1996) *Using English: From Conversation to Canon*, London, Routledge/Milton Keynes, The Open University.

Mercer, N. and Swann, J. (eds) (1996) *Learning English: Development and Diversity*, London, Routledge/Milton Keynes, The Open University.

Goodman, S. and Graddol, D. (eds) (1996) *Redesigning English: New Texts, New Identities*, London, Routledge/Milton Keynes, The Open University.

The editors for the previously published books were listed in alphabetical order. The list of editors for the present series retains this original order, followed by the additional editors who have worked on the present series. Production of this series, like that of the previously published books, has been a collaborative enterprise involving numerous members of Open University staff and external colleagues. We thank all those who contributed to the original books and to this series. We regret that their names are too many to list here.

Joan Swann and Julia Gillen
Series editors

Biographical information

Book editors

Sharon Goodman is a Lecturer in the Centre for Language and Communication at The Open University, where she has been involved in the writing and production of many of the Centre's undergraduate and postgraduate English Language courses. Her interests include stylistics, media literacy, multimodal communication and academic writing.

David Graddol, director of the English Company (UK) Ltd, produced two influential reports for the British Council, 'The Future of English?' (1997) and 'English Next' (2005). He was formerly a Lecturer at The Open University. His books include *Describing Language* (2nd edn, 1994, Routledge) written with Jenny Cheshire and Joan Swann.

Theresa Lillis is a Senior Lecturer in the Centre for Language and Communication at The Open University. She has published research on academic writing, including *Student Writing: Access, Regulation and Desire* (2001, Routledge), and articles on multilingual scholarly publishing in *TESOL Quarterly* and *Written Communication.* She is co-author of *A Dictionary of Sociolinguistics* (2004, Edinburgh University Press).

Additional contributors

Lesley Jeffries is a Principal Lecturer in English language at the University of Huddersfield. She works on the stylistics of literary and non-literary texts, and she is particularly interested in the language of contemporary poetry, political reporting and the textual creation of opposites. She is author of *The Language of Twentieth Century Poetry* (1993, Macmillan) and *Meaning in English* (1998, Macmillan).

Jane Miller is Professor Emeritus of the University of London Institute of Education, where she taught in the English Department. She is the author of *Many Voices* (1983, Routledge), *Women Writing about Men* (1986, Virago), *Seductions, Studies in Reading and Culture* (1990, Virago), *More has meant Women, the Feminisation of Schooling* (1992, Tufnell Press), *School for Women* (1996, Virago) and *Relations* (2003, Jonathan Cape).

Allan Bell is Professor of Language and Communication and Director of the Centre for Communication Research at Auckland University of Technology. He has published extensively in academic journals, edited collections, and authored or co-edited books including *The Language of News Media* (1991, Blackwell) and *Approaches to Media Discourse* (with Peter Garrett; 1998, Blackwell). He is co-founder and editor of the international *Journal of Sociolinguistics.*

Colin Gardner has taught undergraduate courses in English language and literature and designed and coordinated courses dealing specifically with the arts and the World Wide Web. He has a background in critical theory, focusing on the theoretical implications and practical effects of reading non-linear, hypertext fiction. He is currently studying perspectives on the status of text in early twentieth-century literary theory.

Introduction

Theresa Lillis

The English language appears in many different forms according to the purposes of its users, the material resources available to them and their own creativity. This book focuses on some of the key ways in which English is constantly being *redesigned* as both a verbal and visual resource for shaping texts and identities. The concept of multimodality – attention to the visual and other potential dimensions of texts besides the verbal – is often viewed as a new topic. Yet the materiality of language – how it sounds, looks and feels – has always been intrinsic to its effects. So users of language, especially when aiming for lasting effects as in literature, have always been concerned to orchestrate available tools and media in their crafting of texts. Together the chapters explore innovative uses of English from early manuscripts to postcolonial literature, creative writing and developments in new media. Drawing on a range of analytical approaches including stylistics, sociolinguistics and multimodality, the book illustrates how English as a resource has evolved historically and is continuing to evolve in the twenty-first century, not least because of its status as an international lingua franca and its prominent role in global communications.

The book begins by considering the kind of writings that we may most commonly think of as being consciously designed: works of literature. Chapters 1 and 2 draw on stylistics and sociolinguistics to illustrate how varieties of English are used in novels, plays and poems. In Chapter 1, Lesley Jeffries illustrates how writers use stylistic features, such as rhyme and rhythm, and linguistic variation, such as accent and dialect, to craft creative texts. Like Jeffries, Jane Miller in Chapter 2 focuses on English as a resource for creating literature around the world and illustrates how, through global use, its very nature as a resource is changing. Both Chapters 1 and 2 ask readers to consider what is special about the way English is used in poetry, novels, plays, stories, songs and various kinds of live performance that makes them works of art or 'artful'.

Chapter 3 continues the focus on English use in international contexts, but moves away from literature to explore a different written genre, that of the newspaper 'news story'. Allan Bell examines the changing structure of time in news stories, from a straightforward chronological narrative to a complex story design which responded to new institutional production processes and changed reading preferences at the end of the late nineteenth century. Bell also shows how news stories illustrate a number of textual qualities that have become more frequent in other genres in the twentieth and early twenty-first century. These include the bringing together of many voices – sources, witnesses and earlier stories on the same topic – which leads to forms of heteroglossic text in which the concept of authorship is rendered problematic.

While Chapters 1, 2 and 3 focus on the verbal linguistic resources of English, Chapter 4 shifts our attention to the visual nature of English and to how words, typography, music and movement are woven together to create multimodal texts. Sharon Goodman provides many examples of the different varieties of multimodal texts and offers ways of analysing such complex texts.

This interest in the multimodal nature of English texts is continued in Chapter 5, which provides readers with an opportunity to pause and consider from a historical dimension the key themes from both preceding and subsequent chapters. David Graddol traces the history of visual English from early runic engravings up to and through medieval illustrated manuscripts and considers their historical influence on orthographies of English. He brings to bear a socially and politically informed understanding on the finely nuanced choices facing scribes and authors when crafting texts, and demonstrates that even in medieval times in England book production was an international business.

Both Chapters 4 and 5 illustrate a point of key relevance to contemporary concerns: the technologies available at any historical moment significantly shape the 'stuff' of English – the use of rock, parchment ink and paper shaped the material nature of English just as much as the use of billboards and the internet today. These chapters serve as a reminder that while it is often suggested that the visual dimension of texts may be increasing in salience in the twenty-first century, it has always been a significant part of textual practices.

Chapter 6 focuses on the ways in which new technologies, particularly the internet, are contributing to the development of changed practices in English across the globe. Colin Gardner considers the extent to which English is the dominant language of the internet and the emergence of new 'varieties' of English used on the internet. He also considers how new practices resulting from the use of new media, notably digitisation, are facilitating remote access to English artefacts housed in many institutions around the world.

Chapters 5 and 6 together indicate how technologies of design and production vary historically, from being in the hands of the specialist skilled few (for example, scribes in the Middle Ages) to being in the hands of many (in the use of internet and computer software). However, they also illustrate how design and production practices are always stratified; for example, there are significant differences in access to new technologies – not everyone has access to the internet.

To end, there is an explicit examination of a theme that has run throughout the book: the position of English as a resource for shaping texts and identities across the world. In Chapter 7, David Graddol explores some of the conflicting trends in global English, from its potential as a lingua franca meeting the communicative interests of both monolingual and multilingual participants, to its role in the global restructuring of social and economic inequality. Graddol shows that while the English language may be perceived as a dominant force in globalisation, there is strong evidence of the resilience of local and national cultures and languages alongside resistance to any globally imposed uniform culture. And *redesigning* English will, if anything, become an even more powerful imperative as its users continue to diversify in terms of their resources, settings, challenges and opportunities.

Each chapter is accompanied by at least one reading, which represents an additional 'voice' or viewpoint on one or more of the principal themes or issues raised in the chapter. The volume's overall coherence is enhanced by the inclusion of these voices, which serve to broaden the reader's understanding of the rich range of perspectives available in this dynamic field of study.

I would like to thank Anna Magyar for carrying out background research for Chapter 7.

Each chapter includes:

activities to stimulate further understanding or analysis of the material

text boxes containing illustrative or supplementary material

key terms which are clearly explained as soon as they appear in order to increase the reader's familiarity with the subject.

A note on representing the sounds of language

The distinctive sounds of a particular language, or more precisely of a particular variety of a language, are known as phonemes, and phonemes are conventionally signalled by being enclosed in diagonal brackets / /. The sound of each phoneme is always clearly explained or illustrated by placing it in a familiar context. The important thing to remember is that when you see diagonal brackets, the symbols inside represent sounds and not letters.

What makes English into art?

Lesley Jeffries

1.1 Introduction

In this chapter I examine what is special about the way English is used in poetry, novels, plays, stories, songs and various kinds of live performance, which makes them into a form of art. Is it a question of particular linguistic techniques cleverly used by accomplished authors, or is there something more difficult to define about the creative and artistic uses of language? Can we talk about art purely in terms of a text or performance, or do we also need to look beyond the text at cultural expectations and conventions? How far should we consider art as a particular kind of social practice rather than in abstract aesthetic terms? In Activity 1.1, you have the opportunity to reflect on your own ideas on such topics before continuing with the chapter.

ACTIVITY 1.1

Allow about 10 minutes

Which of the following might you describe as 'art'? (For the purposes of this activity, it is not necessary to be familiar with all of these texts.) What factors seem to be important in deciding whether an oral or a written text counts as art?

1   Shakespeare's *Romeo and Juliet*
2   a poem written in dialect
3   a list of immigration laws
4   the song 'Sergeant Pepper's Lonely Hearts Club Band' by The Beatles
5   an anonymous traditional ballad
6   Jane Austen's *Pride and Prejudice*
7   Wole Soyinka's *Ake* (twentieth-century Nigerian dramatist's autobiography)
8   an improvised twenty-first century theatre piece
9   a conversation with a friend while shopping together.

Comment

You probably immediately identified numbers 1 and 6 from the list as 'art'; as part of the English literature canon, their quality and value seems incontrovertible. You may have decided that, although the song by The Beatles and the traditional ballad might not have been accepted by everyone as 'art' when they first appeared, they have now stood the test of time and can safely be included. You probably wanted to know more about numbers 2 and 8 in order to decide whether they can be counted as art. They also raise issues about whether an artistic text can be written in any variety of English and whether a work of art in English needs a permanent script. What counts as art is influenced by conceptions of 'literature', which often means printed fiction (poetry, plays and novels), but it is already clear that language often combines with other media to produce artistic effects. What about texts on the borders of fiction and non-fiction, like number 7? Numbers 3 and 9 are not immediately obvious as art in themselves but, as we see later in the chapter, technical documents and everyday talk can be contextualised within artistic performances.

You may have found in this exercise that the factors determining whether a text is art were not as distinct as you expected. Often, when we try to categorise our experience, we find that we are left with many grey areas. Art is a term which has many different and sometimes contentious interpretations, but there are a number of linguistic and social factors which can help us answer the question: what makes English into art?

In this chapter I look from a linguistic point of view at some of the ways in which English has been used to achieve special artistic effects. I also examine the way artistic uses of English are shaped both by the contexts in which they are created and by the contexts in which they are received. My focus in this chapter is mainly on poetry, novels and drama.

1.2 Language art in written English texts

Focusing on language

In this section I draw on a form of linguistic analysis known as **stylistics** to try to pinpoint a number of language features commonly found in artistic uses of English. Stylisticians have focused mainly on written texts, partly because these are more accessible for detailed study. However, the emphasis on written texts also arises because those theories of language dominant in the Western world have, at least until recently, treated language as a self-contained symbolic system which is revealed more clearly in writing than in speech. (For an introduction to stylistics, see Widdowson, 1975; Toolan, 1998; Wales, 2001.)

One key idea used by stylisticians, which comes from a school of Russian scholars of the 1920s and 1930s who are known as the Russian formalists, is the notion that literary language is different from everyday language because it draws attention to some property of the language itself, and highlights or foregrounds it. This **foregrounding** surprises the reader into a fresh perception and appreciation of the subject matter. Foregrounding can be achieved by focusing on sounds, grammar, or meanings, and will be a central theme throughout this chapter.

Rhyme, rhythm and repetition

One fairly obvious example of foregrounding is the way in which literary language, especially poetry, uses regular controlled patterns of rhythm, rhyme and repetition.

ACTIVITY 1.2

Allow about 10 minutes

The poem below, by English poet William Blake, was published in 1789 in his collection *Songs of Innocence*. In what ways does his use of rhythm, repetition and rhyme foreground particular qualities of language? (Reading the poem aloud may help you recognise these features.) How do they appeal to the senses and give some kind of form to the ideas and meaning in the poem?

The Tyger

Tyger! Tyger! burning bright
In the forests of the night,
What immortal hand or eye
Could frame thy fearful symmetry?

In what distant deeps or skies
Burnt the fire of thine eyes?
On what wings dare he aspire?
What the hand dare seize the fire?

And what shoulder, & what art,
Could twist the sinews of thy heart?
And when thy heart began to beat,
What dread hand? & what dread feet?

What the hammer? what the chain?
In what furnace was thy brain?
What the anvil? what dread grasp
Dare its deadly terrors clasp?

When the stars threw down their spears,
And water'd heaven with their tears,
Did he smile his work to see?
Did he who made the Lamb make thee?

Tyger! Tyger! burning bright
In the forests of the night,
What immortal hand or eye
Dare frame thy fearful symmetry?

(Blake, 1970)

Comment

Let us look first at the rhythm: every line has four stressed syllables alternating with three or four unstressed syllables – a rhythm associated in English with songs or ballads, as in the traditional nursery rhyme '*Jack* and *Jill* went *up* the *hill*'. This, together with the repetitive string of questions, gives the lines an unusually obvious 'beat', like the beating of a drum, or in this case, the beating of an anvil, or the powerful tread of a dangerous animal. This apparently excessive emphasis on rhythm actually enhances the sensory appeal of the poem, by imitating the frequency of a hammer striking an anvil, or an animal's foot hitting the ground. The 'beat' is also emphasised by the sounds of the words themselves with their frequent plosive /d/, /t/ or /p/, all suggestive of sounds made by hammering or hitting.

In each four-line stanza, the first two and last two lines rhyme in the pattern aabb. The symmetry of the rhyme scheme in each stanza reflects the 'fearful symmetry' in the design of the tiger which Blake describes. Rhymed or repeated words increase their emphasis and develop in the reader a sense of expectation or inevitability. The last stanza and the first are identical except for one word; this break in the pattern provides the sense of closure, and of a powerful design fulfilled.

Rhythm, rhyme and repetition also contribute to the imagery in the poem: the fire, the blacksmith and the darkness. The formalists saw these different, specialised uses of language working together to create a self-contained and complete work of art. The meaning was believed to be contained within the text, so that the social or historical context in which it was written, or facts about the author's life, or the reader's experience, were all irrelevant.

This belief that a work of language art is complete in itself, with a definitive meaning waiting to be discovered, also underpins what was the dominant twentieth-century British–US approach to literary criticism, known as **practical criticism** (although there is no evidence of contact between the British and US critics and the formalists).

(I am grateful to Robert Abel for permission to draw on his unpublished material in the analysis of 'The Tyger'.)

You may have noticed the foregrounding of repeated sounds, in addition to rhyme, in 'The Tyger'; for instance, the repetition of the sound /t/ at the end of the first two lines of the first and last stanza (brigh*t*, nigh*t*), which symmetrically reflects the initial sound /t/ in '*Ty*ger!, *Ty*ger!' with which each verse opens. Blake also uses alliteration in '*d*istant *d*eeps'. Like rhythm, alliteration and assonance (repeated vowel sounds) give poetry its musical effect and contribute to the overall mood and meaning. For instance, in the following extract from *The Prelude* (Book 1) by English poet William

Wordsworth, the alliterative use of a number of sibilant sounds shows how a build-up of one type of consonant can echo the action being described, in this case the sound of ice-skates on winter ice:

All shod with steel.
We hissed along the polished ice in games

(Wordsworth, 1991 [1850], p. 26)

Rhyme and alliteration

Rhyme is a kind of 'phonetic echo'. In English verse, the most frequently occurring rhyme is the 'end rhyme': units at the end of metrical lines have identical stretches of sound from the vowel to the end of the word (usually stressed), with the initial sound varied; for example, *sight/night*. Rhyme usually depends on phonemes rather than spelling (e.g. *ewe* rhymes with *too*), although sometimes 'eye-rhymes' are used, which are based on sight rather than sound (*bough/cough*). Rhymes within a metrical line are called 'internal rhymes'. Since the nineteenth century, poets have also used 'half rhymes', in which the final consonants are repeated (*bend/sand*).

Before the Norman conquest, Anglo-Saxon used alliteration (repeated initial consonants) rather than rhyme for poetic cohesion, a style which reappeared in the poetry of fourteenth-century England, as, for example, in the following lines from *Sir Gawain and the Green Knight*:

The snaw snitered ful snart, that snayped the wilde

(The snow came shivering down very bitterly, so that it nipped the wild animals)

(cited in Wales, 2001, p. 15)

Alliteration is still widely used in poetic language, as is assonance which is based on the repetition of vowel sounds in adjacent words; for example, the *far star*.

(based on Wales, 2001)

An example of assonance can be seen in the following line from Ruth Padel's poem 'Still Life with Bible' in which she describes the artist (perhaps Van Gogh) painting his madness:

If the sick sun came now it couldn't purge
the mad grappling sky.

(Padel, 1993, p. 20)

The open front vowel, /a/, is repeated in quick succession and is therefore foregrounded, with the effect that the vowel evokes a 'scream' or blood-curdling cry of despair. If you doubt this, see what kind of cry is evoked if you replace the phrase 'mad grappling' with words containing closed vowels like /ɪ/ as in *hit* or /u:/ as in *fool*.

Breaking the rules of English

So far we have been concentrating on how language in poetry highlights or foregrounds particular properties of sound and rhythm. Foregrounding also occurs when particular language rules are played with, or broken.

Every language has rules for combining sounds and words and linguists have pointed out **syntagmatic** and **paradigmatic** relations between words. First, a language has rules for the way in which words are syntactically combined in phrases or sentences; for example, English is a 'determiner adjective noun' language (*the-big-house*). Second, words have paradigmatic relations with other words which could grammatically and semantically replace them. For instance, in the line 'Did he smile his work to see?', *he* has a syntactic relationship to *smile*, while *work* has a paradigmatic relationship with *creation*, *product*, or other words of the same word class which could replace it (Graddol et al., 1994, pp. 73–5). These syntagmatic and paradigmatic rules are often exploited and broken in literary language. In fact, as we shall see, rules governing the sound system (phonology), the writing system (graphology), word structure (morphology), grammar and paragraphing, can all be broken, individually or in combination.

Let us look at some examples where authors and poets deliberately manipulate, or break, rules at various levels. The following passage is from the opening chapter of *The Sound and the Fury* by US novelist William Faulkner. It is narrated by Benjy, a character whose cognitive development is stuck in babyhood, although he is thirty-three years of age when the book opens:

> Through the fence, between the curling flower spaces, I could see them hitting. They were coming toward where the flag was and I went along the fence. Luster was hunting in the grass by the flower tree. They took the flag out, and they were hitting. Then they put the flag back and they went to the table, and he hit and the other hit.

> (Faulkner, 1989 [1929], p. 1)

In this first section of the novel, Faulkner's aim is to show what might be going through Benjy's mind, even though Benjy does not actually speak. This use of English to represent a stream of thought which looks strange in written English, is a challenge which requires the reader to be 'shocked' out of feeling comfortable with the language. For instance, Benjy constantly uses a transitive verb (one that expects to be followed by an object) with no object; for example, *he hit*. This simple device gives us some insight into the way that Benjy fails to make connections between cause and effect; he does not realise that the golfers are hitting the balls into the holes. Benjy visits the golf course frequently, because he likes to hear the name of his beloved sister, Caddie, when the golfers shout to their caddy (the assistant who transports the golf-clubs). The power of Faulkner's text lies in the way it reveals a limited and unrefined mind through language which recreates the freshness and vividness of a human perception unrestricted by learnt cultural and social structures.

Some writers make a particular feature of breaking the rules of English morphology and syntax. For instance, the American poet e e cummings refuses to use upper-case letters (as in the spelling of his own name), changes word classes, adds morphological endings to words that do not normally have them and plays with negation. What is interesting about such radical rule breaking is that cummings's stylistic tendencies are repetitive and thus, once accustomed to his ways, we can understand the poetry quite well. A familiar structure with which cummings plays is where a word is repeated with *by* in the middle, as in the everyday examples: 'one by one', 'side by side', 'year by year'.

In the following extract from the poem 'anyone lived in a pretty how town', cummings uses this structure but subverts paradigmatic rules by choosing words that normally belong in another word-class:

> busy folk buried them side by side
> little by little and was by was

> (cummings, 1969, p. 44)

Here cummings sets the scene with a conventional phrase, *side by side*. He then moves on to the phrase, *little by little*, which normally means 'gradually'. However, since one can hardly bury a body 'gradually' we are forced to understand *little* as a noun. The last phrase turns the past tense form of the verb 'to be' into a noun in *was by was*. The echoes of another noun derived from the verb 'to be', 'has-been', perhaps suggest that these people were never very 'present' in their lives, even before they died.

ACTIVITY 1.3

Allow about
5 minutes

The extracts below come from the opening passages of two novels; the first, from *Bleak House* by Charles Dickens, is set in nineteenth-century England; and the second, from *Midnight's Children* by Salman Rushdie, in twentieth-century India. In each case, what conventions of formal written English are being broken, and to what effect?

1   Fog everywhere ... Fog on the Essex marshes, fog on the Kentish heights.
    Fog creeping into the cabooses of collier-brigs; fog lying out on the yards,
    and hovering in the rigging of great ships; fog drooping on the gunwales of

barges and small boats. Fog in the eyes and throats of ancient Greenwich pensioners, wheezing by the firesides of their wards; fog in the stem and bowl of the afternoon pipe of the wrathful skipper, down in his close cabin; fog cruelly pinching the toes and fingers of his shivering little 'prentice boy on deck.

(Dickens, 1948 [1850], p. 1)

2   I must work fast, faster than Scheherazade, if I am to end up meaning – yes, meaning – something. I admit it: above all things, I fear absurdity.
And there are so many stories to tell, too many, such an excess of intertwined lives events miracles places rumours, so dense a commingling of the improbable and the mundane!

(Rushdie, 1982, p. 11)

Comment

In the first extract, Dickens omits the main verb from each clause, painting a scene in the present tense, drawing the reader into the actual context of the novel. The clauses describing the fog build up and accumulate to create the effect that there is not a corner, nor a person, that can escape its stifling damp and cold. If you know *Bleak House*, you may remember that this fog is a metaphor for the crippling and all-pervasive effects of the nineteenth-century English law courts which are a central theme of the novel. Dickens highlights the importance of particular qualities of the fog (and the legal system) by breaking syntactic rules to catch and focus the reader's attention right at the beginning of the novel.

In the second extract, the way in which Rushdie addresses the reader as an intimate friend is an unusual and striking aspect of his style. The aberrant starting of a new paragraph (let alone a new sentence) with *And* contravenes traditional written conventions, but is in keeping with the highly colloquial and rather chaotic opening of the novel. This chaos is echoed when Rushdie breaks the graphological convention of putting commas between the listed items in the last sentence. The reader is surprised into recognising the lack of separateness of these items; they are, as Rushdie says, densely intertwined and intermingled.

Metaphor and collocation

I have looked at different ways of highlighting the sounds, rhythms and grammatical patterns of English. Another important aspect of literary language is the way in which it plays with, and subverts, relationships of meaning, through metaphors, similes and puns.

The *burning* of the tiger's eyes and the stars' *spears* in Blake's poem, and the fog of the British legal system in Dickens's novel, are metaphors used to highlight particular qualities through direct comparison, sometimes in a surprising way. Metaphors exploit the networks of meaning invoked by particular words and many of the most effective metaphors are 'slipped in' to the text by way of a small deviation from traditional patterns of word combination. This can just as easily happen in spontaneous conversation as in a poem or a short story, but is particularly common in poetry.

An example of metaphor comes from Carol Ann Duffy's poem 'Litany', where she condemns the lives of her parents' generation in the lines:

> The terrible marriages crackled, cellophane
> round polyester shirts ...

> (Duffy, in France, 1993, p. 117)

Duffy uses metaphorically the verb 'crackled' which normally follows an inanimate subject (e.g. sticks crackling in a fire). This, together with her metaphoric comparison of the marriages with cellophane around polyester shirts, evokes images of relationships which are dry, brittle and somehow 'synthetic' – just like the materials which were at that time first being produced and which were replacing natural materials in every area of life.

Simile and metaphor

Simile refers to a device that makes a comparison explicit, as in this example from the American writer Toni Morrison's novel *Jazz*:

> Washing his handkerchiefs and putting food on the table before him was the most she could manage. A poisoned silence floated through the rooms *like a big fishnet* that Violet alone slashed through with loud recriminations.

> (Morrison, 1992, p. 5, emphasis added)

The effect of **metaphor** is akin to that of the simile, but the comparison is not made explicit; for example, *crackled* in the example from Duffy, and, on a broader level, the comparison of God to a blacksmith in 'The Tyger' and the fog in *Bleak House*.

In 'Litany', Duffy is relying on the reader's knowledge of the **collocations** of the word 'crackle' to make sense of her unusual choice of verb. When we hear or read a word a whole range of possible associations may be invoked, drawn from our experience of its use in other contexts. The artist juxtaposes particular words or phrases to highlight unusual and striking associations of meaning. Here is another example of this kind of juxtaposition (notice also the use of alliteration and assonance), taken from Samuel Beckett's *Footfalls*:

> Some nights she would halt, as one frozen by some shudder of the mind, and stand stark still till she could move again.

(Beckett, 1984, p. 242)

Beckett exploits the reader's familiarity with the common collocations 'stock still', 'stark naked' and 'stark staring mad', to make the phrase *stand stark still* particularly concise, evoking both madness and nudity as well as the stillness it conveys more directly.

The effect is achieved by exploiting the reader's/hearer's usual collocational expectations. For example, the verb *awaken* is normally constrained to occur with an animate object such as a person or an animal. The effect of placing an inanimate object after it, as the poet Sujata Bhatt does in the following lines from 'The Langur Coloured Night', is to suggest that the cry was loud enough to wake objects normally considered unwakeable:

> It was a cry
> to awaken the moon

(Bhatt, 1991, p. 11)

Collocation

Collocation refers to the combining tendencies of words. We know, for example, that *coffee* and *dining* are often to be found in the company of *table*. Some words are subject to slightly looser restrictions. For example, *eat* normally requires an object that is edible such as *sandwich* or *apple*, while *snap* requires an object brittle enough to break in this way. Poetic effects often depend on unusual juxtapositions of words where collocations are invoked to create a metaphor, as in *marriages crackled* and *stark still*.

More systematic study of the collocations of words has been made possible through the amassing on computer of large numbers of spoken and written English texts, which can then be analysed to show the kinds of context in which particular words are likely to occur. The extraction from a large collection of texts of all the instances where a particular word appears is called a **concordance**. Concordancing can throw up some surprising results; for instance, some apparently neutral words can be shown to have consistently negative, or consistently positive, connotations. Sinclair (1987) describes how the phrase *set in* almost always refers to a negative state of affairs, being commonly found in association with words such as *decay, ill-will, impoverishment, bitterness, rigor mortis* and *disillusion*, for example (cited in Louw, 1993).

Analysts claim that concordances can explain some of the more subtle nuances that particular words or phrases may have for us. Bill Louw has used computer concordancing to investigate the semantic associations of phrases used by Philip Larkin, whose poetry is well known for its ironic melancholy. Louw computed a concordance for the phrase *days are* in Larkin's poem 'Days', by extracting all the instances where the phrase appears from an 18 million-word corpus of English texts:

Days

What are days for?
Days are where we live.
They come, they wake us
Time and time over.
They are to be happy in:
Where can we live but days?

Ah, solving that question
Brings the priest and the doctor
In their long coats
Running over the fields.

(Larkin, 1964, p. 27)

Concordance for 'days are'

1	t it yourself the prices these	days are	absolutely astronomica
2	ite 'The world is wide, no two	days are	alike, not even two ho
3	ays are gone whenel. But those	days are	almost twenty years go
4	glass extinction when the grey	days are	done but who are reason
5	omen for unequal pay. But the	days are	gone whenel. But those
6	or do I. The big beer drinking	days are	gone. They drank becau
7	nd cry for peace. My political	days are	good and over. I'm not
8	ople making these things these	days are	making money out of th
9	erage trawler when its fishing	days are	over – as the Morning
10	it was before. Those good old	days are	over because trout fis
11	Lourenco Marques. Alas those	days are	over. What did he die
12	o walk means that his babying	days are	over. The stroking cea
13	ade me regret that my dancing	days are	over. Rudolph couldn't
14	fate of Czechoslovakia. These	days are	over, and that is what
15	ng after me Grandad's working	days are	past walk along with m
16	a black black sky. But those	days are	rare and usually to be
17	f I had a striking clock. The	days are	stretching out again a
18	ness and constancy of country	days are	the very qualities tha
19	e the only movies I see these	days are	these nights, on the 1
20	finances of old people these	days are	very much better than
21	rate that situation. The hard	days are	with us and they are c

(Louw, 1993, p. 162)

ACTIVITY 1.4

Allow about
10 minutes

The line *Days are where we live* might be expected to produce happy associations, yet it leaves the reader with inexplicable feelings of sadness, foreshadowing the theme of death in the second verse. How might the evidence from the concordance explain the feeling of sadness evoked by the second line?

Comment

Louw points out that in more than two-thirds of the concordance, the phrase *days are* is followed by words like *past*, *over* and *gone*. As he puts it, 'Days are not so much *where we live* as where we *have lived* and where we are likely, possibly sooner rather than later, to die' (Louw, 1993, p. 162). Louw did a further concordance using a 37 million-word corpus of texts where the term *days are* appeared 104 times, and found the same kind of profile as in the concordance above.

This kind of analysis challenges both the idea that a literary work should be treated as a self-contained piece of art, and the belief that literary analysis should focus on how literary language is different from that in other texts. Louw shows that our unconscious understanding of the associations of particular words and phrases in a poem is built up through our previous experience of them in many different kinds of other texts. In 'Days', these collocations are a central vehicle for the poem's effect; the meanings associated with the intertextual collocations swarm into the poem, colouring our reading of *days are*, so that its juxtaposition with *where we live* becomes deeply ironic.

In addition to exploiting the collocations of words, writers sometimes play on different meanings of the same word. You may recall examples of **punning** in extracts earlier in the chapter: the two meanings of *Caddie* in the Faulkner novel tell us that, although Benjy is simple, he is capable of strong human attachment; and the word *Lamb* in Blake's poem refers to an animal associated with gentleness and weakness, but which is also a common metaphor for Jesus Christ.

Punning highlights particular relationships between two different sets of meaning, for dramatic effect, as shown in the following extract from *My Children! My Africa!*, by South African playwright Athol Fugard:

THAMI   But you were good!

ISABEL   Because I happen to feel very strongly about what we were debating. But it was also the whole atmosphere you know. It was so ... so free and easy. The debates at my school are such stuffy affairs. And so boring most of the time. Everything is done according to the rules with everybody being polite and nobody getting excited ... lots of discipline but very little enthusiasm. This one was a riot!

THAMI   *[Finger to his lips]* Be careful.

ISABEL   Of what?

THAMI   That word.

ISABEL   Which one?

THAMI   Riot! Don't say it in a black township. Police start shooting as soon as they hear it.

ISABEL   Oh ... I'm sorry ...

THAMI   *[Having a good laugh]* It's a joke, Isabel.

ISABEL   Oh ... you caught me off guard. I didn't think you would joke about those things.

THAMI   Riots and police? Oh yes, we joke about them. We joke about everything.

(Fugard, 1990, p. 7)

The extract explores a culture clash in South Africa where two high school children, one black and one white, begin to find out about each other's lives when they meet in an interschool debate. The irony here lies in the two opposing meanings of the word *riot* that are being juxtaposed. The more obvious and literal meaning is a real and often frightening experience for township dwellers, while the privileged white girl is brought up sharply when she realises that she uses the same word lightly to mean 'great fun'. The solemnity of her reaction is turned round again by Thami's ironically humorous response.

Iconicity

We have been looking at the way in which meaning can be played with, and highlighted, by invoking particular connotations. Writers also manipulate another layer of meaning by highlighting the manner in which a word relates to the object or process it is representing. For most words, this relationship is purely **symbolic**. There is no intrinsic reason, for example, for calling a tiger 'tiger' – it could just as well be called something else, so long as everyone in the speech community understood. But there are two other kinds of relationship which a sign can have with the object or event it is representing. The relationship may be **indexical** where there is some direct cause and effect: for example, smoke is a sign of fire, and, in the English language, an accent or dialect is a sign that the speaker comes from a particular geographical area or class. The third type of sign, which is particularly significant in literary language, is the **iconic**, where the sounds and shapes of words and phrases imitate particular objects or processes. Words can often function as more than one kind of sign simultaneously. For example, in 'The Tyger', the phrase *What dread hand? & what dread feet?* iconically imitates the sound of the beating of an anvil, while individual words have a symbolic relationship with the thing they are representing (hand, feet).

One of the most easily recognisable examples of iconicity in literary language is **onomatopoeia**, where the sound of a word echoes the action it is describing; for example, in the extract from *The Prelude* we looked at earlier in this chapter, Wordsworth uses the sibilant /s/ sound of the words to describe skating on ice. Another kind of iconicity is the way the patterns of rhyme in 'The Tyger' mirror the symmetry of its stripes.

Iconicity can also be achieved through the manipulation of grammatical rules. In another extract from *The Prelude* (Book 1) Wordsworth describes skating on a frozen lake in midwinter. Notice how he invokes the childhood pleasure of making oneself dizzy. Again, the effect is more marked if you read the poem aloud.

> ... and oftentimes,
> When we had given our bodies to the wind,
> And all the shadowy banks on either side,
> Came sweeping through the darkness, spinning still
> The rapid line of motion, then at once
> Have I, reclining back upon my heels,
> Stopped short; yet still the solitary cliffs
> Wheeled by me – even as if the earth had rolled
> With visible motion her diurnal round!

(Wordsworth, 1991 [1850], p. 26)

Wordsworth's language imitates the movement and dizziness of the narrator so effectively that we can not only remember, but almost feel, the childish exhilaration of the skater. How is this effect achieved? The passage consists of a single, rather long, sentence, whose main subject and verb, *I* and *stopped*, occur very late in its structure. This late placing of subject and verb, the two obligatory clause elements in English, contravenes a general 'rule' of English sentences, in which commonly the main verb appears early in the sentence, with any lengthy and complicated phrases occurring after the verb. The result of this general tendency in English sentences is that speakers of English expect the verb sooner rather than later. When it fails to occur, there is either a feeling of frustration and expectation, or (as in this case) a breathless, headlong rush towards the verb.

Wordsworth's description gives us four adverbial elements, the second of which is very long:

> oftentimes
> When we had given our bodies to the wind ... motion
> then
> at once

They almost begin to spin out of control until suddenly the auxiliary verb and subject, *Have I*, seem to pull the structure back into line. However, there is one more adverbial element, *reclining back upon my heels*, before the main verb finally arrives. It is as though the skater is first of all abandoned to the movement, then decides to take control, but finds this takes a little longer than expected. When he does at last manage to stop, the short, sharp plosives of *stopped short* just have time to echo in the sudden stillness before the sentence continues, like the apparent movement of the landscape to a dizzy skater, for a further two and a half lines.

Iconicity

Iconic describes a word, phrase or other symbol which has some non-arbitrary relationship with the thing it represents. So while the words *male toilets* are arbitrary (symbolic), the sign in the margin is iconic, because it looks like a man. Iconicity at the level of phonology, where a word imitates the sound it represents, is known as **onomatopoeia**; for example, *buzz, miaouw, plop*. Iconic words may echo the sound they are representing within their form; for example, *quick* has a short vowel and a final plosive consonant, while *slow* has a long diphthong and no final consonant. Patterns of rhythm and syntax may mime or enact meaning as in, for example, Wordsworth's description of skating, the symmetrical pattern in 'The Tyger', or the rhythm of the train in W.H. Auden's poem 'Night Mail': 'This is the night mail crossing the border/Bringing the cheque and the postal order' (Auden, 1969, p. 83). Within narrative, chronological sequencing may iconically mimic the order in which participants experience events.

1.3 Narrative and dialogue

So far I have been focusing on how particular aspects of English are highlighted and exploited in poetry. In this section I look at narrative, and the kinds of foregrounding used in this genre. Narrative is basically a story of events which the narrator considers important. Narratives are found in newspapers and histories (non-fiction), and in epic poems, ballads, comic strips, novels and short stories (fiction). They can be oral or written, enacted on stage, or envisioned in film and mime (Wales, 2001, p. 265). I look particularly at the use of detail and dialogue in novels, short stories and plays.

Plot and detail

The formalists distinguished between the series of events on which a narrative is based (which they called the 'fabula'), and the way those events are turned into a story (the 'sjuzhet'). The sjuzhet may include significant emphases, omissions, inferences and flashbacks, for example, which are all part of the narrator's art. The relationships between these two levels can be more or less complex. For instance, the film *Dr Zhivago* begins with an event which occurs long after the main portion of the narrative, and introduces a 'narrator' who is only very peripheral to the main events in the film. We only become aware of the significance of who the narrator is as the plot unfolds, and his interest at the beginning of the film in a particular factory girl is only fully explained at the very end. The fabula, the basic chronology of events, is like a skeleton, given a body and life by the way the sjuzhet is used to explore the relationships between the characters, and the intricacies of the plot.

Another aspect of foregrounding in prose writing is the very explicit or concrete nature of descriptive language use, in contrast to the generally inexplicit nature of English in everyday speech.

ACTIVITY 1.5

Allow about
10 minutes

Read the extract below from the opening of Ambrose Bierce's short story 'Occurrence at Owl Creek Bridge'. What might be the author's purpose in providing such precise details about the height of the bridge, and the nature of the stream?

> A man stood upon a railroad bridge in northern Alabama, looking down into the swift water twenty feet below. The man's hands were behind his back, the wrists bound with a cord. A rope closely encircled his neck. It was attached to a stout cross-timber above his head and the slack fell to the level of his knees. Some loose boards laid upon the sleepers supporting the metals of the railway supplied a footing for him and his executioners – two private soldiers of the Federal army, directed by a sergeant who in civil life may have been a deputy sheriff ...
>
> Beyond one of the sentinels nobody was in sight; the railroad ran straight away into a forest for a hundred yards, then, curving, was lost to view ...
>
> The man who was engaged in being hanged was apparently about thirty-five years of age ...

His face had not been covered nor his eyes bandaged. He looked a moment at his 'unsteadfast footing', then let his gaze wander to the swirling water of the stream racing madly beneath his feet. A piece of dancing driftwood caught his attention and his eyes followed it down the current.

(Bierce, 1970, pp. 305–6)

Comment

Here are comments on Bierce's opening from a contemporary US novelist, Robert Abel:

One purpose of this explicitness is 'authenticating detail', to draw us into the story, so we feel we are actually there ... Bierce goes to the extreme of even giving us precise measurements to help dissolve the barriers between the world he is creating and our own awareness that it is 'only a story', after all. He tells us not that the bridge is 'high above the water', or even 'quite a distance from the water', but 'twenty feet' above. The precision of this detail makes the scene quite vivid. Notice also that the stream beneath the bridge is not just any stream, but contains 'swift water', 'racing madly', which can carry driftwood logs along. All these details seem innocent enough, vivid as they are, but in fact they serve at least two important purposes at this point in the story. One is that the stream's turbulence reflects the psychology of the situation – it is war time, and a man is being hanged for attempted sabotage. His state of mind is also in turmoil. The second purpose these details serve is to make it possible to believe what happens – or seems to happen – in the rest of the story. Such a raging little stream could carry a man along as well as a log, and at a fast pace. Such a little stream, we don't need to be told, but can already sense, could, with a little bit of luck, carry a condemned man to safety. The carefully selected details, therefore, give us not only a sense of time and place, but prepare us nicely to accept and believe what happens next in the story. You might like to play with the details of the story, to see what the consequences would be for the reader. Suppose, for example, the stream was shallow and not so fast moving. Suppose the bridge was only ten feet from the water, or fifty feet above it. Even these apparently trivial adjustments in the 'facts' of this fictional world would make it almost impossible to persuade us that the condemned man would have any chance at all of getting out of his predicament. Caught in a narrow, muddy stream, he would surely be an easy target for the sharpshooters. If he fell fifty feet, he would surely be injured too badly to make a successful flight into the woods beyond. So there is nothing really innocent or haphazard about these details – they establish secretly what is possible in this fictional world, and 'authenticate' the reading experience which follows.

(I am grateful to Robert Abel for his permission to use material from his unpublished work *The Characteristics of Literary English*.)

Constructing dialogues

Authors make explicit decisions about the kind of details they are going to foreground in their descriptions. They also have to make decisions about the ways in which they represent natural speech in their characters' dialogue. They usually conform to a number of conventions that distinguish dialogue from 'real' speech. These include using the minimum of overlaps and interruptions, very few hesitations and almost no self-corrections. Speakers in novels or plays often use complete sentences, as in the next example from *The Radiant Way*, a novel by twentieth-century British writer, Margaret Drabble:

'Well, I don't know,' said Liz. 'I don't know why Charles doesn't move out, until he goes to New York. Wouldn't that be more orthodox, Charles?'

'I think I've lost my grip of orthodoxy. It's too late to be orthodox now,' said Charles: not quite believing his own words.

'Has Henrietta got any children?' asked Aaron. 'Are we about to acquire some new stepbrothers and stepsisters?'

(Drabble, 1987, p. 122)

However, although written dialogue is often 'tidied up', writers can also exploit our knowledge of the apparent inconsistencies and non-sequiturs in ordinary conversation in a fairly direct way, as in this extract from *Minna*, a play by the contemporary British dramatist, Howard Barker:

MINNA   Go away!

FRANCISCA   If you insist.

MINNA   No, don't go away ...

             [She hesitates, then flings herself into Francisca's arms]

             I don't like dancing, I only think I do!

FRANCISCA   Very well, don't dance –

MINNA   But that is true of everything.

(Barker, 1994, p. 95)

From our experience of everyday conversation, we know that people in distressed states of mind sometimes contradict themselves in succeeding utterances, as Minna does at the beginning of this extract. And we understand that the apparently irrelevant last line must be interpreted as a general 'truth' of which the dancing is just one example.

ACTIVITY 1.6

Allow about
10 minutes

The following extract is taken from *Night School*, a play by twentieth-century British dramatist Harold Pinter. In what ways does the dialogue here differ from 'natural' conversation?

WALTER   Marvellous cake.

MILLY   I told her to go and get it.

WALTER   I haven't had a bit of cake like that for nine solid months.

MILLY   It comes from down the road.

WALTER   Here you are, Aunty, here's some chocolates.

MILLY   He didn't forget that I like chocolates.

ANNIE   He didn't forget that I don't like chocolates.

(Pinter, 1979, p. 201)

Comment

Pinter uses no overlaps, interruptions, hesitations or self-corrections. He writes in complete sentences and, while he parodies the tendency of people to repeat each other's words, he stylises these repetitions to create a rhythmic and mesmeric pattern. This pattern implies that people's everyday lives are made up of such humdrum, pointless repetitions.

In prose writing, stretches of dialogue are usually 'framed'. There are particular narrative or aesthetic reasons for the points at which the author chooses to begin and end the dialogue, relating for instance to character, plot, or communicating information to the reader. In the extract below, from *Things Fall Apart*, Nigerian novelist Chinua Achebe provides just enough direct dialogue to convey the ritual politeness commonly used at the beginning of a visit in the community depicted in his novel. Okoye has come to ask Unoka to give him back the quite considerable sum of money Unoka owes him.

One day a neighbour called Okoye came in to see him. [Unoka] was reclining on a mud bed in his hut playing on the flute. He immediately rose and shook hands with Okoye, who then unrolled the goatskin which he carried under his arm, and sat down. Unoka went into an inner room and soon returned with a small wooden disc containing a kola nut, some alligator pepper and a lump of white chalk.

'I have kola,' he announced when he sat down, and passed the disc over to his guest.

'Thank you. He who brings kola brings life. But I think you ought to break it,' replied Okoye passing back the disc.

'No, it is for you, I think,' and they argued like this for a few moments before Unoka accepted the honour of breaking the kola.

(Achebe, 1958, pp. 4–5)

This dialogue 'enacts' the beginning of Unoka and Okoye's encounter and gives us the flavour of the ritual exchange, the rest of which Achebe summarises: 'they argued like this for a few moments'. After this point, Achebe summarises the content of most of the encounter, switching back into direct speech for the final confrontation concerning the money.

In the examples so far, there has been a fairly clear boundary between the author's voice, and those of the characters. Sometimes, however, we are particularly aware of the author's voice behind the character, putting words into their mouth for particular ironic effect. For example, when Uriah Heep in Dickens's *David Copperfield* keeps telling David how humble he is, the reader suspects, because of what Dickens has hinted about Uriah, that this is in fact quite opposite from the truth. Conversely, we can also sometimes hear the voice of a character within the authorial voice. This happens, for instance, in 'stream of consciousness' novels, where the narration is ostensibly in the third person, but reflects the thought processes of particular characters.

In the next example, taken from *To the Lighthouse*, Virginia Woolf uses a kind of internal monologue to describe Minta's feelings:

Besides, she knew, directly she came into the room, that the miracle had happened; she wore her golden haze. Sometimes she had it; sometimes not ... Yes, to-night she had it, tremendously; she knew that by the way Mr Ramsey told her not to be a fool. She sat beside him, smiling.

(Woolf, 1977 [1927], p. 133)

Woolf's novels are renowned for consisting of a series of different perspectives, usually reflecting the thoughts of the major characters in turn. The author does not intervene, but tells the story through the emotions and reactions of the characters themselves. The result is that there are differences of vocabulary and syntax that approximate to the style of whichever character is currently the 'narrator'; for example, the terms *golden haze* and *tremendously* are typical of Minta's speech.

The use of English vernaculars

The use of strongly vernacular language would seem to go against the idea that literary language represents the best or most prestigious forms of English and is distinctly different from everyday usage. Vernacular English is not particularly widespread in traditional English literature, although there are some famous examples of dialect in characters' speech; for example, in Dickens's *Hard Times* and Emily Brontë's *Wuthering Heights*. More recently, there has been a considerable increase in the number and range of writers who feel free to use their own variety or some other non-standard variety of English for characters' voices, or even for whole poems and novels.

The Singaporean writer Catherine Lim, for example, uses vernacular Singaporean English in her short stories to convey a realism that also addresses the issue of linguistic oppression. In her story entitled 'The Teacher', she portrays a teacher obsessed with 'correctness' (i.e. with Standard English) and a secondary-school girl who is clearly very unhappy:

> The teacher read, pausing at those parts which he wanted his colleague to take particular note of. '*My happiest day it is on that 12 July 1976 I will tell you of that happiest day. ... My mother is too sick and weak as she just born a baby.*' Can anything be more atrocious than this? And she's going to sit for her General Certificate of Education in three months' time.'

In the story Lim tells how, in a later essay under the title 'The stranger', the same girl wrote about her father:

> *He canned me everytime, even when I did not do wrong things still he canned me and he beat my mother and even if she sick, he wallops her.*

And the teacher comments:

> This composition is not only grossly ungrammatical but out of point. I had no alternative but to give her an F9 straightaway. God, I wish I could help her!

> (Lim, cited in Platt et al., 1984, p. 191)

The irony (for the reader) of the teacher's comment is underlined at the end of Lim's story when, on hearing of the girl's suicide, he complains, 'If only she had told me of her problems'.

Another writer who directly addresses the subject of linguistic equality is Tony Harrison, a British poet whose Yorkshire dialect was in danger of getting in the way of a 'good' education. In one of his poems on the subject of his dialect and identity, 'Them & [uz]', he recalls his schooldays at Leeds Grammar School, where he was among a minority of boys with a local dialect:

> I doffed my flat a's (as in 'flat cap')
> my mouth all stuffed with glottals, great
> lumps to hawk up and spit out ... *E-nun-ci-ate!*

> (Harrison, 1987, p. 122)

Other poets have also made the decision to write in their own variety of English as a way of making a point about the validity of different varieties within literature. There are, for example, many writers of Caribbean backgrounds, who write at least some of the time in creole. The following example is from Louise Bennett's poem, 'Independance':

> Independance wid a vengeance!
> Independance raisin Cain!
> Jamaica start grow beard, ah hope
> We chin can stan de strain!

(Bennett, in Burnett, 1986, p. 35)

The editor of the *Penguin Book of Caribbean Verse in English*, Paula Burnett, argues that 'it is only in the twentieth century (with one or two exceptions) that poets in the literary, Standard English tradition have begun to explore ways of working the rich ore of dialect in literary contexts' (Burnett, 1986, p. xxv).

ACTIVITY 1.7

Read 'In the vernacular' by Rib Davis (Reading A). What various purposes do authors have, in the different ways they reconstruct vernacular Englishes in written form?

Comment

Davis shows that the choice to use a non-standard variety of English, and the way in which the author represents it on paper, is never 'innocent'. It is not a simple matter of transcribing the sounds and forms of speech; there is always a selection and focus on particular aspects of non-standardness to construct a character or advance a plot. Writers' purposes vary enormously; for instance, they may use an eye-dialect to mark a character as the kind of person who would use non-standard English (with all the social connotations that conveys). In the example from Hoban, we see an invented vernacular variety being used to symbolise iconically the degeneration of a whole society. It could be that use of the vernacular is a new kind of foregrounding, in presenting language which looks strange in the context of established literary conventions.

The stylistic landscape

We have already begun to explore the consistent use of particular forms of English which constitute a genre or, at a more specific level, the personal styles of individual authors. While this has always been an area of interest in literary criticism, the development of fast computers has enabled us to examine in far more detail cumulative effects of style; that is, those effects which are not localised in a phrase or a paragraph but are the result of a gradual build-up of grammatical and semantic choices which characterise the style of an author, rather like an individual fingerprint. It is now possible, for instance, to compare authors' works with databases of texts ranging from the literary to the functional, as a genuine basis of comparison.

Computer studies have shown that many of these 'topographical' features of the textual landscape can only be seen as the researcher rises above the details of a text in order to gain a bird's-eye view. For instance, it has often been assumed that the small words which knit phrases and sentences together, such as articles, pronouns and conjunctions, are not particularly significant in achieving artistic effects. They are often regarded as a kind of inert medium, against which artistic uses of English are highlighted. But the assumption that these 'grammatical' words are of no consequence to a writer's style is challenged by John Burrows (1987), who carried out a computer analysis of the frequency and pattern of occurrence of these words in Jane Austen's novels. Burrows shows that the patterns of use for these grammatical words, which make up between a third and a half of Austen's written output (depending on where one draws the line), are far from arbitrary in her novels. For example, there is a distinct contrast between three of the main protagonists in *Northanger Abbey*, Catherine Morland, Henry Tilney and Isabella Thorpe, in terms of the number of times per thousand words they use *the*, *of*, *I* and *not*. These kinds of differences contribute to each character's **idiolect**, or individual speech style.

Table 1.1 Differences of incidence: four words in three idiolects

	Catherine	Henry	Isabella	Mean[1]	Mean[2]
the	16.34	35.29	25.81	24.61	26.45
of	15.91	29.92	17.32	20.71	23.69
I	56.68	24.56	52.86	43.69	38.75
not	26.99	12.69	19.62	19.12	16.14

Mean[1]: overall incidence per 1,000 words in dialogue of *Northanger Abbey*.

Mean[2]: overall incidence per 1,000 words in dialogue of Jane Austen's six novels.

(Burrows, 1987, p. 3)

Burrows argues that the effects of these differences must colour every speech the characters make, and leave some impression in the mind of the reader. Using information about the incidence of common grammatical words, he builds up a picture of the individual speech styles of particular characters, and tracks how these change during the course of the novel, sometimes moving further apart from the idiolects of other characters, and sometimes almost converging with them, as the characters come together within their own lives in the story.

Some literary scholars are very suspicious of the results produced by computer analysis of texts, because it tends to ignore the kinds of features that generations of critics have identified as the crowning achievement of literary style. However, there is increasing evidence to show that quantitative analyses give us indications of the overall pattern of usage in particular writers, even in texts from different periods of their writing careers.

Leech and Short arrive at the following compromise:

> So let us see quantitative stylistics as serving a role in the 'circle of explanation' as follows. On the one hand, it may provide confirmation for the 'hunches' or insights we have about style. On the other, it may bring to light significant features of style which would otherwise have been overlooked, and so lead to further insights; but only in a limited sense does it provide an objective measurement of style.

> (Leech and Short, 1981, p. 47)

1.4 Authors, audience and context

I looked in the last section at writers' use of vernacular Englishes, how an author's purpose affects the choice of language, and how that choice reflects the society within and about which they write. Although traditional approaches to literary criticism have tended to treat a novel, play or poem as a self-contained work of art with fixed meanings, more recently there has been a growing interest in how the context and process involved in creating language art, and the contexts in which it is read, listened to, or viewed, affect meaning and interpretation.

Context and meaning

The world is not reflected in talk, but refracted, as speakers or writers shape an account according to their own perspective, values and motives. It could be argued that literary language, in its simulation of the language of other discourses and its focus both on what is being represented and on itself, adds additional refractive layers. In this sense all texts, including literary ones, are 'ideological'; they present the reader with a particular view of the subject matter, which is usually the author's view and is deeply embedded and often implicit in the language of the text. In this respect the text cannot help but be a distorting refraction; but it also follows that there is no such thing as the 'perfect' mirror, a text with no ideological basis.

Overt or coercive propaganda in a text is not as common as the more hidden 'common-sense' or 'naturalised' ideologies that take for granted the reader's agreement on certain points. Authors may make implicit assumptions about the 'normal' needs and aims of men and women. Jane Austen played on this technique in the famous opening sentence of *Pride and Prejudice*: 'It is a truth universally acknowledged, that a single man in possession of a good fortune, must be in want of a wife.'

Such statements normally mean that the reader is not in a position to doubt their truth, since their truth is precisely what the sentence asserts. Austen, however, clearly has her tongue in her cheek in presenting the reader with assumptions made by a society where mothers and daughters spend their lives scheming to win the latter the richest husband possible.

The basis for the perception that all texts are ideological is that language (spoken and written) is now usually seen as being shaped by its context, both linguistic and sociopolitical. No text is produced which is not in some way affected by texts, both spoken and written, literary and non-literary, that have gone before it. Based on Bakhtin's idea that every utterance has some kind of dialogic relationship with other utterances which have preceded it (Bakhtin 1986), **intertextuality** in literature refers to the way in which a text may invoke other texts through the use of particular words, phrases or ideas, so the reader's or listener's knowledge of that other text comes into play in their interpretation of what the current author is saying.

ACTIVITY 1.8

Allow about
10 minutes

Read the following extract from the opening of the novel A Chain of Voices by André Brink, a contemporary South African author writing about the slave trade in nineteenth-century Afrikaner society. Consider the kinds of connection this text has with its context, and any references it makes to other texts. The narrator is a woman, Ma-Rose.

> To know is not enough. One must try to understand too. There will be a lot of talking in the Cape these days, one man's word against another's, master against slave. But what's the use? Liars all. Only a free man can tell the truth. In the shadow of death one should walk on tiptoe, for death is a deadly thing.

> (Brink, 1982, p. 19)

Comment

What knowledge of the world or of other texts do you find yourself using in interpreting the passage? You may have noticed a number of hints about the context and intertextual relationships, some of which would be more apparent when you were familiar with the whole book. For example, the word Cape conjures up associations with the southern part of South Africa. These associations may be contemporary thoughts about the establishment of democracy in the country and the abandoning of apartheid, but the reference to masters and slaves may also, depending on the reader's historical knowledge, bring to mind the early nineteenth century and the days of Afrikaans rule.

The phrase the shadow of death is evocative to those familiar with the Christian liturgy, and the twenty-third psalm: 'Yea, though I walk through the valley of the shadow of death, I will fear no evil: for thou art with me; thy rod and thy staff they comfort me'. As we discover later in the novel, Ma-Rose is resistant to the white person's religion, preferring to take counsel from her traditional spiritual world. Here, however, the words so evocative of the Christian 'comfort' are undermined by the rest of the sentence, *one should walk on tiptoe, for death is a deadly thing*, underlining the cultural difference between the white and black participants in the drama that is to unfold in the novel. Ma-Rose would advise caution where the psalmist reassures with knowledge of the after-life. We shall also discover in the story that Ma-Rose is a woman in a man's world, so the repeated use of the masculine generic *man* may be an intentional irony.

A similar intertextuality is exhibited in the poem 'Spring Cleaning' by Jean 'Binta' Breeze, who intertwines extracts from the twenty-third psalm with a description of a woman spring cleaning.

> de Lord is my shepherd
> I shall not want
>
> an she scraping
> de las crumbs
> aff de plate
> knowing ants will feed
>
> Maketh me to lie down
> in green pastures
> leadeth me beside de still
> waters

(Breeze, in France, 1993, p. 71)

In this case the juxtaposition of the two styles underlines the gulf that exists between the words of comfort of the psalm and the hard drudgery of the woman's life.

In the previous paragraphs, almost without noticing, we have taken for granted that the context of any text is the context of its production. We would probably agree that writers are influenced by their background (education, family, wealth) and their social context (country, period, history, tradition). However, many literary and linguistic theorists have also pointed out the importance of the context in which a text is 'received'; for instance, a South African with intimate and direct knowledge of the country's history may respond differently to Ma-Rose than might a student in a far-off place encountering the book on a literature course. And individual South Africans and students will vary in their reaction to the book, depending on their own personal histories and political beliefs. The 'meaning' of any text, then, is a kind of negotiation between producers and receivers, both of whom are to some extent constructed by their own cultural positioning.

The reading of texts is also historically conditioned, as particular periods attach value to particular styles of writing. Once-maligned writers may come back into fashion and be re-established as great 'artists'. For example, the work of English seventeenth-century poet John Donne went out of fashion in the eighteenth century because the expectation of 'correct' or 'polite' usage in literature was not met in his more rugged expression.

Particular cultures place value on different kinds of English language art. Oral literature has lost much of its currency in the dominant literate society of England. But in other cultures, irrespective of literacy, there are highly regarded forms of storytelling with stylistic features deriving from their oral delivery. In Ireland, for example, the tradition of storytelling survives despite the high literacy of the population. Loreto Todd (1989) shows that some features of storytelling also occur in everyday conversation in Ireland including, for example, the Irish love of hyperbole:

> He has a tongue that would clip a hedge

> She could cut beef that thin, you could a blew the slices over a mountain.

> (Todd, 1989, p. 53)

Storytelling is also highly valued in many parts of Africa. In the box below is the opening of one of the stories collected by Loreto Todd in West Africa. It was told in Kantok, an English-related pidgin language that is widely spoken and accepted as a lingua franca in Cameroon; Todd has added a Standard English translation. Notice the use of repetition in the last four sentences, echoing the oral delivery of the story.

Cameroon Folktale

Sehns no bi foh daso wan man

(Wisdom belongs to everyone)

Sohm taim bin bi we trohki bin disaid sei sehns pas mohni, so, i bin bigin foh gada sehns. i tek smohl sehns foh ehni man wei i mitohp. i swipam foh graun an i kasham as i fohl foh di skai. ehni taim we i fain sohm smohl sehns, i tekam, putam foh sohm big pohl. i gada di ting foh plenti dei. i gadaram foh plenti yia. i gadaram sotei i poht dohn fulohp foh sehns. trohki tink sei i geht ohl di sehns foh di hol graun foh i poht.

At one time Tortoise decided that wisdom was more precious than wealth, so he began to collect wisdom. He took a little from everyone he met. He swept it up from the ground and caught it as it fell from the sky. Every time he found a piece of wisdom he took it and put it in a large pot. He gathered it for many days. He gathered it for many years. He gathered it until his pot was full of wisdom. Tortoise believed he had all the wisdom of the world in his pot.

(Todd, 1979, pp. 84–5)

Some contexts have seen a transmutation of oral tradition into modern settings. The African tradition of oral songs and rhymes was exported to the Caribbean and America with the slaves, and on the plantations the ability to improvise satirical lyrics ridiculing the slave owners was highly prized. This tradition has influenced more recent phenomena such as 'dub' poetry, a highly rhythmical improvised verse form where performers are admired for their ability to invent witty and often politically astute verses to the accompaniment of instrumental music.

1.5 Conclusion

I have looked in this chapter at some of the ways in which English is used to achieve specific artistic effects in literary texts, through different kinds of foregrounding, the manipulation of rules, iconicity and the exploitation of relations of meaning within the English language system. I have looked at particular artistic techniques within narrative, including different ways of representing and framing vernacular dialogue. I have also explored how various aspects of context and intertextuality are invoked by authors, and how they influence the reader's/audience's understanding and appreciation of oral and written artistic texts.

ACTIVITY 1.9

Allow about
15 minutes

Figure 1.1 shows the different levels of language in the organisation of a text. Many of the examples we have discussed in this chapter have involved foregrounding or breaking the rules and conventions of English in relation to one or more of these levels.

Choose two examples from the chapter and, if possible, a couple of examples of your own and consider how they illustrate artistic uses of language, using any of the levels shown in the figure.

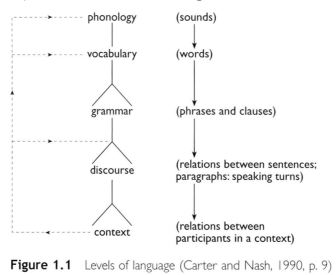

Figure 1.1   Levels of language (Carter and Nash, 1990, p. 9)

We have seen through the course of this chapter that artistic uses of English achieve their effect by creating meanings on a number of different levels simultaneously; for example, through collocation, iconicity, metaphor and irony. A further layer of meaning may be added through invoking intertextual references, or through the combination of language with visual effects, body language and movement. We can't explain art, or a particular style, with reference to any one of these levels on its own. It is the complex combination of manipulating the properties of language and context at different levels that turns English into art. This is then interpreted by readers and viewers, who bring a whole range of new contextual information to bear in their appreciation of the text and its meaning.

READING A: In the vernacular

Rib Davis
(Rib Davis is a freelance playwright and scriptwriter.)

Specially commissioned for Jeffries (1996, pp. 162–97). (Revised by the chapter author.)

> 'Why do you speak Yorkshire?' she said softly.
>
> 'That! That's non Yorkshire. That's Derby.'
>
> He looked at her with that faint, distant grin.
>
> 'Derby, then! Why do you speak Derby? You spoke natural English at first.'
>
> 'Did ah though? An' canne Ah change if Am'm a mind to't? Nay, nay, let me talk Derby if it suits me. If you'n nowt against it.'
>
> (Lawrence, 1970 [1928], p. 254)

In this extract from *Lady Chatterley's Lover* it was not in fact the 'Derby' speech of Mellors which offended his upper-class lover's sister: it was that he was clearly using it out of choice. Here was a working-class man, a gamekeeper – but nevertheless one with some education – *choosing* to use the vernacular of that part of the north Midlands of England when he was capable of using 'Standard English'. So in this novel we are at once involved with some of the key issues connected with use of the vernacular language as a reflection of class, as a statement of identity and as a means of control.

Representing regional speech

English is spoken in different ways by people in Newcastle, Aberdeen, Belfast or Swansea, in Perth, Cape Town, Toronto or Kansas City. There is a wide variety of English *accents*, so that the English sounds different, and there is a range of *dialects* – varieties of English with distinctive local vocabulary and non-standard grammar. There are also various kinds of 'slang', which may or may not be regionally defined. Yet despite what is *spoken* by most people in those places the *written* language of most fictional writing is Standard English. A surprising amount of dialogue, representing the speech of 'ordinary' people, is not written in an obviously vernacular form. However, some authors have attempted to represent the speech of their characters in ways which reflect particular aspects of accent, dialect and idiom. To most authors – as for Mellors – the use of Standard or non-standard English on each occasion is a matter of choice. The choices that the writer makes, and the apparent reasoning behind those choices, as well as the results, reflect not only upon those individual writers and their work but also on the societies from which they have emerged. But before examining further the possible reasons for writing in non-standard forms, let us look at a few more examples of how it is done. The first is from *Trainspotting* by Irvine Welsh, a contemporary novel set in Scotland.

> Ali's doon tae see aboot her rent arrears. She's pretty mad, like, screwed up and tense; but the guy behind the desk's awright. Ali explains that she's oaf the gear n she's been for a few job interviews. It goes quite well. She gits given a set amount tae pay back each week.

> (Welsh, 1993, p. 274)

The second is a depiction of black American life, *The Color Purple* by Alice Walker.

> Dear God,

> Me and Sofie work on the quilt. Got it frame up on the porch. Shug Avery donate her old yellow dress for scrap, and I work in a piece every chance I get. It a nice pattern call Sister's Choice. If the quilt turn out perfect, maybe I give it to her, if it not perfect, maybe I keep.

> (Walker, 1983, p. 53)

The third is from one of Thomas Hardy's novels set in 'Wessex' (the rural Dorset of nineteenth-century England), *Under the Greenwood Tree*.

> 'Mayble's a hearty feller enough,' the tranter replied, 'and will spak to you be you dirty or be you clane. The first time I met en was in a drong, and though 'a didn't know me no more than the dead 'a passed the time of day.'

> (Hardy, 1985 [1872], p. 92)

In each of these extracts the writer has gone to some lengths to convey the vernacular. In *Trainspotting* we have a first-person narrator, using both in his own speech and in his narration essentially the same language as the other characters in the book. The invented spelling conveys the sound of spoken language and, in the process, the very particular identity of this group of people, which includes the narrator. In the extract from Alice Walker's *The Color Purple*, on the other hand, we have a character, Celia, who is writing letters to God. Here the character's own pronunciation cannot be deduced: as she is writing letters rather than conveying the sound of speech. But her grammar is non-standard, reflecting her black working-class background in the southern states of America. In *Under the Greenwood Tree* we have a third-person narrator represented in Standard English, but a number of the characters speak in a dialect which the author attempts to write 'as it sounds'. As in the first extract, the spellings are of course not completely altered to represent the sounds of speech: in *Trainspotting* 'pretty' is not spelt 'pritty', as it would probably be pronounced, and 'enough' does not become 'enuff'. It seems that only where the author considers pronunciation to differ significantly from Received Pronunciation (RP) is the spelling changed and therefore highlighted.

Speech and characterisation

There are a number of different ways, then, to represent non-standard accents and dialect in fictional writing. As well as giving regional authenticity to a character, use of vernacular can convey particular messages about the kind of person that character is. In *Waving*, for example, by Scots writer William McIlvanney, almost the whole touching story is presented in Standard English, but the character of Duncan has a very gently noted vernacular speech, which seems to add to his naivety.

'McQueen.'

'Sur!'

The governor felt that McQueen's respect was subtly disrespectful. He invariably addressed the governor as 'Sir' but he invariably used the inflection of his West Scotland dialect, as if reminding him that they didn't quite speak the same language. 'Sur' was the fifth-column in the standard English McQueen affected when speaking to the governor.

(McIlvanney, 1990, p. 58)

In an entirely different example, Richmal Crompton uses non-standard speech for William and his friends in her 'William' novels (enduringly popular among British children, even though they are set in a lost middle-class world of the 1930s).

'Gotter bit of money this mornin',' explained William carelessly, with the air of a Rothschild.

(Crompton, 1972, p. 12)

The representation of William's speech as non-standard (in contrast to that of the rest of his family) is part of his characterisation as a nonconformist rascal.

Some authors give a character what is called an 'eye-dialect', where a word is written as non-standard, when its pronunciation is actually the same as the spoken standard; for example, *wot* and *what*. *Wot* is then a symbol, rather than an accurate representation, of non-standardness, and is often used by authors for less intelligent, less socially prestigious characters. Conversely, Dickens uses flawless Standard English for Oliver in *Oliver Twist*, despite the fact that he was brought up in poverty in the workhouse. Oliver's standard speech conveys an impression of his innate respectability and incorruptible goodness – and of course at the end of the novel he does indeed turn out to have been of high birth.

Here is an example of a vernacular being used for a different purpose again, in Raymond Chandler's depiction of the archetypal American private eye, Philip Marlowe, in *The Big Sleep*.

> I let my breath out so slowly that it hung on my lip. 'Regan?' I asked.
>
> 'Huh? Who? Oh, you mean the ex-legger the eldest girl picked up and went and married. I never saw him. What would he be doing down there?'
>
> 'Quit stalling. What would anybody be doing down there?'
>
> 'I don't know, pal. I'm dropping down to look see. Want to go along?'
>
> 'Yes.'
>
> 'Snap it up,' he said. 'I'll be in my hutch.'

> (Chandler, 1948, p. 47)

There is little resort to modified spelling, but the vocabulary and the snappy sentences create a fictional vernacular which helps to authenticate the world created by Chandler.

Invented vernaculars

Other writers have invented a new vernacular, as part of a futuristic world. In Russell Hoban's *Riddley Walker* (Figure 1), English in a post-holocaust future has undergone a frightening transformation – it has degenerated, and become corrupted in its vocabulary, its grammar, its spelling, and its meaning.

> Wunnering who ben the las to look at Greanvine befor me. That red and black stripet hard clof it wer old but not as old as Greanvine. Did it come from a Punch mans fit up or a Eusa show mans? Ben there Punch back then in what ever time Greanvine come from? How far back did Greanvine go? Ben he there when them jynt music pipes ben making ther music?

> (Hoban, 1982, p. 163)

Just as the language of the culture has mutated, so have its myths; the people are now coming to terms with their existence through new myths strangely forged from, among others, the traditional tale of Punch and Judy and the Christian legend of St Eustace (referred to in 'a Eusa showmans'). Sometimes we can guess the meanings of his words without difficulty; the significance of others we only gather after a number of uses. This is not an easy world to enter, but, like other linguistic worlds, once we are in it and have gained a little confidence, then the overcoming of further difficulties only makes us feel more a part of the whole experience, an initiate. Yet for all the logic of corruption (nouns mutating into verbs, the fairly regular shifting of one consonant to become another) this is a story about a disintegrating society. The language both tells us about that disintegration and represents it in the

On my naming day when I come 12 I gone front spear and kilt a wyld boar he parbly ben the las wyld pig on the Bundel Downs any how there hadnt ben none for a long time befor him nor I aint looking to see none agen. He dint make the groun shake nor nothing like that when he come on to my spear he wernt all that big plus he lookit poorly. He done the reqwyrt he ternt and stood and clattert his teef and made his rush and there we wer then. Him on 1 end of the spear kicking his life out and me on the other end watching him dy. I said, 'Your tern now my tern later.' The other spears gone in then and he wer dead and the steam coming up off him in the rain and we all yelt, 'Offert!'

The woal thing fealt jus that littl bit stupid. Us running that boar thru that las littl scrump of woodling with the forms all roun. Cows mooing sheep baaing cocks crowing and us foraging our las boar in a thin grey girzel on the day I come a man.

The Bernt Arse pack ben follering jus out of bow shot. When the shout gone up ther ears all prickt up. Ther leader he wer a big black and red spottit dog he come forit a littl like he ben going to make a speach or some thing til 1 or 2 bloaks uppit bow then he slumpt back agen and kep his farness follering us back. I took noatis of that leader tho. He wernt close a nuff for me to see his eyes bur I thot his eye ben on me.

Coming back with the boar on a poal we come a long by the rivver it wer hevvyer woodit in there. Thru the girzel you cud see blue smoak hanging in be tween the black trees and the stumps pink and red where they ben loppt off. Aulder trees

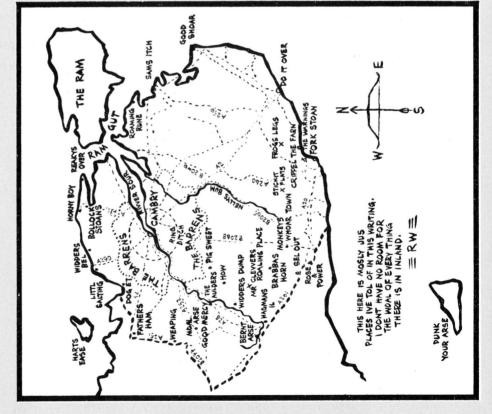

Figure 1   Map and first page from *Riddley Walker* by Russell Hoban

forms of words and phrases. As Jean-Jacques Lecercle has pointed out in
The Violence of Language, this strange language is continually reminding the
reader of the processes of corruption, and of the relationship between past
and present (Lecercle, 1990).

Hoban's vernacular has something in common with the use of language in
Anthony Burgess's *A Clockwork Orange*. Here too we are in the future, but
nadsat, the Russian-sounding vernacular of Alex and his 'malchicks', is a
vernacular expression that emphasises wilful defiance. *Nadsat* is contrasted in
the novel with something very close to Standard English – it has not
superseded it.

> The Doctor said:
>
> 'Come on, gentlemen, we don't want any trouble, do we?' in his very
> high-class goloss, but this new prestoopnick was really asking for it. You
> could viddy that he thought he was a very big bolshy veck ...

> (Burgess, 1965, p. 70)

From representation to reconstruction

In some ways the boundary between authors' representation of 'authentic'
dialects and their use of invented vernaculars is not as clear-cut as it might at
first seem. *Huckleberry Finn* (Figure 2) is one of the most influential models
of non-standard usage in English literature. It has a first-person narrator, the
young white American boy, who draws us into the world of a homeless,
rootless child on the edges of respectable society in the USA of the late
nineteenth century. Here he describes part of his wanderings, aboard a raft on
the Mississippi:

> It must 'a' been close on to one o'clock when we got below the island at
> last, and the raft did seem to go mighty slow. If a boat was to come along
> we was going to take to the canoe and break for the Illinois shore.

> (Twain, 1976 [1884], p. 41)

Although it has always been assumed that Huck spoke poor white non-
standard American, Fishkin (1993) raises some interesting questions about
Twain's sources for the character. She presents a convincing case that the
model for Huck and Huck's language was in fact a black boy, a certain
'Sociable Jimmy' whom Twain met in the early 1870s. There were, of course,
elements of the speech of other, white, boys mixed into this, yet it seems that
Huck's energetic, powerful, utterly memorable non-standard speech is based
on nineteenth-century black American vernacular speech, not on the speech
of poor whites.

What the example illustrates is the power of the vernacular in fiction writing
to add a very special kind of authenticity to the characters, the setting and the

EXPLANATORY

IN this book a number of dialects are used, to wit: the Missouri Negro dialect; the extremest form of the backwoods Southwestern dialect; the ordinary "Pike County" dialect; and four modified varieties of this last. The shadings have not been done in a haphazard fashion, or by guesswork; but painstakingly, and with the trustworthy guidance and support of personal familiarity with these several forms of speech.

I make this explanation for the reason that without it many readers would suppose that all these characters were trying to talk alike and not succeeding.

THE AUTHOR

CHAPTER I

Civilizing Huck–Miss Watson–Tom Sawyer waits

You don't know about me without you have read a book by the name of *The Adventures of Tom Sawyer;* but that ain't no matter. That book was made by Mr. Mark Twain, and he told the truth, mainly. There was things which he stretched, but mainly he told the truth. That is nothing. I never seen anybody but lied one time or another, without it was Aunt Polly, or the widow, or maybe Mary. Aunt Polly–Tom's Aunt Polly, she is–and Mary, and the Widow Douglas is all told about in that book, which is mostly a true book, with some stretchers, as I said before.

Now the way that the book winds up is this: Tom and me found the money that the robbers hid in the cave, and it made us rich. We got six thousand apiece–all gold. It was an awful sight of money when it was piled up. Well, Judge Thatcher he took it and put it out at interest, and it fetched us a dollar a day apiece all the year round–more than a body could tell what to do with. The Widow Douglas, she took me for her son, and allowed she would sivilize me; but it was rough, living in the house all the time, considering how dismal regular and decent the widow was in all her ways; and so I lit out.

I got into my old rags and my sugar-hogshead again, and was free and satisfied. But Tom Sawyer he hunted me up and said he was going to start a band of robbers, and I might join if I would go back to the widow and be respectable. So I went back.

The widow, she cried over me and called me a poor lost lamb, and she called me a lot of other names, too, but she never meant no harm by it. She put me in them new clothes again, and I couldn't do nothing but sweat and sweat, and feel all cramped up. Well, then the old thing commenced again. The widow rung a bell for supper, and you had to come to time. When you got to the table, you couldn't go right to eating but had to wait for the widow to tuck down her head and grumble a little over the victuals, though there warn't really anything the matter with them–that is, nothing only everything was cooked by itself. In a barrel of odds and ends it is different; things get mixed up, and the juice kind of swaps around, and the things go better.

After supper she got out her book and learned me about Moses and the Bullrushers, and I was in a sweat to find out all about him. But by and by she let it out that Moses had been dead a considerable long time; so then

Figure 2   Explanatory and opening page of Chapter 1 from *Huckleberry Finn* by Mark Twain

story which may not directly map on to the 'real world' being depicted. In this example, as in others throughout this reading, the author's representation of speech reflects not just the features of a particular variety of spoken English, but also specific authorial purposes, to do with plot and character development as well as imaginative authenticity. And the way in which authors use vernacular to represent a particular kind of character, or a particular sort of setting, reflects both their own attitudes and values towards different varieties of spoken English, and also those values of the society from which they have sprung.

References for this reading

Burgess, A. (1965) *A Clockwork Orange*, Harmondsworth, Penguin.

Chandler, R. (1948) *The Big Sleep*, Harmondsworth, Penguin.

Crompton, R. (1972) *Just William*, London, Collins.

Fishkin, S.F. (1993) *Was Huck Black?*, Oxford, Oxford University Press.

Hardy, T. (1985 [1872]) *Under the Greenwood Tree*, Oxford, Oxford University Press.

Hoban, R. (1982) *Riddley Walker*, London, Picador.

Lawrence, D.H. (1970 [1928]) *Lady Chatterley's Lover*, Harmondsworth, Penguin.

Lecercle, J.-J. (1990) *The Violence of Language*, London, Routledge.

McIlvanney, W. (1990) *The Prisoner in Walking Wounded*, London, Sceptre.

Twain, M. (1976 [1884]) *Huckleberry Finn*, Maidenhead, Purnell.

Walker, A. (1983) *The Color Purple*, London, The Women's Press.

Welsh, I. (1993) *Trainspotting*, London, Secker and Warburg.

A tongue, for sighing

Jane Miller

2.1 Introduction

In this chapter my aim is to explore the views of some writers about writing in English. Writers who reflect on the business of writing and on their own entry into the activity have a good deal to tell us about language and culture. As writers, they have needed to develop knowledge about language and, as a rule, an ear for its meanings, more acute and subtler than that possessed by the rest of us. Yet theirs is also a heightened version of communal, shared language use; and for the most part their reflections on writing and becoming a writer focus on the complex and changing relations which exist in any society between the spoken and written forms of the language, or languages, of that society. The written language is always the product of some form of schooling, and most writers work within tensions between the schooled character of writing and the less formal ways in which we first learnt to speak and articulate ourselves within conversations. Such reflections by writers are often incorporated into their novels and poems: as central preoccupations and as metaphors for the connections that may exist between individual consciousness and shared assumptions and values. Many writers have also lectured and written about these questions. In this chapter I consider examples of that sort of writing too.

If such reflections by writers are likely to express ambivalence and contradiction about language and, especially, about the relations between spoken and written language, we should not be surprised by that. Since ancient times, writing has mimicked and incorporated speech into all its forms: drama, epic poetry, narrative, and so on. Yet the role of the writer and the activity of writing have also been perceived as specialised, different, in some respects constraining, but in other ways susceptible to new possibilities of form and playfulness. For many writers there is a complex process of negotiation between the rich resources of memory and childhood, and public expectations of their writing. Writers rarely discuss such issues as if they were primarily academic or abstract ones. Indeed, issues of language such as these are lived as aspects of history, politics and social relations; and it is characteristic of such discussion to dwell on division and polarity.

In 'Belfast' the Irish poet Seamus Heaney, for instance, writes of one such division positively, as something at the very heart of his work. History, language, culture and consciousness are implicated in this for him:

> I speak and write in English, but do not altogether share the
> preoccupations and perspectives of an Englishman. I teach English

literature, I publish in London, but the English tradition is not ultimately home. I live off another hump as well ...

One half of one's sensibility is in a cast of mind that comes from belonging to a place, an ancestry, a history, a culture, whatever one wants to call it. But consciousness and quarrels with the self are the result of what [D.H.] Lawrence called 'the voices of my education'.

Those voices pull in two directions, back through the political and cultural traumas of Ireland, and out towards the urgencies and experience of the world beyond it ...

If you like, I began as a poet when my roots were crossed with my reading. I think of the personal and Irish pieties as vowels, and the literary awarenesses nourished on English as consonants. My hope is that the poems will be vocables adequate to my whole experience.

(Heaney, 1980, pp. 34–7)

Yet for Samuel Beckett, another Irish writer, a move from writing in English to writing in French seems to have released something vital in him and to have allowed for the rupture from his childhood, Ireland and even the particular poetic potential of English, which his work required. Writers may come to express proprietorial interests in the language in which they write, but they have usually approached that language with some anxiety about their own rights to it and to the traditions of writing which can seem to haunt the language itself.

There are tensions and contradictions at the heart of the compulsion to write at all, and their source lies in the contradictions intrinsic to all language. No speaker is ever, as Russian literary theorist Mikhail Bakhtin once wrote, 'the first speaker, the one who disturbs the eternal silence of the universe' (Bakhtin, 1986, p. 69). There has always been another speaker, just as any utterance is bound to be followed by another utterance. Every writer is similarly preceded and followed. Thus every writer writes within and against some notion of a tradition, however inhospitable that tradition may be. But every writer also endeavours and needs to contribute something else, something more, something new: to break with tradition as well as to extend and remake it. The tension lies here: in the dialogue a writer engages in with other writers, in the shared, recognisable character of language, *but also* in the equally strong impulse a writer feels to go against what is constraining, determining.

In this chapter, I focus on what have sometimes been called 'the new English literatures', and specifically on a number of writers for whom dilemmas over the language have been pressing ones, since they approached writing and English through schooling within a colonial or ex-colonial society. I then explore a contemporary woman writer, Maxine Hong Kingston, who writes from experiences of exile and dislocation, and from the strengths as well as the drawbacks of becoming a writer in English. I conclude by returning to

Seamus Heaney and to the continuities that exist between writers entering English from the peripheries, as it were, and writers whose relation to what Edward Said (1993), the Palestinian American writer, called 'the metropolitan centres' seems less problematic.

2.2 Decolonising the mind

Figure 2.1   Ngũgĩ wa Thiong'o

In 1981 Ngũgĩ wa Thiong'o, a Kenyan writer, delivered a paper called 'The language of African literature' at a conference of African writers. It is a piece he has returned to and which has been published in a number of forms and places. That paper, now a chapter in a collection of important essays called *Decolonising the Mind* (Ngũgĩ, 1986a), explains the promise he made, when his novel *Petals of Blood* was published in 1977, to stop writing in English and to write from that point onwards in either Gĩkũyũ, his first language, or Kiswahili, the Kenyan national language. A statement preceding the essays ends with the words: 'I hope that through the age old medium of translation I shall be able to continue dialogue with all.'

ACTIVITY 2.1

Read the extract from 'The language of African literature' by Ngũgĩ wa Thiong'o (Reading A). How far do you feel Ngũgĩ's decision to stop writing in English is justified?

A complex history and politics lie behind Ngũgĩ's decision to give up writing in English, and much painful drama and contention have come in its wake. Ngũgĩ was arrested and imprisoned in 1978 as a consequence of some of the anti-government views expressed in his English writing. Other writers all over the world have been moved to explain or justify their own use of English, where it stood for them as the language of imperialism, of racism, of Western assertions of cultural superiority, as well as (for some of them) having the status of a second or third language, a language learnt in school rather than at home.

It is significant that Ngũgĩ starts from his first language, from his childhood memories of its music, its meanings, its narrative riches and the linguistic awareness and values he learnt as a speaker of it. Any consideration of which language a writer may choose to write in will involve complex questions about power and culture, about the status of the language in the community where it is spoken as well as in the wider world, and about traditions of writing and the social relations to which a writer may hope to refer and contribute. But the choice of language is also an intensely personal issue. For Ngũgĩ, the language of family, of work, of stories, of literature and of pleasure was also the language in which he and many other children began their schooling. Later, he went to a school where it was banned, literally forbidden. English became, as he puts it, *the* language. Success in English was more important than success in all other areas of the curriculum. It brought with it the potential for 'colonial elitedom' and it also brought knowledge of the work of writers in English – admired writers – many of whom knew nothing of Africa or African life, though they might casually, or deliberately, cast aspersions on its institutions, inhabitants, languages, culture. As Ngũgĩ says, 'Thus language and literature were taking us further and further from ourselves to other selves, from our world to other worlds.'

Writers may be said to write from what they know but to rely on a capacity for recognition in their readers. For Ngũgĩ, his hard-won mastery of an English of great expressiveness and precision remains hopelessly contaminated by the politics of its acquisition, by the history of Kenya's colonial past, by the part played by English in education and other forms of social control, by the fact that the poorest, most oppressed groups and individuals in the country are unable to read English, by the continuing exploitation of Africa by the West and by Africa's need, in Ngũgĩ's eyes, of its own writers and their articulation and analysis of people's current experience in the literature they produce. To use English is, for Ngũgĩ, to remain mired in 'colonial alienation' and to refuse the all-important task of enabling the young to transcend the history that produced such alienation. It is to assent to a continuing European theft of African culture, as of its other 'natural' resources.

Ngũgĩ had written four novels in English, as well as essays, plays and short stories, when he decided he would not write in English again, although at first he made a distinction between his creative work and his polemical writing. The language of his early novel, *Weep Not, Child* (first published in 1964), for instance, as of his last in English, *Petals of Blood* (first published in 1977), is a spare and supple English which is able to stand in for dialogue in other languages and to communicate an elaborate and detailed social world to those who are unfamiliar with it, as well as to those whose life it more closely resembles.

Extract from the opening of *Weep Not, Child* (first published in 1964)

Nyokabi called him. She was a small, black woman, with a bold but grave face. One could tell by her small eyes full of life and warmth that she had once been beautiful. But time and bad conditions do not favour beauty. All the same, Nyokabi had retained her full smile – a smile that lit up her dark face.

'Would you like to go to school?'

'O, mother!' Njoroge gasped. He half feared that the woman might withdraw her words. There was a little silence till she said,

'We are poor. You know that.'

'Yes, mother.' His heart pounded against his ribs slightly. His voice was shaky.

'So you won't be getting a mid-day meal like other children.'

'I understand.'

'You won't bring shame to me by one day refusing to attend school?'

O mother, I'll never bring shame to you. Just let me get there, just let me. The vision of his childhood again opened before him. For a time he contemplated the vision. He lived in it alone. It was just there, for himself; a bright future ... Aloud he said, 'I like school.'

He said this quietly. His mother understood him.

'All right. You'll begin on Monday. As soon as your father gets his pay we'll go to the shops. I'll buy you a shirt and a pair of shorts.'

(Ngũgĩ, 1976 [1964], p. 3)

Ngũgĩ does not, as some writers in his position do, mimic the patterns and rhythms of the speech of his characters, or attempt to reproduce their actual language, though in *Petals of Blood* he introduces, without glossary but in helpful context, items of vocabulary from Gĩkũyũ. His novels carry the pain and conflict of the postcolonial experience, and his English smoothly (perhaps too smoothly for Ngũgĩ's own peace of mind) conveys the tensions involved in being schooled out of the culture of childhood and into values and understandings which are explicitly grounded in views of that childhood world as a primitive tribal one, better forgotten and abandoned. Yet the reality of what could be delivered by an English education was often the kind of empty, rootless, isolated existence lived by Ngũgĩ's central characters, men unnourished by what they have so painfully acquired and cut off from the society they hope to serve.

Such a character is Godfrey Munira in *Petals of Blood*, whose training and experience as a teacher have made him unable to meet the real needs of his pupils. The shoddiness of the educational legacy he has inherited is contrasted with the children's intelligence and curiosity. Here, he has just returned from taking them out on a walk to study nature:

> He was pleased with himself. But then the children started asking him awkward questions. Why did things eat each other? Why can't the eaten eat back? Why did God allow this and that to happen? He had never bothered with those kinds of questions and to silence them he told them that it was simply a law of nature. What was a law? What was nature? Was he a man? Was he God? A law was simply a law and nature was nature. What about men and God? Children, he told them, it's time for a break.

(Ngũgĩ, 1986b [1977], p. 22)

Ngũgĩ's novels in English have not only treated the effects of colonialism on Kenyan life. He also acknowledges that he learnt from Western writers (particularly from Joseph Conrad) vital narrative techniques, without which he found it hard to imagine writing fiction.

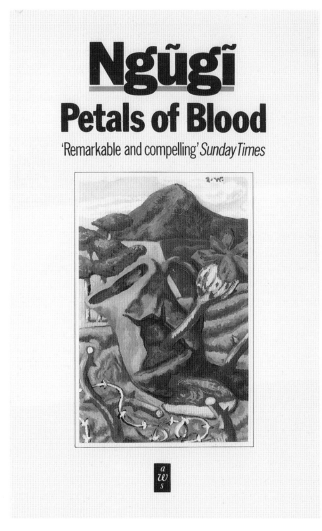

Figure 2.2 Front cover of *Petals of Blood*

When Ngũgĩ decided to write in Gĩkũyũ, which had at that time a relatively undeveloped literature, he could not at first find traditions of written narrative to help him. Then, as he points out in his essay 'The language of African fiction', which was first published in 1984, he looked elsewhere:

> Now my own observation of how people ordinarily narrated events to one another had also shown me that they quite happily accepted interventions, digressions, narrative within a narrative and dramatic illustrations without losing the main narrative thread. The story-within-a-story was part and parcel of the conversational norms of the peasantry. The linear/biographical unfolding of a story was more removed from actual social practice than the narrative of Conrad and [George] Lamming.
>
> (Ngũgĩ, 1986a, p. 76)

In the earlier essay, 'The language of African literature', mentioned above, Ngũgĩ (1986a) recalls a conference of African writers at Makerere University in Uganda, which he attended as a young man in 1962. He wanted above all to show *Weep Not, Child* to Chinua Achebe, the somewhat older and already greatly admired Nigerian writer. Much of Ngũgĩ's argumentative writing has taken the form of a dialogue with Achebe. It is helpful, therefore, to consider the older writer's position on the use of English.

2.3 Appropriating English

Achebe also remembers the famous Makerere conference in his article 'English and the African writer', which was first published in 1965. In this, he argues strongly for a *national* as opposed to what he calls an *ethnic* literature. He too is arguing from what he sees as the *reality* of an Africa where alienation has indeed been an inevitable consequence of the kind of education a carefully selected minority of children received. Achebe's 'reality' has also included the dozens of languages spoken in addition to English. For Achebe, though, the imposition of English, however arbitrary, has made it possible for Africans to talk to one another. If, as he puts it, the British failed to give Africans a song, they 'at least gave them a tongue, for sighing'. He acknowledges that English is a 'world language which history has forced down our throats', but is convinced that to insist that 'any true African literature must be written in African languages ... would be merely pursuing a dead end, which can only lead to sterility, uncreativity and frustration'. He continues:

> What I do see is a new voice coming out of Africa, speaking of African experience in a world-wide language. So my answer to the question, Can an African ever learn English well enough to be able to use it effectively in creative writing? is certainly yes. If on the other hand you ask: Can he ever learn to use it like a native speaker? I should say, I hope not. It is neither necessary nor desirable for him to be able to do so. The price a world language must be prepared to pay is submission to many different kinds

of use. The African writer should aim to use English in a way that brings out his message best without altering the language to the extent that its value as a medium of international exchange will be lost.

(Achebe, 1965, p. 29)

'For me', he goes on, 'there is no other choice. I have been given this language and I intend to use it.'

Figure 2.3 Chinua Achebe

ACTIVITY 2.2

Allow about 10 minutes

What are the relative advantages and disadvantages of Ngũgĩ's and Achebe's positions, in terms of reaching out to a reading audience?

It is possible to see both Ngũgĩ and Achebe as grappling with versions of the same history, the same dilemma. Both see English as loaded with a past, with traditions of writing and of education which are at once damaging and a challenge to them as African writers. Learning English has usually involved contempt for the languages they grew up with, as well as their banning. A successful education was always meant to separate a child from his or her family, to inculcate other, Western values. Both writers know that their entry into English as writers exposes them to criticism on two counts: for betrayal of the people and the values they grew up with and for writing what may then be read as culpably un-English English. To write in English is to use the imperialist language to express the experience of people who have been colonised and exploited in a language more accessible to the colonisers than to the colonised. To write in Gĩkũyũ, as Ngũgĩ now does, is to write for a known readership, while leaving a potentially large international audience to encounter his work through translation. For Achebe, his use of English entails 'altering', 'making new' a language which may have been forced on him but which, by now, he has claimed as his own. That appropriation of the oppressor's language constitutes a strength for Achebe. In a later essay, called 'Colonialist criticism', first published in 1975, he writes: 'And let no one be fooled by the fact that we may write in English for we intend to do unheard of things with it' (Achebe, 1988, p. 50).

The English of Achebe's novels is able to represent a subtle range of language: intimate, ritualistic, fiercely resistant to some aspects of English usage, on the one hand; and infected by varieties of English Englishes and African Englishes, on the other.

Extract from *Things Fall Apart* (first published in 1958)

That year the harvest was sad, like a funeral, and many farmers wept as they dug up the miserable and rotting yams. One man tied his cloth to a tree branch and hanged himself.

Okonkwo remembered that tragic year with a cold shiver throughout the rest of his life. It always surprised him when he thought of it later that he did not sink under the load of despair. He knew he was a fierce fighter, but that year had been enough to break the heart of a lion.

'Since I survived that year,' he always said, 'I shall survive anything.' He put it down to his inflexible will.

His father, Unoka, who was then an ailing man, had said to him during that terrible harvest month: 'Do not despair. I know you will not despair. You have a manly and a proud heart. A proud heart can survive a general failure because such a failure does not prick its pride. It is more difficult and more bitter when a man fails *alone*.'

Unoka was like that in his last days. His love of talk had grown with age and sickness. It tried Okonkwo's patience beyond words.

(Achebe, 1976 [1958], pp. 17–18)

In his essay 'Named for Victoria, Queen of England' Achebe writes of his languages, his bilingualism:

> I don't know for certain but I have probably spoken more words in Igbo than English but I have definitely written more words in English than Igbo. Which I think makes me perfectly bilingual. Some people have suggested that I should be better off writing in Igbo. Sometimes they seek to drive

the point home by asking me in which language I dream. When I reply
that I dream in both languages they seem not to believe it.

(Achebe, 1988, p. 22)

Achebe sees his contribution to Africa in a different way from Ngũgĩ, for
whom, in 'The language of African literature', 'language was the means of the
spiritual subjugation', just as 'the bullet was the means of the physical
subjugation' (Ngũgĩ, 1986a, p. 9). Achebe writes:

I would be quite satisfied if my novels (especially the ones set in the past)
did no more than teach their readers that their past – with all its
imperfections – was not one long night of savagery.

(cited in Dathorne, 1975, p. 67)

These two African writers may have arrived at diametrically opposed solutions
to questions about using English and other languages in their work as writers,
but in doing so they illustrate some central themes about writing: themes that
have occupied monolingual writers too.

2.4 The politics of entry into English

Language is learnt in conversations, and conversations are conducted between
speakers who are unequal, if only temporarily or shiftingly so. If two speakers
were possessed of identical thoughts, knowledge and language there would,
after all, be no need for them to communicate at all. So inequalities are built
into all language use from the beginning, intrinsic to dialogue. Children learn
from their earliest conversations with adults that they are children, and
therefore smaller, younger, less knowledgeable about the world and different
from adults in these and other respects. But in their conversations with adults
they are also learning about conversations and about how adults behave in
them; about difference, inequality and power; and that language enables some
manipulation of those relations, some possibilities for change and
destabilisation of the status quo.

What we may take from the debate between Ngũgĩ and Achebe is that the
inequalities inherent in much language use match larger social and historical
inequalities. Where, for instance, English is learnt as a second or additional
language in parts of the world once colonised by Britain, that language
learning has not been neutral, any more than teaching children who speak a
London or a Caribbean dialect of English to speak and write in Standard
British English is neutral. The languages of schooling will always carry the
ambiguities inherent in the reasons there are for learning them. If they are
potentially 'empowering' they are also potentially undermining and exposing.
There is more to it than that, of course, for Achebe and Ngũgĩ may be thought
to have different visions of the future of African countries, and therefore of
the role that English and other languages will play in them. For Achebe, the

future demands forms of compromise with the rest of the world, in so far as they encourage African unity and productive two-way communication between African and other countries. For Ngũgĩ, the future must start from revolutionary change within a country like Kenya, and with the recovery and remaking of Kenya's own identity.

Another Nigerian writer, Buchi Emecheta, says of the heroine of her first novel, *In the Ditch*:

> Trouble with Adah was that she could never speak good London English, or cockney. Her accent and words always betrayed the fact that she had learned her English via *English for Foreign Students*.

(Emecheta, 1979 [1972], p. 69)

Emecheta's novels are set sometimes in Nigeria and sometimes in London, where she has spent most of her adult, writing life. All the novels tell stories about the pressures there are in both societies on a woman who manages to snatch her own independence out of the unthinking oppressions meted out to her. English and an education become aspects of such a woman's capacity to resist and make a life for herself. Yet traditional storytelling, as it is performed by women to circles of adults and children, and which Emecheta remembers from her own village childhood, provides her with what she has seen as specifically female narrative vantage points: the storyteller as teacher, explainer, rearer of children. She allows her heroines the specialised role of cultural transmitter, even within cultures which undermine women materially and socially. Like other writers in a similar position, she has used that position's ambivalence and the vulnerability it confers on her as focus, subject matter and narrative approach. Adah's 'good' schooled English can never be an unambiguous good in a world where, as a black and single mother on the breadline, she must live within as well as against other people's limiting perceptions of her. Yet Adah's sense of the discrepancy between her 'good' English and the worlds she inhabits, whether in Nigeria or in England, is also at the heart of Emecheta's purpose as a writer.

2.5 Recreating dialogue

The 'good' English of a novel undertakes above all to recreate through fictional narrative the speech and thoughts of its characters. How does English – indeed, how do Englishes – do that? In the novels of Ngũgĩ and Achebe, and in most of Emecheta's, the characters are not – for the most part – having conversations or thinking their thoughts in English. In Achebe's *Arrow of God* (1974 [1958]), a novel about time and generation and the painful evolution of a tribal community towards a compromise with Western values, with Christianity and with English, that process is compressed in the scene in Reading B, as two policemen come to arrest Ezeulu, the chief priest, whose authority is threatened just at the point when he is preparing – disastrously, as it turns out – to make overtures to the local white officials and to the powers they stand for.

ACTIVITY 2.3

Read the extract from *Arrow of God* by Chinua Achebe (Reading B). Notice the kind of English he uses to represent the policemen's and villagers' exchanges in Igbo, in contrast to his representation of the policemen's switch to a variety of English when addressing each other.

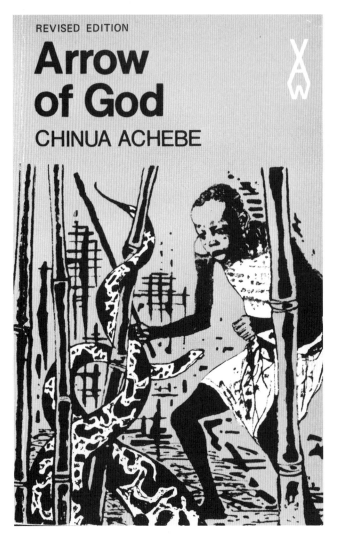

Figure 2.4 Front cover of *Arrow of God*

For the conversation in Igbo, Achebe uses a rather formal Standard English with Igbo idioms (e.g. 'I shall slap okro seeds out of your mouth'). The policemen talking together, however, use a pidgin English and Achebe represents both its grammar ('we no go return back') and pronunciation ('Gi me dat ting') in written form. Here, the language does more than tell us about the penetration of English and of British rule generally into African life. It *enacts* that penetration and the confusions produced by it. What Achebe so ironically achieves here is an impression that the two policemen have literally taken leave of their senses in direct proportion to their reliance on English to disconcert and intimidate their non-English-speaking compatriots. By comparison, the English Achebe uses to represent their speech in Igbo allows them rationality. It is not simply that writers have different histories of writing in English, nor that their reasons for choosing English or another language reflect a different politics or different theories of language. It is also the case that the English they create in their novels enacts quite different kinds of social relations.

Indian writers have also developed a range of techniques for representing dialogue in different languages. In an illuminating essay on the English used by characters in novels by the Indian writers R.K. Narayan and Mulk Raj Anand and by V.S. Naipaul, the Trinidadian East Indian writer, Ann Lowry (1982) usefully distinguishes between their quite different approaches. Whereas the English of Narayan's novels is in some sense 'transparent' – a language for writing about people who for the most part speak forms of non-standard or Standard Tamil, forms which are not represented and are rarely even alluded to by Narayan – the more politically committed Anand assembles an English which acknowledges its complex and everyday proximity to and entanglement with Hindi and the other Indian languages spoken by variously mixed collections of people. For instance, there are in his novels English characters speaking bad Hindi and Indian characters using educated and uneducated varieties of Hindi (see the extract from *Coolie* in the box below).

Extract from *Coolie* (first published in 1936)

Munoo lifted the tray lightly as soon as he heard his mistress answer his question and walked away with a wonderful agility while she abused and warned and threatened with a copious flow of her hard, even chatter.

'Here we are, children!' said Prem, clapping his hands. 'Here is the tea! A bit late, but never mind!'

'The tea! The tea!' exclaimed Sheila, her blue eyes melting, her lips contracting.

'Ooon, aaan! I want the tea, too!' sobbed Lila from where she sat on a table swaying her head to the music, in a ridiculously childish

---

manner, which amused her elder sister, her uncle and her father, when that last worthy was not too embarrassed to come and play with his children.

'Put it down here, you black man!' said Prem, with mock anger in the wrong Hindustani which he sometimes affected, especially in the face of anything so European as a tea tray or when dressed in an English suit, in imitation of the tone in which Englishmen talk to their native servants. 'Put it down on this table, black man, you who relieve yourself on the ground!'

(Anand, 1945 [1936], pp. 23–4)

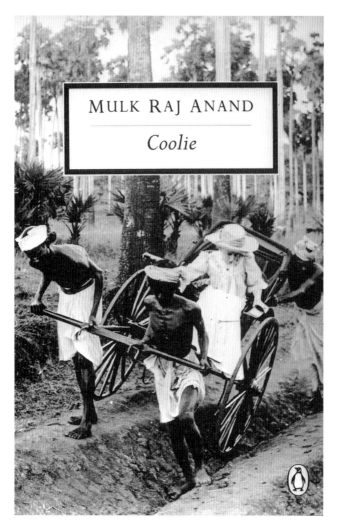

Figure 2.5   Front cover of *Coolie*

All this is written in an English made permeable not just to the particular Indian varieties of English spoken in India, but also to the vast range of separate and overlapping languages and dialects which characterise most urban Indian settings.

Lowry's account of how Naipaul uses English in *A House for Mr Biswas* (first published in 1961) suggests yet more possibilities. She points to three principal ways in which English is modified by Naipaul in order to suggest quite different kinds of language spoken by characters in the novel. In the first, Standard (educated) English dialogue stands in for Hindi speech; in the second, English dialect forms are written as they would be spoken; and finally, 'in a few rare cases [Standard] English dialogue is spoken by one of the characters, but the hesitation and care with which he/she speaks is always noted by the narrator' (Lowry, 1982, p. 291). Naipaul marks these shifts across varieties of West Indian speech by modifying the grammar.

ACTIVITY 2.4

Allow about 10 minutes

In the following extract from his novel *A House for Mr Biswas*, can you identify examples of the three ways in which Naipaul represents the different kinds of language spoken by characters in the novel?

This extract comes from the funeral scene at the beginning of the novel, when Mr Biswas's father is about to be buried.

> The photographer, of mixed Chinese, Negro and European blood, did not understand what was being said. In the end he and some of the men took the coffin out to the verandah and stood it against the wall.
>
> 'Careful! Don't let him fall out.'
>
> 'Goodness. All the marigolds have dropped out.'
>
> 'Leave them,' the photographer said in English. 'Is a nice little touch. Flowers on the ground.' He set up his tripod in the yard, just under the ragged eaves of thatch, and put his head under the black cloth.
>
> Tara roused Bipti from her grief, arranged Bipti's hair and veil, and dried Bipti's eyes.
>
> 'Five people all together,' the photographer said to Tara. 'Hard to know just how to arrange them. It look to me that it would have to be two one side and three the other side. You sure you want all five?'
>
> Tara was firm.
>
> The photographer sucked his teeth, but not at Tara. 'Look, look. Why nobody ain't put anything to chock up the coffin and prevent it from slipping?'
>
> Tara had that attended to.

The photographer said, 'All right then. Mother and biggest son on either side. Next to mother, young boy and young girl. Next to big son, smaller son.'

There was more advice from the men.

'Make them look at the coffin.'

'At the mother.'

'At the youngest boy.'

The photographer settled the matter by telling Tara, 'Tell them to look at me.'

Tara translated, and the photographer went under his cloth. Almost immediately he came out again. 'How about making the mother and the biggest boy put their hands on the edge of the coffin?'

This was done and the photographer went back under his cloth.

'Wait!' Tara cried, running out from the hut with a fresh garland of marigolds. She hung it around Raghu's neck and said to the photographer in English, 'All right. Draw your photo now.'

(Naipaul, 1992 [1961], pp. 33–4)

Comment

In the initial exchange over the placing of the coffin against the wall, Standard English represents speech in Hindi. The photographer's English dialect, however, is written as it would be spoken (notice the grammatical variation from Standard English). For Tara's final remark, Naipaul has her use a grammatically, but not idiomatically, correct Standard English.

In such ways Naipaul is able to produce what are in effect new and hybrid forms of language. The social and language situations they evoke are even more complex than the kinds of mimicry to be found in the fiction of monolingual writers working within purely class or regionally differentiated language communities. They also constitute an aspect of the difficulties that many such writers express concerning the relation of what they write to those they write about: difficulties of distance and dissociation. At best, this produces the exquisite ironies of Narayan and Naipaul. Yet that irony is often imbued with pain and ambivalence; in Naipaul's case the ridicule rarely avoids some element of cruelty. And Narayan, for instance, can seem to be inviting us to laugh at people he understands better than we do, while simultaneously warning us that we mock them at our peril. Yet he gives no sense of having a problem about writing in English and writing novels which are set in a non-English-speaking town in south India. Indeed, he has written:

> English has proved that if a language has flexibility any experience can be communicated through it, even if it has to be paraphrased sometimes rather than conveyed ... In order not to lose the excellence of this medium some writers in India took to writing in English, and produced a literature that was perhaps not first-class; often the writing seemed imitative, halting, inapt, or an awkward translation of a vernacular, mode or idiom; but occasionally it was brilliant. We are all experimentalists. I may straightaway explain what we do not attempt to do. We are not attempting to write Anglo-Saxon English.

(cited in Killam, 1976, p. 131)

Figure 2.6 Front cover of *A House for Mr Biswas*

Figure 2.7 V.S. Naipaul

2.6 English and cultural identity

For many – perhaps most – writers, there is probably no question of having a choice of languages in which to write, as Ngũgĩ and Achebe have. Narayan seems not to have considered writing in Tamil or Kannada, and for Naipaul it appears that Hindi was never a possible language for him to write in. Moreover, slavery, indentured labour and all the other material deprivations of colonialism have often obliterated people's languages; and certainly, for many of those languages, have impeded the development of literacy. In the English-speaking Caribbean, for instance, writers have never had a serious alternative to writing in English. Yet the business of writing at all confronts such writers with parallel issues of identity and of history and power. In the passage from 'Prologue to an autobiography' in Reading C, V.S. Naipaul, whose use of English we have already considered and who grew up in an East Indian, Hindu and rural community in Trinidad, remembers writing the first lines of his first published book, the collection of stories called *Miguel Street*.

ACTIVITY 2.5

Read the extract from *Finding the Centre* by V.S. Naipaul (Reading C). In what ways does Naipaul feel ambivalent about writing and about his own cultural identity?

It is a characteristic irony that Naipaul should have produced those first lines in a BBC office at the heart of an empire whose divisions and depredations underpinned the humorous stories he was writing. These are woven out of his memories of the two years or so when his family moved from the countryside in Trinidad to Port of Spain. Naipaul's emphasis is not on the use of English itself – for, as I have said, despite being brought up in a Hindi-speaking family he seems always to have regarded English as his principal language – but on the crucial nuances of accent and phrasing which characterise the racial and class distinctions that mark out the lives of his characters in *Miguel Street*, and which in their turn reflect a long history of migrations from Africa and India to the Caribbean.

Here the narrator's problems are ones of voice, of point of view, of his own relation to the Trinidad of his childhood and the relation of that experience to the activity of literature, the 'calling' of the writer. That 'calling' – one he has aspired to in emulation of a father who was for a time a journalist as well as a writer of humorous stories about the Indian community in Trinidad, but who seems somehow always to have risked failure and courted ridicule in his son's eyes – occasions for Naipaul the extremes of both ambition and anxiety. The very notion of 'writer' is felt as foreign, imported from the metropolis, unrealisable. Derek Walcott, the St Lucian poet, has said of his initiation into writing: 'I had entered the house of literature as a houseboy' (Walcott, 1973, p. 77). The purveyors of a culture beamed out from the London headquarters of the BBC to the far-flung Commonwealth, and offered as capaciously inclusive of all those parts of the world once governed from Britain, can scarcely have dreamt that the worldwide dissemination of the English language might produce not just readers and listeners of English but writers of English too. Was it ever predicted, one wonders, by those who legislated for the teaching of English literature in India in the early nineteenth century that India might one day produce many of the best writers of English in the world?

Naipaul's father 'dangled all his life in a half-dependence and half-esteem between these two powerful families'. Naipaul's rootlessness, his isolation, can seem wilfully dangling at times, even excessive. But for him that 'calling' of writer has entailed a life of restless movement, of needing to recognise and understand what must necessarily be new and strange, to return again and again to the Caribbean and to other parts of the world to which Indians have moved and tried to make lives for themselves. And then, as he puts it:

> A writer after a time carries his world with him, his own burden of experience, human experience and literary experience (one deepening the other); and I do believe – especially after writing 'Prologue to an Autobiography' – that I would have found equivalent connections with my past and myself wherever I had gone.

> (Naipaul, 1984, p. 10)

The exalted and even heroic role of writer accompanies something like a settled pessimism in Naipaul's view of the society he has left and the societies to which he has been – provisionally – drawn. The complex world of the Caribbean, in which he grew up, is unable within this view to provide 'mature social experience'. So it is only as a rootless wanderer that Naipaul can find a role for himself as a man and as a writer, or, as he puts it, 'a looker' (Naipaul, 1984, p. 11). His language aspires to be universally communicative, alluding to the local, the particular, the specialised, but forever determined on keeping its distance from the idiomatic, the oral, the hybrid, the colonial, all that he deemed to be second-rate.

There are useful parallels as well as contrasts here with the work of Barbadian poet Edward Kamau Brathwaite, for whom the immigrant (indeed, the *emigrant*) – a two-way fugitive and an essential figure, actual and metaphoric, of West Indian culture – is quite differently understood. However, in his essay 'Caribbean critics' (first published in 1969), a generous and illuminating reading of Naipaul's early novels, Brathwaite writes:

> In the very process of rejecting West Indian society, Naipaul, in *Miguel Street* (1951) and *A House for Mr. Biswas* (1961), embraces and examines it most intimately. This is the real source of Naipaul's irony. It is the literary expression of a deeply rooted cultural dichotomy. The apparently Eurocentric East Indian remains a West Indian.

(Brathwaite, 1993, p. 124)

Figure 2.8   Kamau Brathwaite

2.7 Marginality and language

The desire to articulate new ways of life, new truths, can seem to conflict with the learning of rules, with what may even be the subservience required for the learning of another language or a language which is learnt as another's. And all language is another's as well as our own. Obedience to rules and conventions is part of how we relate to language, but notions of theft and appropriation have their place too. For we also need to appreciate how writers attempt to alter language, as Achebe puts it, to remake it, in order to say what has not yet been said, to represent or reflect experiences and points of view which have been absent or subsumed within more familiar discourses.

'The new English literatures' may be read as by and large a legacy of British colonialism. Their writers have highlighted issues related to the choice of writing in English or in the other languages of a community. But they have done more than that. They have focused on the status of writers and of writing in societies with an oral rather than a literate culture, where an emphasis on English is associated with aspirations towards modernity and internationalism, and with education, science and technology. Most of all, writers have demonstrated that confronting these conflicts is a source of extraordinary vitality in itself.

Figure 2.9 Maxine Hong Kingston

Many women have written of dilemmas like these as specifically ones of gender, and Maxine Hong Kingston has seen gender as indivisibly implicated in racial and linguistic identity. She was brought up in a Chinese community in San Francisco. Her two novels about the history of Chinese emigration to America: a woman's novel and a man's, are distinguished by their narrative forms. *The Woman Warrior* (first published in 1977) relies on her mother's stories, on what she calls 'talk-stories', tales and sagas which move between her past in China, a more distant past there, and episodes from the present world of ghosts: white Americans, among whom Chinese people move invisibly and inaudibly.

The history of Chinese emigration to America is of men leaving China for the 'Gold Mountain' to look for work and either returning or sending for their wives and children. So men and women do, quite literally, have different stories to tell. But the story of the exploitation of Chinese men's labour, usually in order to build the railway, is one the men are either too 'frail' or too bludgeoned to tell the girl. In *China Men*, Maxine Hong Kingston (1981a

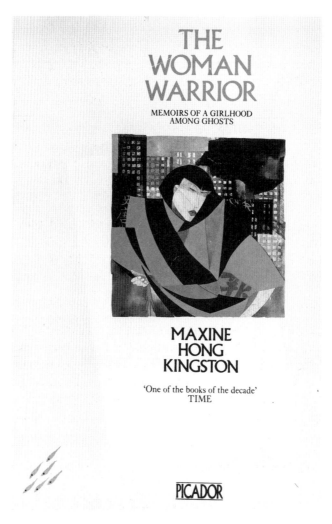

Figure 2.10 Front cover of *The Woman Warrior*

[1980]) writes a history parallel to the one she has constructed from her own stories and her mother's. The prose changes. She works in libraries, ferrets out of history books what has usually been ignored by them, fills in the details imaginatively. So little does she hear from men about their feelings and thoughts that she is obliged to invent for them.

Language, speech and writing become mandatory for survival in *The Woman Warrior*. How is the girl at its centre to become visible, audible? In Reading D all the terrors surrounding the voice are rehearsed, as it chants and mimics, vanishes and contorts itself, gives itself away. And then, even in Chinese school, where the children shriek and play freely, she realises that 'You can't entrust your voice to the Chinese, either; they want to capture your voice for their own use. They want to fix up your tongue to speak for them' (Hong Kingston, 1981b [1977], p. 152).

ACTIVITY 2.6

Read the extract from *The Woman Warrior* by Maxine Hong Kingston (Reading D). How do you interpret the significance of Hong Kingston's initial silence at the American school, and her ambiguous feelings about her own voice?

It seems to me there are few metaphors more vivid than Hong Kingston's for the compulsion to write, the hazards of doing so and the need to forge a language which will carry what V.S. Naipaul called 'my very particularity' and which Maxine Hong Kingston invokes elsewhere in the novel with the question:

> Chinese-Americans, when you try to understand what things in you are Chinese, how do you separate what is peculiar to childhood, to poverty, insanities, one family, your mother who marked your growing with stories, from what is Chinese? What is Chinese tradition and what is the movies?

(Hong Kingston, 1981b [1977], p. 13)

Through all the whirling and conflicting stories that the novel's nameless heroine hears, tells herself or participates in she is also making herself, and in two languages: 'And all the time I was having to turn myself American-feminine, or no dates' (Hong Kingston, 1981b [1977], p. 49). The pressure is on her to speak and to hear herself speak, for 'insane people were the ones who couldn't explain themselves' (p. 166).

2.8 Conclusion

I began with the words of the contemporary Irish poet Seamus Heaney, and with his offer of a poetry which springs from the experience of division and tension between the inherited and the learnt. I shall now return to Heaney, and to his engagement with the St Lucian poet Derek Walcott in his essay 'The murmur of Malvern', where he discusses Walcott's collection of poems *The Star-Apple Kingdom*.

ACTIVITY 2.7

Read the extract from 'The murmur of Malvern' by Seamus Heaney (Reading E). How does Heaney link Walcott with J.M. Synge, the Irish playwright who used the speech of the west coast peasants in his plays, and with William Langland, a fourteenth-century English poet?

This is Heaney's first characterisation of Walcott's achievement:

> I imagine he has done for the Caribbean what Synge did for Ireland, found a language woven out of dialect and literature, neither folksy nor condescending, a singular idiom evolved out of one man's inherited

divisions and obsessions, an idiom which allows an older life to exult in itself and yet at the same time keeps the cool of 'the new'.

(Heaney, 1988, p. 23)

Heaney insists on Walcott's fine ear for both speech and written language, and on his capacity to make new forms through the exploration and the bridging of these diverse traditions. But he goes further than this, further than a consideration of what Walcott has taken from the speech of the Caribbean and the traditions of English poetry. His comparing of Walcott with J.M. Synge is intended to remind us of the language Synge brought to the plays he wrote about the Irish peasantry, and to reinforce Heaney's elegant formulation that Walcott 'made a theme of the choice and the impossibility of choosing'. The substance of both writers' work emerges from the tensions inherent in attempting to reconcile forms of English which carry the history of colonial hostilities.

Heaney's interest is also in the kind of contribution Walcott makes to poetry written in English. His reading of Walcott's poem 'The Schooner Flight' returns it to what he traces as the poem's 'origins' in *Piers Plowman*, the fourteenth-century poem by William Langland. Heaney makes a boldly resonant move as he argues for Walcott's poetry becoming, as he puts it, 'a common resource', a language deriving its strength and texture from a history of struggle and offering quite new connections. It is fitting that two contemporary poets writing in English, one Irish, the other Caribbean, should come together, as the friends they are, but also as poets who share a sense of difference and a language able to generate forms of literature from what has first been heard as a ringing in the ear.

We have been listening to voices and reading the written language which invokes and comments on those voices. Far from the efficient, transparent tool it is sometimes thought to be, language is the stuff of pain and pleasure, fear and confidence, allegiance and furious rejection. As Guyanese poet David Dabydeen has put it in his essay 'On not being Milton: nigger talk in England today', 'It's hard to put two words together in creole without swearing. Words are spat out from the mouth like live squibs, not pronounced with elocution' (Dabydeen, 1990, p. 3). Languages can seem to stand for authority and regulation while simultaneously inviting us to regard them as malleable, permeable, responsive to our needs.

Towards the end of his book *Culture and Imperialism*, Edward Said offers this as a proposal for the future:

> Texts ... are tied to circumstances and to politics large and small, and these require attention and criticism. No one can take stock of everything, of course, just as no one theory can explain or account for the connections among texts and societies. But reading and writing texts are never neutral activities: there are interests, powers, passions, pleasures entailed no matter how aesthetic or entertaining the work. Media, political economy,

mass institutions – in fine, the tracings of secular power and the influence of the state – are part of what we call literature. And just as it is true that we cannot read literature by men without also reading literature by women – so transfigured has been the shape of literature – it is also true that we cannot deal with the literature of the peripheries without also attending to the literature of the metropolitan centres.

(Said, 1993, p. 384)

To many people in the world a lifetime's poverty, disenfranchisement or exile can make the notion of 'the hybrid' no more than a fashionable and luxurious imperative, attractive to those who are bored by the excesses and the barriers of nationalism or sectarianism. Yet ultimately, I think, Said must be right to insist that:

Exile, far from being the fate of nearly forgotten unfortunates who are dispossessed and expatriated, becomes something closer to a norm, an experience of crossing boundaries and charting new territories in defiance of the classic canonic enclosures, however much its loss and sadness should be acknowledged and registered.

(Said, 1993, p. 384)

It is possible to understand some of the energy of the writers we have been considering as emerging, nourished, from such a struggle. There is more to it than that, though. Said not only directs us to the modern world and its characteristic disjunctions and redistributions. He also reminds us of history, of geography and of those patterns of language change and renewal which have so regularly signalled new vitalities among writers as well as new functions for literature. An understanding of the geography of language, of its relation to landscape and to the lives lived within these physical worlds is essential to Said's picture of a culture in which the metropolitan centres depend on and are revived by the traffic with the rest of the world that language makes possible.

READING A: Extract from 'The language of African literature'

Ngũgĩ wa Thiong'o
(Ngũgĩ wa Thiong'o is a highly acclaimed Kenyan novelist, essayist, playwright and teacher of African writing.)

Source: Ngũgĩ wa Thiong'o (1986a) *Decolonising the Mind: The Politics of Language in African Literature*, London, James Currey, pp. 10–12, 27–8.

I was born into a large peasant family: father, four wives and about twenty-eight children. I also belonged, as we all did in those days, to a wider extended family and to the community as a whole.

We spoke Gĩkũyũ as we worked in the fields. We spoke Gĩkũyũ in and outside the home. I can vividly recall those evenings of story-telling around the fireside. It was mostly the grown-ups telling the children but everybody was interested and involved. We children would re-tell the stories the following day to other children who worked in the fields picking the pyrethrum flowers, tea-leaves or coffee beans of our European and African landlords.

The stories, with mostly animals as the main characters, were all told in Gĩkũyũ. Hare, being small, weak but full of innovative wit and cunning, was our hero. We identified with him as he struggled against the brutes of prey like lion, leopard, hyena. His victories were our victories and we learnt that the apparently weak can outwit the strong. We followed the animals in their struggle against hostile nature – drought, rain, sun, wind – a confrontation often forcing them to search for forms of co-operation. But we were also interested in their struggles amongst themselves, and particularly between the beasts and the victims of prey. These twin struggles, against nature and other animals, reflected real-life struggles in the human world.

Not that we neglected stories with human beings as the main characters. There were two types of characters in such human-centred narratives: the species of truly human beings with qualities of courage, kindness, mercy, hatred of evil, concern for others; and a man-eat-man two-mouthed species with qualities of greed, selfishness, individualism and hatred of what was good for the larger co-operative community. Co-operation as the ultimate good in a community was a constant theme. It could unite human beings with animals against ogres and beasts of prey, as in the story of how dove, after being fed with castor-oil seeds, was sent to fetch a smith working far away from home and whose pregnant wife was being threatened by these man-eating two-mouthed ogres.

There were good and bad story-tellers. A good one could tell the same story over and over again, and it would always be fresh to us, the listeners. He or she could tell a story told by someone else and make it more alive and dramatic. The differences really were in the use of words and images and the inflexion of voices to effect different tones.

We therefore learnt to value words for their meaning and nuances. Language was not a mere string of words. It had a suggestive power well beyond the immediate and lexical meaning. Our appreciation of the suggestive magical power of language was reinforced by the games we played with words through riddles, proverbs, transpositions of syllables, or through nonsensical but musically arranged words. So we learnt the music of our language on top of the content. The language, through images and symbols, gave us a view of the world, but it had a beauty of its own. The home and the field were then our pre-primary school but what is important, for this discussion, is that the language of our evening teach-ins, and the language of our immediate and wider community, and the language of our work in the fields were one.

And then I went to school, a colonial school, and this harmony was broken. The language of my education was no longer the language of my culture. I first went to Kamaandura, missionary run, and then to another called Maanguuῦ run by nationalists grouped around the Gīkūyū Independent and Karinga Schools Association. Our language of education was still Gīkūyū. The very first time I was ever given an ovation for my writing was over a composition in Gīkūyū. So for my first four years there was still harmony between the language of my formal education and that of the Limuru peasant community.

It was after the declaration of a state of emergency over Kenya in 1952 that all the schools run by patriotic nationalists were taken over by the colonial regime and were placed under District Education Boards chaired by Englishmen. English became the language of my formal education. In Kenya, English became more than a language: it was *the* language, and all the others had to bow before it in deference.

Thus one of the most humiliating experiences was to be caught speaking Gīkūyū in the vicinity of the school. The culprit was given corporal punishment – three to five strokes of the cane on bare buttocks – or was made to carry a metal plate around the neck with inscriptions such as I AM STUPID or I AM A DONKEY. Sometimes the culprits were fined money they could hardly afford. And how did the teachers catch the culprits? A button was initially given to one pupil who was supposed to hand it over to whoever was caught speaking his mother tongue. Whoever had the button at the end of the day would sing who had given it to him and the ensuing process would bring out all the culprits of the day. Thus children were turned into witch-hunters and in the process were being taught the lucrative value of being a traitor to one's immediate community.

The attitude to English was the exact opposite: any achievement in spoken or written English was highly rewarded; prizes, prestige, applause; the ticket to higher realms. English became the measure of intelligence and ability in the arts, the sciences, and all the other branches of learning. English became *the* main determinant of a child's progress up the ladder of formal education.

As you may know, the colonial system of education in addition to its apartheid racial demarcation had the structure of a pyramid: a broad primary base, a narrowing secondary middle, and an even narrower university apex. Selections from primary into secondary were through an examination, in my time called Kenya African Preliminary Examination, in which one had to pass six subjects ranging from Maths to Nature Study and Kiswahili. All the papers were written in English. Nobody could pass the exam who failed the English language paper no matter how brilliantly he had done in the other subjects. I remember one boy in my class of 1954 who had distinctions in all subjects except English, which he had failed. He was made to fail the entire exam. He went on to become a turn boy in a bus company. I who had only passes but a credit in English got a place at the Alliance High School, one of the most elitist institutions for Africans in colonial Kenya. The requirements for a place at the University, Makerere University College, were broadly the same: nobody could go on to wear the undergraduate red gown, no matter how brilliantly they had performed in all the other subjects unless they had a credit – not even a simple pass! – in English. Thus the most coveted place in the pyramid and in the system was only available to the holder of an English language credit card. English was the official vehicle and the magic formula to colonial elitedom.

Literary education was now determined by the dominant language while also reinforcing that dominance. Orature (oral literature) in Kenyan languages stopped. In primary school I now read simplified Dickens and Stevenson alongside Rider Haggard. Jim Hawkins, Oliver Twist, Tom Brown – not Hare, Leopard and Lion – were now my daily companions in the world of imagination. In secondary school, Scott and G.B. Shaw vied with more Rider Haggard, John Buchan, Alan Paton, Captain W.E. Johns. At Makerere I read English: from Chaucer to T.S. Eliot with a touch of Graham Greene.

Thus language and literature were taking us further and further from ourselves to other selves, from our world to other worlds ...

I started writing in Gĩkũyũ language in 1977 after seventeen years of involvement in Afro-European literature, in my case Afro-English literature. It was then that I collaborated with Ngũgĩ wa Mĩriĩ in the drafting of the playscript, *Ngaahika Ndeenda* (the English translation was *I Will Marry When I Want*). I have since published a novel in Gĩkũyũ, *Caitaani Mũtharabaini* (English translation: *Devil on the Cross*) and completed a musical drama, *Maitũ Njugũira* (English translation: *Mother Sing for Me*); three books for children, *Njamba Nene na Mbaathi i Mathagu*, *Bathitoora ya Njamba Nene*, *Njamba Nene na Cibũ Kĩng'ang'i*, as well as another novel manuscript: *Matigari Ma Njirũũngi*. Wherever I have gone, particularly in Europe, I have been confronted with the question: why are you now writing in Gĩkũyũ? Why do you now write in an African language? In some academic quarters I have been confronted with the rebuke, 'Why have you abandoned us?' It was almost as if, in choosing to write in Gĩkũyũ, I was doing something abnormal. But Gĩkũyũ is my mother tongue! The very fact that what common sense dictates in the literary practice of other cultures is being questioned in an African writer is a measure of how far imperialism has distorted the view of African realities. It has turned reality upside down: the abnormal is viewed as normal and the normal is viewed as abnormal. Africa actually enriches Europe: but Africa is made to believe that it needs Europe to rescue it from poverty. Africa's natural and human resources continue to develop Europe and America: but Africa is made to feel grateful for aid from the same quarters that still sit on the back of the continent. Africa even produces intellectuals who now rationalise this upside-down way of looking at Africa.

I believe that my writing in Gĩkũyũ language, a Kenyan language, an African language, is part and parcel of the anti-imperialist struggles of Kenyan and African peoples. In schools and universities our Kenyan languages – that is the languages of the many nationalities which make up Kenya – were associated with negative qualities of backwardness, underdevelopment, humiliation and punishment. We who went through that school system were meant to graduate with a hatred of the people and the culture and the values of the language of our daily humiliation and punishment. I do not want to see Kenyan children growing up in that imperialist-imposed tradition of contempt for the tools of communication developed by their communities and their history. I want them to transcend colonial alienation.

READING B: Extract from *Arrow of God*

Chinua Achebe
(Chinua Achebe, poet and novelist, is considered to be one of the most important contemporary African writers.)

Source: Achebe, C. (1974 [1958]) *Arrow of God* (2nd edn), London, Heinemann, pp. 152–4.

Meanwhile the policemen arrived at Ezeulu's hut. They were then no longer in the mood for playing. They spoke sharply, baring all their weapons at once.

'Which one of you is called Ezeulu?' asked the corporal.

'Which Ezeulu?' asked Edogo.

'Don't ask me which Ezeulu again or I shall slap okro seeds out of your mouth. I say who is called Ezeulu here?'

'And I say which Ezeulu? Or don't you know who you are looking for?' The four other men in the hut said nothing. Women and children thronged the door leading from the hut into the inner compound. There was fear and anxiety in the faces.

'All right,' said the corporal in English. 'Jus now you go sabby which Ezeulu. Gi me dat ting.' This last sentence was directed to his companion who immediately produced the handcuffs from his pocket.

In the eyes of the villager handcuffs or *iga* were the most deadly of the white man's weapons. The sight of a fighting man reduced to impotence and helplessness with an iron lock was the final humiliation. It was a treatment given only to violent lunatics.

So when the fierce-looking policeman showed his handcuffs and moved towards Edogo with them Akuebue came forward as the elder in the house and spoke reasonably. He appealed to the policemen not to be angry with Edogo. 'He only spoke as a young man would. As you know, the language of young men is always *pull down and destroy*; but an old man speaks of conciliation.' He told them that Ezeulu and his son had set out for Okperi early in the morning to answer the white man's call. The policemen looked at each other. They had indeed met a man with another who looked like his son. They remembered them because they were the first people they had met going in the opposite direction but also because the man and his son looked very distinguished.

'What does he look like?' asked the corporal.

'He is as tall as an iroko tree and his skin is white like the sun. In his youth he was called Nwa-anyanwu.'

'And his son?'

'Like him. No difference.'

The two policemen conferred in the white man's tongue to the great admiration of the villagers.

'Sometine na dat two porson we cross for road,' said the corporal.

'Sometine na dem,' said his companion. 'But we no go return back jus like dat. All dis waka wey we waka come here no fit go for nating.'

The corporal thought about it. The other continued:

'Sometine na lie dem de lie. I no wan make dem put trouble for we head.'

The corporal still thought about it. He was convinced that the men spoke the truth but it was necessary to frighten them a little, if only to coax a sizeable 'kola' [bribe] out of them. He addressed them in [Igbo]:

'We think that you may be telling us a lie and so we must make quite sure otherwise the white man will punish us. What we shall do then is to take two of you – handcuffed – to Okperi. If we find Ezeulu there we shall set you free; if not ...'

He completed with a sideways movement of the head which spoke more clearly than words. 'Which two shall we take?'

READING C: Extract from *Finding the Centre*

V.S. Naipaul
(V.S. Naipaul is a creative writer and has been awarded a number of
literary prizes, among them the Booker Prize in 1971.)

Source: Naipaul, V.S. (1984) *Finding the Centre: Two Narratives*,
Harmondsworth, Penguin, pp. 16, 26–9.

It was in that Victorian-Edwardian gloom, and at one of those typewriters, that
late one afternoon, without having any idea where I was going, and not
perhaps intending to type to the end of the page, I wrote: *Every morning*
when he got up Hat would sit on the banister of his back verandah and
shout across, 'What happening there, Bogart?' ...

So I became 'writer'. Though to myself an unassuageable anxiety still attached
to the word, and I was still, for its sake, practising magic. I never bought paper
to write on. I preferred to use 'borrowed', non-rustle BBC paper; it seemed
more casual, less likely to attract failure. I never numbered my pages, for fear
of not getting to the end ... And on the finished manuscripts of my first four
books – half a million words – I never with my own hand typed or wrote my
name. I always asked someone else to do that for me. Such anxiety; such
ambition.

The ways of my fantasy, the process of creation, remained mysterious to me.
For everything that was false or didn't work and had to be discarded, I felt that
I alone was responsible. For everything that seemed right I felt I had only
been a vessel. There was the recurring element of luck, or so it seemed to me.
True, and saving, knowledge of my subject – beginning with Bogart's street –
always seemed to come during the writing.

This element of luck isn't so mysterious to me now. As diarists and letter
writers repeatedly prove, any attempt at narrative can give value to an
experience which might otherwise evaporate away. When I began to write
about Bogart's street I began to sink into a tract of experience I hadn't before
contemplated as a writer. This blindness might seem extraordinary in someone
who wanted so much to be a writer. Half a writer's work, though, is the
discovery of his subject. And a problem for me was that my life had been
varied, full of upheavals and moves: from my grandmother's Hindu house in
the country, still close to the rituals and social ways of village India; to Port of
Spain, the Negro and G.I. life of its streets, the other, ordered life of my
colonial English school, which was called Queen's Royal College; and then
Oxford, London and the freelances' room at the BBC. Trying to make a
beginning as a writer, I didn't know where to focus.

In England I was also a colonial. Out of the stresses of that, and out of my
worship of the name of writer, I had without knowing it fallen into the error
of thinking of writing as a kind of display. My very particularity – which was
the subject sitting on my shoulder – had been encumbering me.

The English or French writer of my age had grown up in a world that was more or less explained. He wrote against a background of knowledge. I couldn't be a writer in the same way, because to be a colonial, as I was, was to be spared knowledge. It was to live in an intellectually restricted world; it was to accept those restrictions. And the restrictions could become attractive.

Every morning when he got up Hat would sit on the banister of his back verandah and shout across, 'What happening there, Bogart?' That was a good place to begin. But I couldn't stay there. My anxiety constantly to prove myself as a writer, the need to write another book and then another, led me away.

There was much in that call of 'Bogart!' that had to be examined. It was spoken by a Port of Spain Indian, a descendant of nineteenth-century indentured immigrants from South India; and Bogart was linked in a special Hindu way with my mother's family. So there was a migration from India to be considered, a migration within the British Empire. There was my Hindu family, with its fading memories of India; there was India itself. And there was Trinidad, with its past of slavery, its mixed population, its racial antagonisms and its changing political life; once part of Venezuela and the Spanish Empire, now English-speaking, with the American base and an open-air cinema at the end of Bogart's street. And just across the Gulf of Paria was Venezuela, the sixteenth-century land of El Dorado, now a country of dictators, but drawing Bogart out of his servant room with its promise of Spanish sexual adventure and the promise of a job in its oilfields.

And there was my own presence in England, writing: the career wasn't possible in Trinidad, a small, mainly agricultural colony: my vision of the world couldn't exclude that important fact.

So step by step, book by book, though seeking each time only to write another book, I eased myself into knowledge. To write was to learn. Beginning a book, I always felt I was in possession of all the facts about myself; at the end I was always surprised. The book before always turned out to have been written by a man with incomplete knowledge. And the very first, the one begun in the freelances' room, seemed to have been written by an innocent, a man at the beginning of knowledge both about himself and the writing career that had been his ambition from childhood.

READING D: Extract from *The Woman Warrior*

Maxine Hong Kingston
(Maxine Hong Kingston is a highly acclaimed writer of both fiction and non-fiction.)

Source: Hong Kingston, M. (1981b [1977]) *The Woman Warrior: Memoirs of a Girlhood Among Ghosts*, London, Picador, pp. 150–1.

It was when I found out I had to talk that school became a misery, that the silence became a misery. I did not speak and felt bad each time that I did not speak. I read aloud in first grade, though, and heard the barest whisper with little squeaks come out of my throat. 'Louder,' said the teacher, who scared the voice away again. The other Chinese girls did not talk either, so I knew the silence had to do with being a Chinese girl.

Reading out loud was easier than speaking because we did not have to make up what to say, but I stopped often, and the teacher would think I'd gone quiet again. I could not understand 'I'. The Chinese 'I' has seven strokes, intricacies. How could the American 'I', assuredly wearing a hat like the Chinese, have only three strokes, the middle so straight? Was it out of politeness that this writer left off strokes the way a Chinese has to write her own name small and crooked? No, it was not politeness; 'I' is a capital and 'you' is a lower-case. I stared at that middle line and waited so long for its black centre to resolve into tight strokes and dots that I forgot to pronounce it. The other troublesome word was 'here', no strong consonant to hang on to, and so flat, when 'here' is two mountainous ideographs. The teacher, who had already told me every day how to read 'I' and 'here', put me in the low corner under the stairs again, where the noisy boys usually sat.

When my second grade class did a play, the whole class went to the auditorium except the Chinese girls. The teacher, lovely and Hawaiian, should have understood about us, but instead left us behind in the classroom. Our voices were too soft or nonexistent, and our parents never signed the permission slips anyway. They never signed anything unnecessary. We opened the door a crack and peeked out, but closed it again quickly. One of us (not me) won every spelling bee, though.

I remember telling the Hawaiian teacher, 'We Chinese can't sing "land where our fathers died".' She argued with me about politics, while I meant because of curses. But how can I have that memory when I couldn't talk? My mother says that we, like the ghosts, have no memories.

After American school, we picked up our cigar boxes, in which we had arranged books, brushes and an ink box neatly, and went to Chinese school, from five to seven thirty p.m. There we chanted together, voices rising and falling, loud and soft, some boys shouting, everybody reading together, reciting together and not alone with one voice. When we had a memorization test, the teacher let each of us come to his desk and say the lesson to him privately, while the rest of the class practised copying or tracing. Most of the teachers were men. The boys who were so well behaved in the American school played tricks on them and talked back to them. The girls were not mute. They screamed and yelled during recess, when there were no rules; they had fistfights. Nobody was afraid of children hurting themselves or of children hurting school property. The glass doors to the red and green balconies with the gold joy symbols were left wide open so that we could run out and climb the fire escapes. We played capture-the-flag in the auditorium, where Sun Yat-sen's and Chiang Kai-shek's pictures hung at the back of the stage, the Chinese flag on their left and the American flag on their right. We climbed the teak ceremonial chairs and made flying leaps off the stage. One flag headquarters was behind the glass door and the other on stage right. Our feet drummed on the hollow stage. During recess the teachers locked themselves up in their office with the shelves of books, copy-books, inks from China. They drank tea and warmed their hands at a stove. There was no play supervision. At recess we had the school to ourselves, and also we could roam as far as we could go – downtown, Chinatown stores, home – as long as we returned before the bell rang.

READING E: Extract from 'The murmur of Malvern'

Seamus Heaney
(Seamus Heaney is a highly acclaimed poet, writer and lecturer.)

Source: Heaney, S. (1988) *The Government of the Tongue: The 1986 T.S. Eliot Memorial Lectures and Other Critical Writings*, London, Faber & Faber, pp. 23–5.

'The Schooner Flight', the long poem at the start of the book [*The Star-Apple Kingdom* (Walcott, 1979)], is epoch-making. All that Walcott knew in his bones and plied in his thought before this moves like a swell of energy under verse which sails, well rigged and richly cargoed, into the needy future. I imagine he has done for the Caribbean what [J.M.] Synge did for Ireland, found a language woven out of dialect and literature, neither folksy nor condescending, a singular idiom evolved out of one man's inherited divisions and obsessions, an idiom which allows an older life to exult in itself and yet at the same time keeps the cool of 'the new'. A few years ago, in the turbulent and beautiful essay which prefaced his collection of plays, *Dream on Monkey Mountain*, Walcott wrote out of and about the hunger for a proper form, an instrument to bleed off the accumulated humours of his peculiar colonial ague. He has now found that instrument and wields it with rare confidence:

> You ever look up from some lonely beach
> and see a far schooner? Well, when I write
> this poem, each phrase go be soaked in salt;
> I go draw and knot every line as tight
> as ropes in this rigging; in simple speech
> my common language go be the wind,
> my pages the sails of the schooner *Flight*.

The speaker fixes his language in terms that recall Walcott's description of an ideal troupe of actors, 'sinewy, tuned, elated', and the language works for him as a well-disciplined troupe works for the dramatist ...

For those awakening to the nightmare of history, revenge – Walcott had conceded – can be a kind of vision, yet he himself is not vengeful. Nor is he simply a patient singer of the tears of things. His intelligence is fierce but it is literary. He assumes that art is a power and to be visited by it is to be endangered, but he also knows that works of art endanger nobody else, that they are benign. From the beginning he has never simplified or sold short. Africa and England are in him. The humanist voices of his education and the voices from his home ground keep insisting on their full claims, pulling him in two different directions. He always had the capacity to write with the elegance of a [Philip] Larkin and make himself a ventriloquist's doll to the English tradition which he inherited, though that of course would have been an attenuation of his gifts, for he also has the capacity to write with the murky voluptuousness of a [Pablo] Neruda and make himself a romantic tongue, indigenous and awash in the prophetic. He did neither, but made a theme of the choice and the impossibility of choosing. And now he has embodied the theme in the person of Shabine, the poor mulatto sailor of the *Flight*, a kind of democratic West Indian Ulysses, his mind full of wind and poetry and women. Indeed, when Walcott lets the sea-breeze freshen in his imagination, the result is poetry as spacious and heart-lifting as the sea-weather at the opening of [James] Joyce's *Ulysses*, a poetry that comes from no easy evocation of mood but from stored sensations of the actual:

> In idle August, while the sea soft,
> and leaves of brown islands stick to the rim
> of this Caribbean, I blow out the light
> by the dreamless face of Maria Concepcion
> to ship as a seaman on the schooner *Flight*.
> Out in the yard turning gray in the dawn,
> I stood like a stone and nothing else move
> but the cold sea rippling like galvanize
> and the nail holes of stars in the sky roof,
> till a wind start to interfere with the trees.

It is a sign of Walcott's mastery that his fidelity to West Indian speech now leads him not away from but right into the genius of English. When he wrote these opening lines, how conscious was he of another morning departure, another allegorical early-riser? The murmur of Malvern is under that writing, for surely it returns to an origin in *Piers Plowman*:

> In summer season, when soft was the sun,
> I rigged myself up in a long robe, rough like a sheep's,
> With skirts hanging like a hermit's, unholy of works,
> Went wide in this world, wonders to hear.
> But on a May morning, on Malvern Hills,
> A marvel befell me – magic it seemed.
> I was weary of wandering and went for a rest
> Under a broad bank, by a brook's side;
> And as I lay lolling, looking at the water,
> I slid into a sleep ...

The whole passage could stand as an epigraph to Walcott's book in so far as it is at once speech and melody, amorous of the landscape, matter-of-fact but capable of modulation to the visionary. Walcott's glamorous, voluble Caribbean harbours recall [William] Langland's field full of folk. Love and anger inspire both writers, and both manage – in [T.S.] Eliot's phrase – to fuse the most ancient and most civilized mentality.

Reference for this reading

Walcott, D. (1979) *The Star-Apple Kingdom*, New York, Farrar, Straus & Giroux.

Text, time and technology in news English

Allan Bell

3.1 Introduction

This chapter considers some of the ways in which the English language is used in international news. The English language dominates the exchange of news around the world, particularly through the major international agencies such as Reuters and Associated Press. Translation into other languages is time-consuming and expensive, and although the agencies do a lot, the need for translation cuts news flows by at least half (Boyd-Barrett, 1980; Boyd-Barrett and Rantanen, 1998). In short, if you do not have access to English, you miss out on most of the news disseminated throughout the world.

The use of the English language in news stories is termed **news English**. This chapter focuses mainly on how news stories are published in daily newspapers. It looks especially at the discourse structure of news stories, **news discourse** – that is, how the various language elements that make up a news text are put together. In particular, it focuses on time as one crucial dimension of the news story, and how this is expressed in news English, through different levels of language structure. The chapter examines how the time structure of news stories is different from the treatment of time in other kinds of story. In particular, it considers how shortness of time affects the way news stories are actually put together, and how news workers embed stretches of text from a wide range of sources to produce a story.

3.2 English, news and time

The most far-reaching technological development in the history of news distribution – the telegraph – became widespread in the mid nineteenth century. In that period, it combined with other developments, such as the creation of international news agencies, to become a crucial technological influence on news practices and forms. It established the era in which news and news work assumed its modern pattern: a quest to get the story first, before one's competitors, and the use of a non-chronological format for writing stories. Technological developments in the pursuit of timeliness continue to impel news coverage towards 'present-ation' – that is, closing the gap between the event and its telling, with the goal of displaying events in 'real time'.

The pattern of news work operates to the rhythm of (usually) daily deadlines. On these are imposed shorter and longer cycles, with different hours of the day producing different mixes of news, and different days of the week producing differently defined news for publication or broadcast. In the

Western model, which dominates world media, the basic cycle of news is one of twenty-four hours. Newspapers appear daily, and even broadcast media that transmit hourly bulletins also have flagship news programmes that serve to recapitulate the previous twenty-four hours' news.

Time is a defining characteristic of the nature of news English. It is a major compulsion in news gathering, and has an influence on the structure of news discourse. The journalist's basic rubric of 'the facts' to be included in a story holds time as a primary element. *When* is high among the 'five Ws and an H' that journalists are taught to cover: who, what, when, where, why and how.

The news is one particular kind of story, and I approach it primarily in terms of the way news stories (especially in the press) order the events they report. Time is a basic element of any story, and stories are arguably central to human experience. They come in many forms, including romances, Westerns, fables, parables, gospels, legends and sagas. One feature of stories, however, appears to be so shared across cultures that it is practically a defining characteristic of what counts as a story: events tend to be told in the chronological order in which they occurred. Cognitive psychologists, such as William Brewer, who study the ways in which people understand stories, make the distinction between event structure and discourse structure – between the order in which events actually happened and the order in which they are told in a story (Brewer, 1985, p. 167). There is only one real-world event structure, but many possible discourse structures. Telling a story in chronological order is apparently the 'natural' way because it matches the discourse structure to the event structure.

A useful way to begin examining news stories is to look at the extent to which they differ from other kinds of story. To do this, I make some comparisons with the way people tell stories of their own personal experience in face-to-face conversation. Personal narratives have been studied by, in particular, American sociolinguist William Labov (Labov and Waletzky, 1967, pp. 12–44; Labov, 1972), who has analysed the structure of personal narratives and separated them into six elements:

1   The *abstract* summarises the central action and main point of the narrative. A storyteller uses it at the outset to pre-empt the questions: What is this story about? Why is it being told?

2   The *orientation* sets the scene. It addresses the questions of who, when, what and where, establishing the initial situation or activity of the story, and sometimes sketching out events before or alongside the main narrative events.

3   The *complicating action* is the central part of the story proper, answering the question: Then what happened?

4   The *evaluation* addresses the question: So what? Narrative has a point, and it is the narrator's prime intention to justify the value of the story they are telling, to demonstrate why these events are reportable.

5 The *resolution* – What finally happened? – concludes the sequence of events and resolves the story.

6 Lastly, many narratives end with a *coda* – And that was that. This is an additional remark or observation that bridges the gap between narrative time and real time, and returns the conversation to the present.

These six elements occur in the above order in personal narratives, although evaluation can be dispersed throughout the other elements. Only the action and some degree of evaluation are obligatory components of the personal narrative. By applying the personal narrative framework, we can see the ways in which news differs from other stories. I will take as an example a typical story from an international news agency.

Figure 3.1 (overleaf) shows the text of a story from the Associated Press (AP). The story originated in Argentina, and is given here as it was published in Auckland by the *New Zealand Herald* on 10 August 2005. The time structure of the story's events is listed in the column on the right. Time zero (0) is the present tense of the story, which I define as the time of the lead event in the lead sentence: Lukić's arrest. Times prior to this are labelled time –1 for the event immediately preceding, moving back to time –6 in this story, the earliest occurrence in the reported background. The story also reports on events subsequent to time 0, labelled time +1 for the first (police statement after the arrest), and so on.

Let's now examine in more detail the elements of the time structure of the news story.

Abstract

The first sentence of a news story – known as the 'lead' or 'intro' – functions as the story's abstract. It summarises the central action and establishes the point of the story. The story in Figure 3.1 has a dual abstract in that it covers two events: Lukić's arrest in Argentina and his earlier indictment by the war crimes tribunal in The Hague. Double abstracts are frequent in news stories, and triple abstracts are not uncommon in the drive to pack maximum news impact into the lead sentence. Abstracts are typically linked by time expressions, often *after* for a sequence and *as* for simultaneous events. These time expressions commonly imply a cause-and-effect link. In S1 of Figure 3.1, this causal link is indicated by the subordinate clause *wanted by the United Nations war crimes tribunal* – the tribunal's indictment is the grounds for Lukić's arrest.

In press news, there is also the headline – an abstract of the abstract. The lead sentence is the journalist's primary abstract of a story, although to the reader the headline appears as the first abstract. The headline is in fact a last-minute insertion, written by a subeditor rather than the journalist. Time is almost never expressed in headlines, so it is not surprising to find no time expression in the headline in Figure 3.1. The absence of time expression in the lead

Sentence number		Time structure
	Serb militia gang leader captured in Argentina	
S1	**BUENOS AIRES** – A former Bosnian Serb militia leader, wanted by the United Nations war crimes tribunal, has been captured in Argentina.	−2 0
S2	Milan Lukic, who was indicted in The Hague in 2000 for crimes against humanity, was this year sentenced in absentia to 20 years in prison by a Serbian court for his role in the abduction of 16 Muslims in 1992.	−2 −1 +5 −5
S3	Lukic, as a reputed member of paramilitary group the Avengers, allegedly helped snatch the woman and 15 men from a bus in eastern Serbia.	−5
S4	They were taken to Bosnia, tortured at a hotel and executed.	−5
S5	Their bodies were dumped in the Drina River.	−5
S6	Argentinian police said Lukic was awaiting questioning by a judge.	+1 +3
S7	He had been on the run since the late 1990s.	−3
S8	The war crimes indictment says Lukic in 1992 organised a group of paramilitaries who between May 1992 and October 1994 'committed, planned, instigated and ordered the executions' of Bosnian Muslims in Visegrad and other Bosnian Serb-controlled areas.	−2 −6 −6 −4
S9	He is charged with cruel and inhumane acts against non-Serbs, persecution on political, racial and religious grounds, crimes against humanity, unlawful detention, humiliation, terrorising and psychological abuse of Bosnian Muslims.	−2 −6 −4
S10	In June 1992, Lukic and others led seven Bosnian Muslim men to the Drina River where Lukic shot them with automatic weapons, killing five.	−5
S11	Also in June, Lukic and other militiamen allegedly took seven Bosnian Muslim men from a furniture factory in Visegrad to a riverbank where they were shot and killed.	−5
S12	Lukic was involved in two other executions in the same month.	−5
S13	In Belgrade, the Government said Lukic would be extradited to The Hague – as the tribunal's authority overrides national judiciaries. – AP	+2 +4

Figure 3.1 International news agency story as published in the *New Zealand Herald*, Auckland, 10 August 2005

sentence here is itself also not uncommon. 'Today' plus past tense is routine in lead sentences in press news, but the use of the present perfect *has been captured* without time expression as here is also frequent.

Orientation

For journalists, the basic facts are who, what, when and where; and they are given in concentrated form at the beginning of a story, but may be expanded further down. Where other kinds of story routinely take time out at the beginning to set the scene, describing the characters and the setting, news stories present their orientation while they are already telling the story events.

In this story, time zero is the time of Lukić's arrest, which is carried in the lead sentence in Figure 3.1. While other earlier or later time points are specified in later sentences (see Table 3.1), time zero itself has no time specification. That is, the story does not tell us how immediate its central events are. Because this is 'the news', we assume that Lukić's arrest has just happened – probably the day before publication, 9 August 2005. Our presumption of 'recency' in news is such that we assume the arrest occurred within the past twenty-four hours, but it could have been earlier. Nowhere in the story is there direct reference to the calendar time of the immediate events, which means the news could in fact be several days old.

Some time references in news stories situate events in calendar time by reference, for example, to a particular month or year; in our news story, see *in June 1992* in S10 or *since the late 1990s* in S7 (Table 3.1). Others place events in relation to each other, such as *in the same month* in S12. Still others are **deictic** – that is, they refer to time in its relation to the present, such as *this year* in S2.

Table 3.1 Time expressions in the story in Figure 3.1

Sentence number	Story time	Time expression
S2	−2	in 2000
	−1	this year
	+5	20 years (prison sentence)
	−5	in 1992
S7	−3	since the late 1990s
S8	−6	in 1992
	−6	between May 1992
	−4	and October 1994
S10	−5	in June 1992
S11	−5	also in June
S12	−5	in the same month

International agency stories such as that in Figure 3.1 are 'datelined' at the top for place, and sometimes time, of origin. As noted, this story does not specify the calendar time at which the events occurred or when the story was reported. Often the deictic *today* will occur in the lead sentence. Deictics take their meaning from the viewpoint of the speaker or writer who uses them. It is noticeable that *today* in many international news items published in New Zealand has a different meaning for the journalist who wrote the story than for the story's readers. *Today* refers to when the story was written, but the story may be published in New Zealand one or two days later.

ACTIVITY 3.1

Allow about
40 minutes

Choose a short news story (up to ten sentences long) from an English language newspaper with which you are familiar. Identify and list the time expressions it contains in the way shown in Table 3.1. Try to establish the chronological order of the events in the story.

Action

At the heart of a narrative is the chain of events that occurred: the action. In a personal narrative, this is always told in chronological order, as you'll now see from Labov's definition.

Labov's definition of personal narrative

We define narrative as one method of recapitulating past experience by matching a verbal sequence of clauses to the sequence of events which (it is inferred) actually occurred. For example, a pre-adolescent narrative:

1   a   This boy punched me

    b   and I punched him

    c   and the teacher came in

    d   and stopped the fight.

An adult narrative:

2   a   Well this person had a little too much to drink

    b   and he attacked me

    c   and the friend came in

    d   and she stopped it.

In each case we have four independent clauses which match the order of the inferred events. It is important to note that other means of recapitulating these experiences are available which do not follow the same sequence; syntactic embedding can be used:

3   a   A friend of mine came in just

in time to stop

this person who had a little too much to drink

from attacking me.

Or else the past perfect can be used to reverse the order:

4   a   The teacher stopped the fight.

b   She had just come in.

c   I had punched this boy.

d   He had punched me.

Narrative, then, is only one way of recapitulating this past experience: the clauses are characteristically ordered in temporal sequence; if narrative clauses are reversed, the inferred temporal sequence of the original semantic interpretation is altered: *I punched this boy/and he punched me* instead of *This boy punched me/and I punched him.*

With this conception of narrative, we can define a *minimal narrative* as a sequence of two clauses which are *temporally ordered*: that is, a change in their order will result in a change in the temporal sequence of the original semantic interpretation. In alternative terminology, there is temporal juncture between the two clauses, and a minimal narrative is defined as one containing a single temporal juncture.

The skeleton of a narrative then consists of a series of temporally ordered clauses which we may call narrative clauses. A narrative such as 1 or 2 consists entirely of *narrative clauses*. Here is a minimal narrative which contains only two:

5   a   I know a boy named Harry.

b   Another boy threw a bottle at him right in the head

c   and he had to get seven stitches.

This narrative contains three clauses, but only two are narrative clauses. The first has no temporal juncture, and might be placed after *b* or after *c* without disturbing temporal order. It is equally true at the end and at the beginning that the narrator knows a boy named Harry. Clause *a* may be called a *free clause* since it is not confined by any temporal juncture

(Labov, 1972, pp. 359–61).

Labov found that a defining characteristic of personal narrative as a form is the temporal sequence of its clauses. That is, the action is invariably told in the order in which it happened – 'matching a verbal sequence of clauses to the sequence of events' (Labov, 1972, pp. 359–60). Telling it in a different order would mean that it had happened in a different order.

News stories, by contrast, are seldom if ever told in chronological order. The time structure of the story in Figure 3.1 is very complex, with twelve points in time identified in my analysis. The story as a whole can be divided into five sections: S1, S2–5, S6–7, S8–12 and S13. The lead sentence covers two events and time points, as we have seen. The chronological order of events in Figure 3.1 is shown in Table 3.2.

Table 3.2 Chronology of events in the story in Figure 3.1

Story time	Calendar time	Action
–6	May 1992	Lukić organises paramilitary group
–5	June 1992	atrocities alleged to have been committed
–4	(May 1992) until October 1994	end of paramilitary group's operations
–3	late 1990s until present	Lukić on the run
–2	2000	Lukić indicted by war crimes tribunal
–1	earlier in 2005	Lukić sentenced in absentia
0	[presumed] yesterday, 9 August	Lukić captured in Argentina
	[Wed 10 August	publication date in New Zealand]
+1	soon after arrest	police statement
+2	after arrest	Belgrade government statement
+3	after police statement	questioning by judge
+4	near but unspecified future	extradition to The Hague
+5	into distant future	20-year sentence

The story cycles through events taking us further back in time. It presents in approximately reverse order of actual occurrence (plus a couple of excursions into the story's future time) the chain of events that have culminated in the lead event of this story. Most of S2–5 and S8–12 are background, covering the earliest time points of the story, that is, the actions which have led to Lukić's indictment on war crimes. Note that in Table 3.2, I treat the episode of June 1992 as one time point –5, but it is in fact much more complex than that. The episode consists of a series of at least four events (distinguished in S3–5 and

S10–12), each itself consisting of a series of actions. For example, the first event for which Lukić is indicted consists of at least five named actions: snatching 16 Bosnian Muslims from a bus (S3), transporting, torturing and executing them (S4), and then disposing of their bodies (S5). Note also that it is unclear when this event took place. Whereas the other events reported later are all specified as occurring in June 1992, the leading event as reported in S3–5 is placed only generally as some time in 1992 (though presumably in May or later).

Sandwiched between the extensive sections of background is a statement by police (S6) made after Lukić's arrest, and background on Lukić's situation between the events of 1992 and the present, August 2005 (S7). Some of the time points are in fact durations rather than points: –3 represents from the late 1990s to the present (Table 3.2), and –6 to –4 represents the outside times of paramilitary group's operations, from May 1992 to October 1994, with the June 1992 incidents which fall between those times being identified as –5.

There is a good deal of looking forward to the future of the judicial process – questioning of Lukić, extradition, potential imprisonment – which occupies several sentences (S2, S6, S13). The story ends (S13) with the foreshadowing of proceedings to have Lukić extradited from Argentina to The Hague. The statements by Argentinian police (S6) and the Belgrade government (S13) have already occurred and are therefore in the past, but my analysis represents both as occurring in story-future time (+1, +2), because they are subsequent to the core news event of Lukić's arrest. The three events timed as +3, +4 and +5 are however in the future in real time as well as in story time. Because of their futurity, precise time of occurrence cannot be specified in Table 3.2. We can probably safely assume that the judge questioned Lukić within a day or two of his arrest, but the extradition may be far into the future given the legal proceedings that the accused may use to avoid being taken to The Hague. 'News of the future' is a completely standard feature of many news stories, which will commonly include an ongoing dimension not just reference to events of the past. Research by Jaworski et al. (2003; 2004) has shown how important the future is as a dimension of news reporting, even though news stories stereotypically deal with past events.

ACTIVITY 3.2

Allow about 30 minutes

Analyse the time structure of the story you used for Activity 3.1 and list its events in chronological order in the way shown in Table 3.2. You may find that having to be explicit about the events and their ordering changes some of the chronology you outlined in Activity 3.1.

Evaluation, resolution and coda

Evaluation is the means by which the significance of a story is established. In personal narrative, evaluation is what distinguishes a directionless sequence of clauses from a story with a point and a meaning. In the case of the fight stories studied by Labov, the point is often the self-aggrandisement of the narrator. Evaluation pre-empts the question: So what? It gives the reason why the narrator is claiming the floor and the audience's attention.

News stories also require evaluation, and its function in them is identical to that in personal narrative: to establish the significance of what is being told, to focus the events and to justify claiming the audience's attention. Like all news stories, the news story in Figure 1.1 stresses repeatedly the importance of what has happened, particularly in the lead sentence with its vocabulary of news value: *militia leader, wanted, war crimes, captured.* The lead sentence is a nucleus of news evaluation, because the function of the lead is not merely to summarise the main action. The lead focuses the story in a particular direction. It forms the lens through which the remainder of the story is viewed.

Most kinds of story move to a resolution: the fight is won, the accident survived. News stories often do not present such clear-cut results (although journalists prefer the conclusiveness that a result offers).When they do, as noted above, the result will be in the lead rather than at the end of the story. In this example, the nearest thing to a resolution will be Lukić's deportation and sentencing at The Hague, but that remains in the future. It is of course only the latest step in a continuing saga: the news is more like a serial than a short story. While the beginning of a news story is everything, the ending is nothing. This is a challenge to the 'storyness' of news, because we expect stories in general to end at the end. Brewer (1985) found that narrative sequences that lacked an outcome were not even classed as stories by his (US) informants.

Nor is there a coda to the news story. As I noted earlier, in personal narrative, the coda serves as an optional marker of the story's finish, returning the floor to other conversational partners, and returning the tense from narrative time to the present. None of these functions is necessary in the news, where the floor is not open, and where the next contribution is another story.

The way it was

Labov's analyses show that in personal narrative if you change the order of narrative clauses, you change the order of events. In news English, order is everything but chronology is nothing. As news consumers we are so accustomed to this approach that we forget how 'deviant' it is compared both with other kinds of narrative and with earlier norms of news reporting. Research on news narrative styles by US sociologist Michael Schudson shows that the non-chronological format emerged in American journalism in the late nineteenth century. Stories of the 1880s covering presidential State of the Union addresses did not summarise the key points at the beginning, but by 1910 the lead as summary was standard (Schudson, 1989).

3.3 Discourse structure of news English

By analysing the structure of news stories compared with that of other stories, we can see that the most striking characteristic of news discourse is the non-chronological order of its elements. Dutch discourse analyst Teun van Dijk has called this the 'instalment method' (1988b, p. 43), by which an event is introduced, and then returned to in more detail two or more times. We can see this pattern in the way in which the story in Figure 3.1 introduces Lukić's wanted status in the lead sentence (time –2) and expands on the details of his indictment throughout the remainder of the story, but particularly in S2, S8 and S9. The radical discontinuity of time between many sentences imparts a general lack of cohesion to the news story. This is typified by the fact that each news sentence is usually also its own paragraph, so there is no larger unit of text organisation.

In many kinds of writing it is common to link one sentence to another with time adverbs such as *then*, or markers of cause and effect such as *therefore*, or conjunctions such as *however* or *and*. Words such as these mark the cohesion of a text. They serve to flag continuity from one sentence to the next and help the reader to understand the development of the narrative or argument. News stories usually lack these signposts, so that cohesion between sentences is unclear or nonexistent. As in Figure 3.1, there is often no flow of time sequence from one sentence to the next, and a lack of devices such as adverbs to express linkages between sentences. The news story jumps from one statement to the next, offering somewhat isolated chunks of information in each sentence. It may be genuinely in doubt what events within the story belong together (as in the relation of the S2–5 incident to those reported in S10–12), at what point location actually shifted, or what material is attributed to whom. The lack of cohesion is accompanied by a lack of resolution at the end of the story, as I have already noted.

Time is not the only dimension that structures news stories in English; I briefly describe here a more general framework for analysing the discourse structure of news, using an approach adapted and expanded (Bell, 1991) from van Dijk (e.g. 1988b). A news story normally consists of an abstract, an attribution and the story proper (Figure 3.2).

- The *abstract* consists of the lead sentence of the news story and, for press news, also a headline (as in Figure 3.1). The lead covers the main event, and possibly one or more secondary events. This necessarily entails giving some information on actors and settings involved in the event.
- The *attribution* – where the story came from – is not always explicit. It can include a credit to a news agency (for example to the Associated Press news agency at the end of S13 in Figure 3.1) and/or a journalist's byline. It may also state place and occasionally time (as the dateline *BUENOS AIRES* does in that story).

- *Episodes* and *events*: the body of the story itself consists of one or more events. Related events may be grouped together and treated as a more general episode. Events must describe the actors involved and the action that takes place. They also usually express the setting (time and place), and may have an explicit attribution.

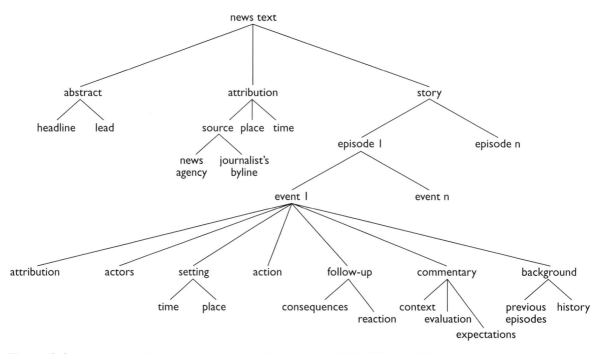

Figure 3.2 Outline model discourse structure of a news text (Bell, 1991, p. 171)

As well as the above elements, which present the central occurrences, there are three additional categories of material in a news story: background, commentary and follow-up. These represent the past, the (non-action) present and the future of the events described in the main action of the story. The category of background covers any events prior to the current action – the story's past time. These are frequently previous events that probably figured as news stories in their own right at an earlier stage of the situation, as undoubtedly did the contents of Lukić's indictment in 2000. If the background goes back beyond the near past, it is classed as 'history'. Most of the Figure 3.1 story is in fact concerned with the history of 10–13 years before (S2–5, S7–12), not the immediate events.

Commentary provides the journalist's or news actor's observations on the action in the present time period; it is an assessment of and a comment on events as they happen (rather than the actual narration of the events themselves, or other parties' verbal reaction to them). In Figure 3.1 it is represented by the explanation in S13 of why the extradition will be to The Hague rather than Belgrade.

Follow-up covers the story's future time – any action subsequent to the main action of an event. It can include verbal reaction by other parties or nonverbal consequences – for example, the statements by Argentinian police (+1, S6) and the government in Belgrade (+2, S13). More of this story is devoted to the future (S6, S13) than to the immediate past. Because it covers action that occurred after what a story has treated as the main action, follow-up is a prime source of subsequent updating stories – which are themselves called 'follow-ups' by journalists.

ACTIVITY 3.3

Allow about 20 minutes

Choose another story from an English language newspaper, longer than the one you chose before (it should be about 15–25 sentences). Can you identify examples of background, commentary or follow-up in this story? Describe how they relate to the main events. Do you think the background represents the main point of a previously published story? If so, write a lead sentence that might have been used on that earlier story.

The structures of news stories also seem to be quite standardised in cultures other than Anglo-American ones, and in languages other than English. Van Dijk's (1988a) analysis of newspaper stories in many languages found few significant differences in news values or structure. In a comparison between different treatments of the assassination of Lebanese President-elect Gemayel in 1975, van Dijk found that stories in Spanish, Chinese and Swedish all followed a similar pattern to that of English language news. There were some differences between newspapers in the first and third worlds. The greatest differences, however, were between 'quality' and 'popular' papers, for instance within West Germany and the UK; for example, the popular *Bild Zeitung* (literally 'picture paper') used a more chronological news order for dramatic effect. The similarities are clearly in part or in whole due to the domination of English language models of news stories, and global patterning on Western (particularly Anglo-American) models.

3.4 Time in news work

I have discussed the non-chronological order of news stories, and the discourse structures that they follow, and pointed out that news was not always written like this. That raises an obvious question of why modern news stories are written with this deviant time structure. Why are they written in an order that both research and intuition indicate is harder to understand, when one of the main features of a news story is supposed to be that it is easily understandable? The answer lies in a combination of news values and practices relating to deadlines and cycles, and I now turn to look briefly at these factors.

News values

The values of the media control the way in which news is presented. We can account for the way news stories are structured only with reference to the values by which one 'fact' is judged more newsworthy than another. The foundation study of news values was undertaken by Scandinavian media researchers Galtung and Ruge (1965), and their categories have been found to be valid and enlightening for a wide range of news types in many countries. I adapted and added to their categories (Bell, 1991; 1998), distinguishing between content-related and process-related values. Time is important in a number of them.

Recency or immediacy means that the best news is something that has only just happened. Recency is related to the concept of frequency – how well a story conforms to news work cycles, how close something falls to an achievable deadline. Events whose duration or occurrence fits – or can be made to fit – into twenty-four hours are more likely to be reported than other events. So the murder is more newsworthy than the police investigation, the verdict more than the trial.

Unexpectedness, however, means that the unpredictable or the rare is more newsworthy than the routine. It is the reverse of frequency, which attempts to tame the rhythm of events to fit the cycle of media deadlines. Closely related to unexpectedness is novelty. 'New' is a key word in advertising, and novelty is one of the main factors in selecting what is newsworthy.

ACTIVITY 3.4

Read 'Extract 1 from "When? Deadlines, datelines, and history"' by Michael Schudson (Reading A). As you read, think about how news values affect the reporting of events and what kinds of stories journalists find easier to cope with and which ones they find more challenging, and why.

Comment

Schudson notes that the best news has an ending that can be anticipated. Journalists have difficulty with complex stories that have no clear end point; they like to be able to identify where they are in a story – at the beginning, the middle or the end. This is closely linked to the issue of journalistic cycles.

Practices: deadlines and cycles

To say that immediacy, novelty and other time-related concepts are news values is not, however, a sufficient explanation of their importance in news and news work. Why is time such a dominating news value? To shed light on this issue we need to look at the practices of news work, the processes by which news is produced, rather than the content of the news text. In

Section 3.5, I detail some of the processes by which news workers create a story, and the sources on which they draw. First, I identify several news values that relate to the production and processing of news rather than to its content. They all have a time element – either present (co-) or future (pre-) time. Among the most important are: continuity, competition, predictability and prefabrication.

Continuity means that once something is in the news, it tends to stay there. Stories have a life cycle, a time period during which they can stay alive in the news. Politicians and other would-be news makers know well that news breeds news. Once one news outlet has a good story, all its competitors want it too.

Competition is the urge to be first with the news. Every news outlet wants a first, an exclusive, or at least wants not to miss out on the stories that other media have. There is a paradox here between the desire of the media to get a scoop, and their desire to cover what other media are covering – continuity.

ACTIVITY 3.5

Read 'Extract 2 from "When? Deadlines, datelines, and history"' (Reading B), Schudson's account of the newsroom's obsession with the scoop. Note who and what is behind the drive to achieve the scoop.

The drive to get the news first – by a few minutes or even a few seconds – is embedded deep in the news ethos. Getting it first is a reason for self-congratulation, and being scooped a cause for mourning. Yet the rush of the deadline is largely self-inflicted. It is a fetish of the profession, as sociologist Philip Schlesinger shows in his participant observation study of news practices in the BBC (Schlesinger, 1987). There is no evidence that the audience really expects such timeliness, but news workers expect it of themselves and expect to be evaluated by it. As Schudson says in Reading B, the audience couldn't care less who gets the scoop.

Predictability is important for news operations, because it enables the planning of future work time. An event is more likely to be covered if it can be prescheduled for journalists than if it turns up unheralded. The canny news maker uses this knowledge to schedule the timing of an event according to news deadlines. Paradoxically, the predictable nature of much news gathering is in contrast to the high value placed on news as the unexpected.

Finally, there is the factor of prefabrication – the pre-existence of ready-made text such as press releases, speech notes, reports and, particularly, earlier news stories on a topic. Journalists can take these over to process them rapidly into a story. The more closely these prefabricated texts conform to news style, the more likely it is that they will appear in the news. I look in more detail below at how journalists use prefabricated text to make new stories. In the visual channel, the existence of high-value news footage of an otherwise low-rating story can take it onto the television news.

Time dominates news work in a way it does in few other professions: the product must be ready by a set time or it is useless. Schlesinger's study rightly characterises news work as 'a stop-watch culture' (Schlesinger, 1987, p. 83). All newsrooms are the same in this respect. They operate against the clock, measuring daily achievement by the ability to produce a required number of stories for the deadline. The stimulus of the deadline helps compensate for the humdrum nature of most news work, but deadlines also encourage high productivity, the maximum number of stories being produced in the minimum time. Journalistic deadlines are genuinely terminal. The paper must be put to bed, or the bulletin broadcast at a certain time.

3.5 Producing news English

Having examined some of the features of English language news texts, I now turn to look at how news English is produced. The process by which news is generated has an effect on the nature of the product. News English is production-line language: it is a response to the demand for productivity against the clock, and the outcome of the involvement of a chain of news workers who handle the news text as it moves along that production line.

The news is seldom a solo performance. News media offer the classic case of language produced by multiple parties. Journalists, editors, printers, newsreaders, sound technicians and camera operators are just some of the people who can directly influence the form of news discourse. Scholars in a number of communication-related fields, particularly sociologist Erving Goffman (1981), have taken an interest in the different roles that people may take in producing composite discourse such as news. The composite nature of news stories is a very explicit example of what Soviet literary theorist Mikhail Bakhtin (1981) has called **heteroglossia** – the mixing of many voices – to which we will return in a moment.

Authoring

The 'author' is the main character involved in producing discourse. All news production focuses on an individual journalist writing stories. I distinguish this originating, usually sole, author of a text from 'editors' – those numerous others who operate on what an author has drafted, whether or not they have 'editor' as part of their job title. Authorship is seldom genuinely shared, but describing the journalist as the originating author of a story is an extreme idealisation. After all, the basic stuff of news is what people tell a reporter. Much of what a reporter writes is therefore paraphrased or quoted from somebody else's words. That much is obvious, but journalists draw on written as well as spoken sources. Very few stories consist entirely of wording newly generated by journalists from their own observations or audio interviews. Much news comprises updates and rewrites of previous stories. In some media the basic news-gathering practice is the following up of stories that were 'diaried ahead' (noted for a follow-up story) the last time they were covered. In addition, many stories contain material selected and reworked from documents generated by news makers or other media. Journalists draw on both spoken and written inputs for their stories. My own analyses and experience yield the following classification of input sources:

- interviews, either face to face or by telephone
- public addresses
- press conferences
- written text of spoken addresses
- organisationally produced documents of many kinds – reports, surveys, letters, findings, agendas, minutes, proceedings, research papers, etc.
- press releases
- earlier stories on a topic, either from the journalist's own newspaper or from other media
- news agency copy
- the journalist's notes from all the above inputs, especially the spoken ones.

The journalist's main spoken source is the interview (and notes taken from it), and most interviews are conducted over the telephone rather than face to face. Secondary sources are public addresses of all kinds, and press conferences, which are a combination of both address and interview. Some stories are entirely cut-and-paste jobs from such sources.

Editing

The processing of news involves the complex and rapid movement of copy (the actual text of the news story) between individuals within a newsroom. Even in a small newsroom, stories are handled by perhaps four different individuals and may follow a complex and often cyclical route: from the chief reporter who assigns the story, to the journalist, to the subeditor, back to the chief reporter, to the newspaper editor, and back to the subeditor again. The role of editors is crucial because of the number of them who handle a journalist's story. On a standard, medium-sized daily newspaper, a journalist's story may pass through the hands of up to eight news workers, each making alterations and producing a new version.

While copy movement within a newsroom may seem complex enough, most news in fact weaves a much more intricate path to its consumers. News media publish more copy that has been generated by other, external, news agencies than by their own in-house journalists. The average international news item published anywhere in the world has probably been through at least four separate newsrooms. At each stage, copy is received, put through the newsroom's editing process and transmitted to the next receiver, where the cycle is repeated.

Heteroglossia in news English

Bakhtin viewed texts and utterances as being made up of multiple 'voices' from all kinds of genres, styles and dialects within a language. His concept of heteroglossia was developed in particular through his study of the many styles of voice used in the novel (Bakhtin, 1981). The term covers everything from the explicit, sourced quotation of others' voices within a text or speech, to the subtle hints of their origins that words continue to carry with them, which flavour the utterances in which they are used. Bakhtin examines the variety of voices that are drawn on in the nineteenth-century comic novel, and the ways in which they are incorporated in the novelist's text. But he also argues more widely that 'at any given moment of its historical existence, language is heteroglot from top to bottom' (Bakhtin, 1981, p. 291). The social history of a word remains present even when the word is spoken in a context very different from previous ones. The diversity of voices might be concealed below the surface of a discourse, or be more openly drawn upon, as in Charles Dickens's parodies of the speech modes associated with official, commercial, ceremonial and other spheres. Bakhtin (1981, p. 303) cites as an example the 'parodic stylization of the language of ceremonial speeches (in parliaments and at banquets)'. This passage is from Dickens's *Little Dorrit*: 'Mr. Merdle came home, from his daily occupation of causing the British name to be more and more respected in all parts of the civilised globe, capable of the appreciation of world-wide commercial enterprise and gigantic combinations of skill and capital' (Dickens, 1979 [1855–57], p. 386). Here the use of elevated vocabulary and expressions such as *the British name* and *all parts of the civilised globe* flag this as drawing on a ceremonial speech-making style.

News text provides a clear illustration of Bakhtin's concept of heteroglossia. Inputs to the finished text can range from overt and acknowledged direct quotation, to the subtle and unacknowledged use of wording from a bureaucratic document. When journalists reproduce unacknowledged wording from bureaucratic reports or meeting agendas, they carry into the news text the taste of those original contexts just as surely as when they quote sources openly. The journalist, therefore, is as much a compiler as a creator of language, and much news English consists of previously composed text reworked into new texts. This intertextuality or **hybridity** of media genres is the focus of Östman and Simon-Vandenbergen (2004), who bring together several studies which look at how discourse styles mix in the media.

Intertextuality is, of course, a main means by which journalists meet the productivity demands of their employer. A standard quota of stories ranges between four and ten per day. Generating that amount of fresh text is impossible, so the generous adoption of old text is required. The usually smooth, unified surface of most news stories thus conceals a variety of origins. But the individual journalist remains the main channel through which diverse sources converge into a single flow of copy. Editors hold journalists responsible for wording that they reuse, as well as wording that they generate themselves. A journalist sanctions the language culled from other sources simply by adopting it.

Embedding in the news text

The way in which journalists insert into their stories text that already exists is only one example of a basic feature of media communication, which I label **embedding**. Embedding is a type of heteroglossia in which one speech event is incorporated into another. This happens most obviously in broadcasting, where recording technology enables actual strips of a news maker's speech to be embedded into a newscaster's or reporter's script instead of being quoted at second hand.

The concept of embedding draws on Goffman's notion of 'footing' (1981) – that is, a speaker's alignment to what he or she is saying. Even in everyday conversation, speakers are constantly quoting other speakers or representing other voices. In doing so, the alignment that speakers take is different from the alignment taken by the represented speakers. They embed words from these other speakers in their own talk, but they may not fully own the opinions expressed in such embedded statements. Indeed, they may embed another's statement specifically to disown its sentiments. Goffman's book *Forms of Talk* is concerned in large measure with the embedding of one kind of utterance within another. He writes: 'a speaker can quote himself [*sic*] or another directly or indirectly, thereby setting into an utterance with one production format another utterance with its own production format, albeit now merely an embedded one' (Goffman, 1981, p. 227). Narrators of all kinds of story are constantly embedding strips of others' talk and quotations from others' speech into their stories. The narrative structures of novels as analysed by literary theorists are obvious sites of embedding.

So far I have described the production of news language as taking place in a linear fashion, with news copy being passed from one news worker to the next along the assembly line. However, we can view the process in another way: as layered in the vertical dimension rather than segmented horizontally. From this point of view we can regard all earlier versions of a story as embedded within the final text. Each successive handling of the copy produces a potentially different text, which is input to the next stage of the process. Each layer implies not just the text and its content but the full speech event that generated it. The speech event includes the participant sender and receiver, and the time and place it occurred.

The many layers of editing are not generally evident in final news copy, since editors aim to produce a unified text that conceals their intervention. But the final text may bear detectable traces of the embedded texts from which it came. For example, copy generated by an international news agency may express a distance in miles, with an exact conversion to kilometres given in parentheses. Recipient subeditors in a country that uses metric units may use only the converted value and describe a place as being *129 kilometres west of London*. Such exactitude reads strangely. It is explicable as the conversion of *80 miles* to a precise metric equivalent. Since *80* in the original copy was assuredly a rounded number in the first place, an approximation (*130 km*) would read more naturally in the metric conversion.

The concept of embedding is extraordinarily important for understanding the language of news discourse. Journalists are rarely on the spot for unscheduled news events, so other people's accounts are the journalists' stock-in-trade for reporting events. Further, news is what people say more than what they do. Much – perhaps most – of what journalists report is talk not action: announcements, opinions, reactions, appeals, promises, criticisms. Most news copy is therefore reported speech – although it may not be overtly attributed as such.

ACTIVITY 3.6

Allow about
20 minutes

For one of the stories you selected in a previous activity, try to identify the sources of information that have an explicit attribution (e.g. people quoted). Identify the parts of the story that seem to come from each of these sources. Is all the information in the story credited to a particular source? Where do you think the information that is not obviously attributed to a specific source has come from?

Prefabricated text

Although talking to news makers forms a major part of reporting the news, documents play a large part, too. The documentary inputs are of two main kinds: those already written in the style of news, and those not written in the style of news. The second group consists mainly of official documents of some sort – reports, agendas, judgements and the like.

Journalists favour written sources that are already prefabricated in an appropriate news style and that therefore require the minimum of reworking. These come in three kinds: news agency copy, press releases and earlier stories on the same topic. News agencies provide most of the copy on any newspaper. Most agency stories will be run almost verbatim, but some will be assigned to a journalist to find a new or local angle using the agency story as a basis. The press release was invented in the USA at the beginning of the twentieth century. Now it is a staple of journalism, openly despised but heavily used by news workers, and providing the basis of a high proportion of published news stories. Still more highly favoured are earlier stories on the same topic. These may be from the journalist's own newspaper, but often come from other media. News media feed voraciously on each other's stories. While always trying to find something new to update and begin the story, an evening newspaper will often reproduce the bulk of a story published by its morning competitor. Text from a continuing story may come round again and again in a format that has changed little.

Pre-existing text can play an important role in news workers' judgements about what is news. Texts that are already cast in news format and style stand a much better chance of selection than texts that are not appropriately packaged. I have worked as an organisational press officer and have often seen journalists ignore a suggestion about a story that they might follow up themselves. They will, however, reproduce the story faithfully when it is supplied as a ready-made press release a week or two later.

The three kinds of pre-packaged news described above have a head start on other news inputs. A story that is marginal in news terms but that is already written and available may be selected ahead of a much more 'news worthy' story that has to be researched and written from the beginning. So the usability of press releases gives the advantage to those potential news makers who can afford to pay someone to write for them – generally official and commercial entities. In addition, the use of earlier news copy embedded into updated stories favours publication of something that has already been in the news – continuity, in terms of the news values outlined earlier.

How journalists use sources

Apart from stories published verbatim from press releases or agency copy, most stories are, then, based on more than one input. Covering a speech by a government minister is a frequent news-gathering routine. In constructing a story from the speech the journalist will draw on sources such as:

- the written text of the minister's prepared speech
- (the journalist's notes of) the minister's speech as actually delivered, which may diverge anywhere between 0 and 100 per cent from the prepared speech
- a press release containing those points of the speech the minister wants reported
- an interview after the speech with the minister.

To these four main sources may be added briefing materials written in advance, prior verbal indications from the minister's press secretary on the content of the speech, an official report released at the time of the speech, subsequent telephone calls to interested groups for comment on the minister's statement, and so on. The situation is further complicated because most source documents are themselves composite productions, with text from earlier documents embedded within them.

A record of an interview or spoken address is kept by the journalist. The record may be verbatim in the form of a tape recording, a selective but more or less verbatim shorthand transcript, or highly selective longhand notes. This material may appear in a story in the form of direct quotation, indirect quotation, or unattributed information. It may be paraphrased or summarised.

Direct quotation – text that is enclosed between quotation marks – is supposed to be verbatim. Much that appears in the form of indirect quotation is paraphrased, and much unattributed information draws heavily on what a news maker has said. Written documents may similarly be used either for quotation or to provide background information.

Researching how journalists work and what inputs they use is not easy: getting access to the material is an obvious problem. I have been able to take advantage of records of my own work as a journalist. In one fairly ordinary story I wrote, concerning the introduction of the gorse mite into New Zealand to control gorse, I found I had dealt with two main persons as sources, a scientist and his research group leader, and used no fewer than eight inputs:

1   Notes from a brief preliminary face-to-face interview with the leader of the group of scientists who had been researching the introduction of the mite.

2   Notes from a later telephone interview with the same group leader.

3   The 350-page Environmental Impact Assessment (EIA) on the effects of introducing the gorse mite. This is itself a highly composite document, drawing heavily on earlier reports. In particular it stresses that three previous impact assessment documents 'should be consulted before reading this EIA' – and it embeds these as appendices.

4   A draft press release written by the main scientist involved in doing the work.

5   A covering letter from this scientist, which accompanied the press release.

6   A copy of a press release (and published clips) issued the previous year at an earlier stage of the assessment.

7   Notes from my telephone interview with the scientist (and follow-up questions in subsequent phone calls).

8   Amendments to my draft story made by both the scientist and the group leader.

The story was twenty-four paragraphs. Of these, nine were based mainly on the spoken inputs (interviews) and fifteen on written inputs. Figure 3.3 gives the first few paragraphs of this story as published (verbatim) in one newspaper, and shows how the eight inputs were used to build the text of the news item. The processes I see at work in Figure 3.3 include the following:

1   Selection from the available inputs and corresponding rejection of most of the written material in order to handle the size of the EIA and the number of other inputs.

2   Reproduction of source material. I found that the later paragraphs, which provide detail and background, tend to reproduce wording from input texts in contrast to the wholesale blending and rewriting evident in the early paragraphs.

3   Summarisation in early paragraphs of information to be detailed later (compare S7 and S9).

4   Generalisation and particularisation. We see a shift from the particular to the general in S7, and from the general to the particular in the description in S5.

5   Frequent restyling and translating of information expressed in scientific phraseology to less technical wording.

INPUTS

FINAL COPY

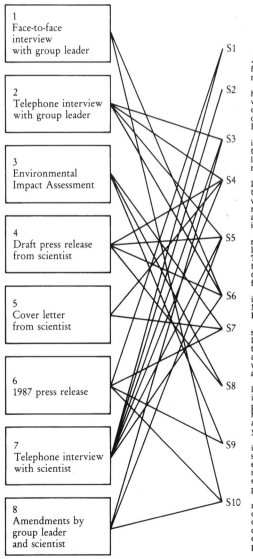

Mite leads gorse war

A TINY mite has arrived in New Zealand to lead the fight against the country's most costly weed, gorse.

A consignment of several hundred gorse spider mites was flown into Christchurch by the Department of Scientific and Industrial Research.

The mites were imported in sealed containers from the CABI Institute for Biological Control at Ascot near London.

They were taken to DSIR's maximum quarantine facility at Lincoln and will be released for multiplication in August and throughout the country in the spring.

The mites are a brick-red colour and measure less than a millimetre. They live in colonies of thousands inside webs spun on to gorse branches and feed heavily on the plant.

The importation follows issue of a permit by the Ministry of Agriculture and Fisheries.

DSIR Entomology Division director John Longworth said introduction of the mite culminates a decade of research, environmental assessment and public consultation.

"Because releasing biological control agents is an irreversible step, the impacts, costs and benefits have been carefully assessed over several years," he said.

Detailed tests carried out in England since 1980 had shown the mite would estabish only on gorse and not damage other native or economically important plants in New Zealand.

A 350-page environmental impact assessment circulated last November concluded there were no compelling economic or environmental reasons to prevent introduction.

Figure 3.3   Embedding of inputs to construct the text of a news story (adapted from *The Daily News*, New Plymouth, 4 August 1988, by Bell, 1991)

3.6 Time and technology in news English

I began this discussion of the nature of news processing by looking at the technological development that first made rapid news dissemination possible – the telegraph. In this section I look at changes in news technologies, their relation to time, and their effects on the character of news English.

At the beginning of this chapter I indicated that the invention of the telegraph was the first crucial step in the development of modern news practices and forms in the pursuit of immediacy and productivity. US media sociologist James Carey (1987) traces the rise of modern forms of news English in nineteenth-century America, particularly the concept of time. He argues that the penny press, which began in the USA in the 1830s, took its concept of time from trade and business, the cycle of which is the day, with its never-ending repetition of prices, goods and transactions. It imposed this daily cycle of commerce on other spheres of social life. By the 1860s, the telegraph cemented what the penny press had begun, as the turnaround time on news shortened radically. So journalistic achievement became defined as being the first rather than the best.

ACTIVITY 3.7

Read 'Extract from "Why and how? The dark continent of American journalism"' (Reading C), James Carey's account of the links between the development of the telegraph and news practices. As you read, note the emergence of the influence of 'when' at the expense of 'why' and 'how'.

Comment

Carey considers that such a concept of time – orientation to the daily, to the most recent, to being first – is a key factor in the news's non-attention to the question of 'why', to its lack of explanation and context. So the journalistic concept of *when* – of immediacy as a news value, of the scoop as the professional goal – defeats the coverage of the 'why' and 'how'.

The computerisation of news writing and processing has redefined the work practices of journalists. The recycling of existing news text in new stories is increasingly likely to occur. Print journalists input their stories direct to their newspaper's central computer system. Typesetting is eliminated, and with it several distinct steps in news production. News copy received from external news agencies or correspondents can also be fed straight into a newspaper's computer, with no need for rekeying on site. In addition, the computer archiving of previously published issues enables journalists to reduce turnaround time and increase their productivity.

A combination of technological advances in and legislative deregulation of the broadcasting industry is leading to more outlets and more competition, and this is also reshaping broadcast forms and styles. Deregulation, primarily of frequencies and ownership, is opening the television spectrum to private operators in countries where public television has been the norm. In this highly competitive environment the way in which news is framed and presented is changing. The old public-service approach to programming was to set off one programme from the next, marking the junctions and encouraging audiences to choose whether or not to watch. Stig Hjarvard (1994) describes how public television scheduling in the UK and other European countries is moving away from this kind of segmented programming format to a commercially oriented flow of programmes designed to lock in the attention of viewers to a particular station.

This process was further along in New Zealand, where public television has always carried advertising. It is at its most obvious in the placement of advertisements. Although there may be as many as five advertising breaks (each several minutes long) within an hour-long programme, no advertising is screened between programmes. The end of one programme leads straight into the start of the next. The intention is blatantly commercial – to avoid giving the 'consumers' a chance to get away during the transition between programmes. It is the exact opposite of a purely public-service approach, which would offer the audience maximum uninterrupted viewing by running advertisements between rather than within programmes.

What effects do such practices have on broadcast news? News has long been regarded by both audiences and media personnel as significant far beyond the rather small amount of time it actually occupies (generally less than 10 per cent of a station's air time). News bulletins structure programming and audience time, and are scheduled at transition points in the personal day. News has become a serial, along the lines of fictional television forms like soap operas or situation comedies (Hjarvard, 1994). It is shifting from recapitulating the day's events to continuous updating, with television adopting the practice of hourly bulletins that has long been used on radio. This reaches its peak in the continuous news services, again part of the radio scene for at least twenty years, but comparatively recent in television.

The emphasis on getting the news first impels news work towards the ultimate goal of offering coverage in real time. Development of the technology for this is closely linked with war and war reporting. It took its first major step with the telegraph during the American Civil War, and attention is now focused on the technology of the satellite. Coverage in real time – initially in CNN's reporting of the 1991 Gulf War, then of the 11 September 2001 attacks – is closer, although it requires further qualitative technological developments to make it more common. Having said this, though, live coverage requires the predictability of situation that I listed earlier as one of the factors in news selection, and most news is not specifically foreseeable in this fashion. In Bell (2003) I examine a case study of the reporting of expeditions to the South

Pole to show how technology and time interweave in the development of news reporting towards live presentation.

The move to live coverage in broadcast news takes news reporting from the past tense to the present. Studio presenters interview news sources and journalists live on air. The role of scripting is diminished, and with it the tightly developed format of the modern news story. Ironically, the achievement of real-time coverage would mean that the inverted news chronology and structure I have described would become obsolete. But such coverage is of course only partial, provides a small minority of regular broadcast coverage, and is by definition impossible in print. So the classic news story, with its violation of chronological order and fragmented paragraphs, will remain a staple as long as we have printed news and as long as most broadcast news remains retrospective rather than live coverage.

The internet, however, is reshaping the accessibility of news, and is important in at least three ways. First, it makes news published in other ways more accessible, for instance making the text of a daily newspaper, or the transcript of a broadcast interview, available online. Second, it provides access to more of the raw material of reporting, for example, presenting the verbatim transcript of a print journalist's interview with a politician which appeared in abbreviated, edited and commentated form in the paper itself. Third, websites are themselves sources of news available both to the general public and to media workers and are used, for example, by terrorist groups to announce – in close to real time – claims to having carried out particular attacks. With the growth of new media, particularly those which are based on the internet, scholars have begun to research language use in these forms. Richardson (2001) examines news and internet newsgroups, Richardson and Meinhof (1999) investigate how channels running twenty-four hours affect news, and Aitchison and Lewis (2003) cover a range of work on the language of new media. (You will find discussion of global media practices in Chapter 7.)

3.7 Conclusion

This chapter has dealt with the way in which news stories in English are written, particularly in relation to time. A feature common to all kinds of story is their chronological time structure: events tend to be told in the order in which they happened. But news stories follow a radically different ordering. They generally begin with the most recent event and cycle back through earlier events, giving information in instalments. Modern news discourse has developed this time structure through a combination of the news values of recency and novelty, the journalistic practices of the deadline and the scoop, and technology that increasingly allows coverage to be live, in real time.

News media also offer the classic case of language produced by multiple parties. The processing of news involves the complex and rapid movement of stories through the hands of many news workers. Much of the news consists of previously composed text embedded and reworked into new texts. This composite character is a very explicit example of Bakhtin's heteroglossia – the mixing of many voices. The push to offer coverage live, or in as close to real time as possible, took its first major step with the telegraph 140 years ago. Attention is now focused on the technology of the internet and the satellite, with repercussions for the format the news will take.

READING A: Extract 1 from 'When? Deadlines, datelines, and history'

Michael Schudson
(Michael Schudson is Professor of Communication and Adjunct Professor of Sociology at the University of California.)

Source: Schudson, M. (1987) 'When? Deadlines, datelines, and history' in Manoff, R.K. and Schudson, M. (eds) *Reading the News*, New York, Pantheon, pp. 97–9.

Nearly everything else may vary, but this is constant in hard news: an orientation to the past twenty-four hours. Time is the scaffolding on which stories are hung, and the day is the chief unit of time. The result, of course, is that events in the world that are or can be made to appear timely, that is, linked to some development of the preceding day, are more reportable than events that move by less discernible rhythms. These events are more easily justified for front-page attention by an editor who does not have room for all the stories he or she would like to include.

But it is clear that the fact that something happened yesterday is not sufficient to make it news. Sometimes newsworthiness has to do not only with timeliness but with the ease with which an event can be placed in a cycle or rhythm of time. Election stories are easy to report, not so much because something newsworthy happens each day in an election campaign (although, of course, candidates do their best to see that this is so), but because journalist and reader alike know the election date and know when the story will *end*. Because everyone knows the story will end the first Tuesday after the first Monday in November, every speech, every poll, every alliance, every debate, every gaffe can be weighed and measured against a day of judgment. The reporter, the editor, and the reader all know *where they are* in the story – near the beginning, the middle, or the end. The election story has a cadence, a rhythm, and is easier to read and absorb because readers can tap out the beat.

The most notorious consequence of journalism's love for stories whose ending they can anticipate is the 'horse race' style of covering elections. Sometimes, even in the best of newspapers, the result is a caricature of itself:

> Sen. Gary Hart of Colorado made it two in a row Sunday, with a come-from-behind victory that snatched away Walter F. Mondale's front-runner status.

> Hart's upset victory in Maine's Democratic caucuses gave him vital additional momentum just five days after his surprise triumph in the New Hampshire primary and nine days before the crucial Super Tuesday contests in nine states.

(Los Angeles Times, March 5, 1984)

Election reporting can always count on an end point to give news a location in time that most reports do not have.

Reporting on legislative activity is correspondingly more difficult much of the time. This is well illustrated in a *Los Angeles Times* story of May 25, 1985, headlined, 'Did Senate Vote Deal Fatal Blow to Future of MX?' The answer is: the reporters cannot be sure. They write, 'The lopsided Senate vote to limit deployment of the MX missile to 50 unless the Reagan Administration can find another basing plan dealt a profound and perhaps fatal blow to the future growth of the MX program'. *Perhaps* fatal? Well, the Pentagon portrayed the vote as a victory, since some senators had sought to limit deployment to forty missiles, not fifty. 'But,' the reporters tell us, 'the Senate decision Thursday represents one of the extremely rare occasions in which Congress has made a clear – and possibly successful – effort to sharply curtail a major weapons program already underway.' But defense appropriations have a way of returning to the floor of Congress. A bill once introduced and defeated may be introduced again. Compromises can be made. Adjustments can be arrived at. A story about failed or failing legislation, especially budgetary legislation where judgment is not 'yes or no' but 'more or less' is not a story with beginning, middle, and end. It is a P.D.Q. Bach spoof of a Beethoven symphony: how many endings are there? How many times will it roar to a climax only to return for one more reprise of the opening theme?

The sense of an ending that gives body and rhythm to a story need not be a date like the first Tuesday in November. It can be a clear-cut finish without a date. In hostage crises, the hostages will either be released safely or killed. The Iranian hostage crisis was mentioned every night on the evening news for fifteen months. It was not *timely* news – it was old hat. Most days it was not timely *news* because nothing new or different had happened. But the gravity of the opposition of the two outcomes – freedom or death, rescue or humiliation – provided a dramatic structure that kept the story a story.

This is what the press handles best: stories that are timely, that have anticipatable end points, and that have end points that figure in simple, binary possibilities – the election or the game will be won or lost, the Dow-Jones will go up or down, the defendant will be judged guilty or not guilty, the criminal is apprehended or at large, the patient survives or dies, the child is missing or has been found. Stories that are more complex than this – the budget, for instance – if they are to be covered well at all, are translated into a binary opposition of this sort: the president is going to get his way or he is going to lose to the Congress. The media found a comfortable way to report President Reagan's tax revision initiative when they discovered in Representative Dan Rostenkowski a skillful and attractive antagonist to set against the president.

READING B: Extract 2 from 'When? Deadlines, datelines, and history'

Michael Schudson
(Michael Schudson is Professor of Communication and Adjunct Professor of Sociology at the University of California.)

Source: Schudson, M. (1987) 'When? Deadlines, datelines, and history' in Manoff, R.K. and Schudson, M. (eds) *Reading the News*, New York, Pantheon, pp. 81–2.

Getting the news fast and, ideally, getting it *first* is of passionate interest to journalists. On November 22, 1963, the UPI White House reporter, Merriman Smith, sat in the middle of the front seat of the pool car in the presidential motorcade in Dallas. When he heard gunshots, he jumped to the phone and started dictating. His Associated Press rival, Jack Bell, seated in the backseat, was helpless to get out a story. Bell demanded the phone, but Smith said he wanted the Dallas operator to read the story back to him because the connection was faulty. This was obviously a dodge to keep hold of the phone. 'Bell started screaming and trying to wrestle with Smith for the receiver. Smith stuck it between his knees and hunched up into a ball, with Bell beating him wildly about the head and shoulders. UPI beat the AP by several crucial minutes on the story, and Smith won a Pulitzer for his coverage of the Kennedy assassination.'

Daniel Schorr's on-the-scene radio reporting from disastrous floods in Holland in 1953 brought him to the attention of Edward R. Murrow, who then hired him at CBS News. Dan Rather began his rise to prominence at station KHOU Houston with live coverage of Hurricane Carla. 'Live coverage,' Rather writes in his autobiography, 'is the mark of a really good local news station.'

But why?

Why should this emphasis on getting the story minutes or seconds faster than a rival bulk so large in journalism? Once upon a time, when a dateline could be two or three or ten days past and when newspapers could differ by days or weeks, not hours or minutes, 'when' mattered. Andrew Jackson fought the battle of New Orleans because news had not reached him from the East Coast that the war with Britain was already over. That is not something that could happen today. Now, when news is a constant commodity – the wire always ticking, the radio always talking, the TV cameras nearly always available – the question of 'when' is a question journalists care about infinitely more than their readers. The pressure journalists are under to be first is generated internally in news organizations. No one in the audience gives a damn if ABC beats CBS by two seconds or not. The journalist's interest in immediacy hangs on as an anachronistic ritual of the media tribe. Getting the story first is a matter of journalistic pride, but one that has little to do with journalistic quality or public service. It is a fetishism of the present, an occupational perversion, and one peculiarly American. The American editor E.L. Godkin noted this as long ago as 1890: 'The stories which Parisian journalists tell each other in their cafés are not of their prowess as reporters, but of the sensation they have made and the increase in circulation they have achieved by some sort of editorial comment or critique; the American passion for glory in beats – meaning superiority over rivals in getting hold of news – they do not understand, or thoroughly despise.'

The American focus on the scoop serves, in part, to cover up the bureaucratic and prosaic reality of most news gathering. The news organization is, as Philip Schlesinger put it, a 'time-machine.' It lives by the clock. Events, if they are to be reported, must mesh with its temporal spokes and cogs. Journalists do not seek only timely news, if by 'timely' one means 'immediate' or as close to the present as possible. Journalists also seek coincident and convenient news, as close to the *deadline* as possible. News must happen at specified times in the journalists' 'newsday.' Politicians adept at 'making news' are well aware of reporters' deadlines. They schedule press conferences and public appearances to coincide with reporters' filing times. The astute press secretary in government or in the private sector schedules events to accord with the weekly round of the press, knowing on which days there will be the least number of stories competing for front-page attention. Much of the news the press reports is given to it by public officials who can pass it out routinely or with fanfare, urgently or casually, all at once or in pieces, depending on what kind of effect they want to achieve. The more the media emphasize the immediacy of news, the more subject journalists are to manipulation by public officials who know how to prey on people with stopwatch mentalities.

This reality – that news gathering is normally a matter of the representatives of one bureaucracy picking up prefabricated news items from representatives of another bureaucracy – is at odds with all of the romantic self-conceptions of American journalism. The insistence on getting the latest news and getting it first, the headlong lunge, the competitive rush that comes with a breaking story, all this is an effort to deny and to escape the humdrum of daily journalism. Moreover, the race for news – a race whose winner can easily be determined by a clock – affords a cheap, convenient, democratic measure of journalistic 'quality.' American society is too diverse and American journalism too decentralized for news organizations to measure themselves by criteria of literary elegance or intellectual sophistication. No small circle of intellectuals can influence the culture of journalism in New York and Washington the way it might in Paris. American journalists are left with competition by the clock. Their understanding of their own business focuses on reporting up-to-the-minute news as fully and fairly as possible.

READING C: Extract from 'Why and how? The dark continent of American journalism'

James W. Carey
(James W. Carey is CBS Professor of International Journalism at Columbia University.)

Source: Carey, J.W. (1987) 'Why and how? The dark continent of American journalism' in Manoff, R.K. and Schudson, M. (eds) *Reading the News*, New York, Pantheon, pp. 162–6.

[A] critical fact concerning the partisan press concerns the matter of time. The cycle of business is the cycle of the day: the opening and closing of trade. The press of the eighteenth and early nineteenth centuries was not technologically equipped to report on a timely, daily basis, but it shared with businessmen the understanding that time is of the essence of trade. As a result, the natural epoch of journalism became the day: the cycle of work and trade for a business class. The technological impetus in journalism has been to coordinate the cycle of communication with the cycle of trade.

...

In the 1830s, a cheap, daily popular press–a 'penny press' – was created in the major cities. The penny press did not destroy the commercial press. The latter has continued down to this day not only in the *Wall Street Journal* and the *Journal of Commerce*, *Barron*'s and *Business Week*, *Forbes* and *Fortune*, but in private newsletters and private exchanges that grew after the birth of the penny press. Such publications have edged closer to the popular press with the enormous expansion of the middle class. The *Wall Street Journal* doesn't call itself 'the daily diary of the American dream' for nothing. But the penny press did displace the commercial-partisan press in the 1830s as the model of a daily newspaper.

While scholars disagree over the significance of the penny press, one can safely say three things about it. First, the penny press was a consumer good for a consumer society; it reflected all of society and politics, not just the world of commerce and commercial politics. The retreat from partisanship meant that any matter, however minor, qualified for space in the paper: the details not only of trade and commerce, but the courts, the streets, the strange, the commonplace. The penny papers were filled with the odd, the exotic, and the trivial. Above all, they focused on the anonymous individuals, groups, and classes that inhabited the city. They presented a panorama of facts and persons, a 'gastronomy of the eye'; in another of Baudelaire's phrases, they were a 'kaleidoscope equipped with consciousness.'

Second, the penny press displaced not merely partisanship but an explicit ideological context in which to present, interpret, and explain the news. Such papers choked off, at least relatively, an ideological press among the working class. At its best, the penny press attempted to eliminate the wretched partisanship and factionalism into which the press had degenerated since the Revolution. It tried to constitute, through the more or less neutral support of advertising, an open forum in which to examine and represent a public rather than a merely partisan interest.

Third, the penny press imposed the cycle and habit of commerce upon the life of society generally. Because in business time is money, the latest news can make the difference between success and failure, selling cheap or selling dear. Time is seldom so important in noncommercial activity. The latest news is not always the best and most useful news. Little is lost if the news of politics or urban life is a little old. Nonetheless, the cycle and habit of beginning and ending the day by reading the latest prices was imposed on social activities generally. Beginning in the 1830s, the stories of society were told on a daily basis. The value of timeliness was generalized by the penny press into the cardinal value of journalism.

The events of journalism happen today. The morning reading of the *New York Times* is important because it establishes the salience of stories for the day. It also determines salience for the television networks, the newsmagazines, the journals of opinion issued weekly and monthly. And the stories of books begin in the announcements in news columns: a family named Clutter was murdered in Holcomb, Kansas, yesterday. With the penny press, all forms of writing became increasingly a parasite of 'breaking news.'

The telegraph cemented everything the 'penny press' set in motion. It allowed newspapers to operate in 'real time' for the first time. Its value was insuring that time became irrelevant for purposes of trade. When instantaneous market reports were available everywhere at the same moment, everyone was effectively in the same place for purposes of trade. The telegraph gave a real rather than an illusory meaning to timeliness. It turned competition among newspapers away from price, even away from quality, and onto timeliness. Time became the loss leader of journalism.

The telegraph also reworked the nature of written language and finally the nature of awareness itself. One old saw has it that the telegraph, by creating the wire services, led to a fundamental change in news. It snapped the tradition of partisan journalism by forcing the wire services to generate 'objective' news that papers of any political stripe could use. Yet the issue is deeper than that. The wire services demanded language stripped of the local, the regional and colloquial.

They demanded something closer to a 'scientific' language, one of strict denotation where the connotative features of utterance were under control, one of fact. If a story were to be understood in the same way from Maine to California, language had to be flattened out and standardized. The telegraph, therefore, led to the disappearance of forms of speech and styles of journalism and storytelling – the tall story, the hoax, much humor, irony, and satire – that depended on a more traditional use of language. The origins of objectivity, then, lie in the necessity of stretching language in space over the long lines of Western Union.

Similarly, the telegraph eliminated the correspondent who provided letters that announced an event, described it in detail, and analyzed its substance. It replaced him with the stringer who supplied the bare facts. As the telegraph made words expensive, a language of spare fact became the norm. Telegraph copy had to be condensed to save money. From the stringer's notes, someone at the end of the telegraphic line had to reconstitute the story, a process that reaches high art with the newsmagazines: the story divorced from the storyteller.

Together those developments of the second third of the nineteenth century brought a new kind of journalism, a kind that is still roughly the staple of our newspapers. But, as explained earlier, this new journalism made description and explanation radically problematic: 'penny' and telegraphic journalism divorced news from an ideological context that could explain and give significance to events. It substituted the vague principle of a public interest for 'class interest' as the criterion for selecting, interpreting, and explaining the news. It brought the newsroom a glut of occurrences that overwhelmed the newspaper and forced the journalist to explain not just something but everything. As a result, he [*sic*] often could explain nothing. By elevating objectivity and facticity into cardinal principles, the penny press abandoned explanation as a primary goal. Simultaneously, it confronted the reader with events with which he had no experience and no method with which to explain them. It filled the paper with human interest material that, however charming, was inexplicable. And, finally, it divorced the announcement of news from its analysis and required the reader to maintain constant vigilance to the news if he was to understand anything.

Visual English

Sharon Goodman

4.1 Introduction

Today it is difficult to find a single text which uses solely verbal English. The vast majority of letters, advertisements and even government circulars in most countries use at least some form of visual information alongside verbal language. In this sense, texts in English are becoming increasingly multimodal: they use devices from more than one semiotic mode of communication simultaneously (Morgan and Welton, 1986; Kress and van Leeuwen, 1996; Messaris, 2001; Kress, 2003).

My focus in this chapter is on **visual English**, those many elements in a text which are visual rather than verbal in nature. A key question underlying the chapter is: to what extent can we say that any picture or graphic representation accompanying English words may be called 'visual English'? In particular I explore three main issues:

- the culturally specific nature of visual forms of communication which, despite their 'natural' appearance, are often highly conventionalised;
- the specific ways in which graphics and pictures can communicate, and the extent to which it is possible to make distinctions between English in the visual and verbal channels of communication;
- the specific ways in which visual and verbal English can interact within a text, reinforcing each others' messages or creating potentially conflicting meanings.

4.2 Culture, language and 'seeing'

To what extent is it meaningful to talk of 'visual English' – as opposed to 'visual French', 'visual Arabic', etc? Does the move towards the visual entail a move away from distinct 'languages' – in other words, is the 'Englishness' of English texts disappearing?

There are many forms of visual information that members of a culture seem to decode almost automatically, so effective is the process of internalisation. Many visual **semiotic systems** (systems of signs) – such as road and shop signs – are social constructs (rather than naturally occurring entities) which have become conventional and internationally accepted. Readily comprehensible once learnt, they diminish the amount of decoding time needed, enabling us to function efficiently in the social world. Because sign systems can very quickly take on a 'natural' appearance, it takes a perceptual shift to realise that they have been learnt and internalised. Faced with the signs shown in Figure 4.1, which appear on the lavatory doors in Poland, which would you go into?

Figure 4.1

Guy Cook points out that comprehension is often based on prior knowledge.

> Many signs are believed to be iconic because the perception of a connection between signified and signifier is so habitual that it begins to seem natural ... For a sign to be truly iconic, it would have to be transparent to someone who had never seen it before – and it seems unlikely that this is as much the case as sometimes supposed. We see the resemblance when we already know the meaning.

(Cook, 2001, p. 75)

This can be seen by considering other icons which people meet fairly regularly, as exemplified in Figure 4.2.

Figure 4.2

ACTIVITY 4.1

Allow about
10 minutes

Figure 4.2 shows some signs in use in the UK and elsewhere. What do they mean? Are they instances of visual English (that is, can we pin down the 'Englishness' of them?) or are they related to more than one language? Are they simply conventionalised international symbols? How does the visual symbol relate to a word, sentence or concept (if it does)? What is its function – does it inform, or prescribe behaviour or act as a visual shorthand for an English sentence? Where might you expect to find each of these symbols, and does the context in which you would encounter it influence its meaning?

Comment

The context is obviously crucial for meaningful decoding (how many times have you interpreted ↑ as 'go up' instead of 'go straight on' in a shopping centre?), and the same applies for cultural significance – the symbol 🏖, for example, might be interpreted as, say, 'umbrellas to keep out of the rain during monsoon' in countries where sunbathing on a sunny beach would be unthinkable. Single icons may be understood as a single word (☎ = telephone) or stand in for a concept or sentence (☎ = 'you may telephone from here'). They may also be combined in a visual shorthand intended to be read as a verbal unit (I ♥ N Y = 'I love New York').

It may be that some of these symbols seem more appropriate than others to your cultural context. If you are bilingual, or live in a country where English is used alongside another language, do the visual representations used in each language differ? It occurs to me that the 'knife and fork' symbol, for example, in Figure 4.2 would not be the most obvious one for 'restaurant' in all countries.

Different languages and cultures – even different regions within a single country – often develop different symbols relevant to their own needs. In some rural parts of the UK, for example, you may see a sign at the roadside which means 'beware sugar beet falling from lorries' – something less likely to be signposted in London. A sign such as the one shown in Figure 4.3, displayed in British shops, would be meaningless in a country with no minimum age for the purchase of cigarettes or lottery tickets. New signs are also invented as the need arises – some of the icons are related to computer communication, such as 🕸 meaning the World Wide Web, or ▱ meaning memory stick. The ☺ is an example of an emoticon, one of a wide range of 'smileys' available to users of online chat rooms and used to signify the mood of the writer.

Figure 4.3   'No under-15s' sign

New symbols are often designed in the simplest possible way for them to be readily understood. A useful tool for discussing this is prototype theory. Rosch (1978) defines a prototype as a 'typical instance of' an object or concept. Thus in Britain, a typical instance of 'bird' might be a robin, and a simplified drawing of a robin may come to signify 'bird' in visual British English. This would then come to stand for all birds, regardless of whether or not they really resembled the depiction. The process is culturally specific: a British representation of 'tree' might look something like those shown in Figure 4.4, whereas in certain parts of Africa you might find something more like the spreading branches of the acacia tree, as shown in Figure 4.5.

Figure 4.4   **Figure 4.5**

Morgan and Welton (1986) note that our ideas of perspective and reality are conditioned by the culture and time in which we are living, in other words by the visual and verbal imagery that surrounds us, and also by the training we receive (by various media) in these literacies. So 'tree' in British or in, say, Indian or in Singaporean visual English are potentially radically different.

4.3 Visual or verbal English?

One of the problems we face is in attempting to distinguish between visual and verbal English. A further complication is that the form of verbal English can also be considered as a visual medium: letterforms themselves can convey meaning and information. Are the shapes of the words on the page, and the spelling, part of visual English, or can we safely confine these to the purely verbal? This is a problematic area, which might lead one to consider the whole text as visual. If we admit letter shapes, spelling and punctuation into the realm of English, then we are into the field of graphosemantics – meaning which derives from the text's 'writtenness'. This looks not only at what is written, but at how it is written and at the relationship between the two. This section will consider some examples.

Spelling

Research has shown that orthography can affect the way in which sounds are perceived. Derwing (1992) found that people may perceive phonetic differences between, for example, /rich/ and /pitch/ – an extra sound being assumed for the silent letter. It also seems that people may attach different meanings to different spellings of the same word. Bolinger's early (1946) work in the USA on 'visual morphemes' included the following citation from author and literature professor, Raymond Macdonald Alden, 'To think, as some do, that "gray" and "grey" are quite different colors, and that a ghost which through the triumph of spelling reform has lost its "h" would also have lost its terrors' (quoted in Bolinger, 1946, p. 336).

ACTIVITY 4.2

Allow about
3 minutes

Bolinger tested this phenomenon on his own students. He asked them which spelling of *grey* would fit best with the following sentences:

> She has lovely _____ eyes

and

> It was a _____, gloomy day.

Which spelling would you use for which sentence? Are you able to say why?

Comment

Bolinger's students invariably preferred *grey* for the first (the positive connotation) and *gray* for the second (the negative). This may be a distinction which is meaningful only for speakers of American English – I do not feel strongly about either spelling. However, it does show that spelling is perceived as having a role to play in interpretation. Another example might be to ask yourself whether you can perceive a difference between *hello, hallo* and *hullo*.

The semiotics of typography

The typeface in which a text, or part of a text, is set can convey vast amounts of connotative meaning – it can convey a mood, signal clues as to content or even suggest a point of view (for examples, see Carter et al., 1985, and Swann, 1991).

A glance through some of the design and typography textbooks available can reveal fascinating insights into the perceived importance of the visual presentation of print. If you look at the typeface used for different headlines in different styles of newspaper, for example, you will often find that the typeface has been carefully chosen to suit the content of the article, or the newspaper's opinion of the events being reported. There may be 'wobbly' letter forms above an article about a ghost, or 'jagged' letters for a story about an electrical storm. Handwritten-style fonts are often used by advertisers, to give the receiver the impression of a friendly, handwritten note from a friend. Clues to other languages and cultures can be conveyed typographically, such as using the Cyrillic Я to connote 'Russianness', for products such as vodka. The range of possibilities is endless (for more examples, see Cook, 2001).

Changes of type can be used to convey multiple voices in a text. The impression of the presence of more than one 'speaker' can be implied through the visual presentation. Figure 4.6 is an experimental poem by the typographer Cal Swann, relating a verbal encounter between a headmaster and a pupil.

As you read, note how the type is used to indicate:
- conversational turn-taking
- intonation and changes of tone (shouting, whispering, etc.).

Headmaster
Pupil

you know that i now **know** where you went don't you

we were in the woods
                                        you went to stephen kennedys house

i'm telling you the truth looking at me in the eyes **and all that**

                              ah no d d d don't interrupt me i warned you

i always find out
         now i'm very displeased with you **because you set out to deceive me**

                                              quite deliberately

and as i told you on friday that makes life very difficult

                    cos its means every time you and m you and i talk to

so can i rely on that in future

                    yeah sorry about the whole thing

Swann uses changes of type, and devices for emphasising text such as emboldening, to express the different voices in the interaction. The headmaster's voice is in bold face, and the pupil's in small, fainter letters. The power differential in the exchange between the two speakers is thus reflected by the visual portrayal of the two voices: the pupil's is physically much smaller and less dominant than the headmaster's. Typography, therefore, has a paralinguistic function: it can portray features associated with speech such as intonation and changes of pace. This can be seen also in online computer communication, where the use of upper and lower case letters is often a point of tension: anyone accidentally leaving the 'caps lock' key on, or deliberately typing a message in upper case letters will very quickly be told to stop shouting.

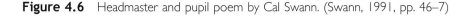

Figure 4.6 Headmaster and pupil poem by Cal Swann. (Swann, 1991, pp. 46–7)

ACTIVITY 4.3

Allow about
5 minutes

An inappropriate typeface can result in, at best, a poorly communicated message and, at worst, total incomprehension. A typeface which appears to 'fit' the information, on the other hand, can give an air of coherence and 'confidence' to the words. In the examples in Figure 4.7, do you think appropriate or inappropriate typefaces have been used? Can you find reasons for your answers?

𝕮𝖔𝖒𝖕𝖚𝖙𝖊𝖗 𝕬𝖎𝖉𝖊𝖉 𝕯𝖊𝖘𝖎𝖌𝖓   – STOP PRESS –

Figure 4.7

Comment

To me, the first example (quoted in Morgan and Welton, 1986, p. 31) seems to be an inappropriate typeface for the concept it is trying to convey: computers are an efficient, modern form of technology which enable people to work and communicate at high speed. Using a typeface such as Old English seems in the UK to connote old-fashioned tea shops and country villages, where little has changed over the centuries. A computer design company using this typeface is not, therefore, presenting the correct image to its customers.

The second example is in Courier, a typeface often associated with the old-fashioned telegraph and telex machines, used to transmit news as it breaks around the world. It therefore seems to fit the information it is being used to present – a press release or urgent report. Even though such machines are barely used now, the connotations and effects remain embedded in the typeface for readers.

ACTIVITY 4.4

Read 'The semiotic construction of a wine label', David Graddol's account in Reading A of the way typefaces can be used to express different voices in another text, the label from a wine bottle. These voices, expressed through the visual semiotics of the typefaces on the label, address the reader in different ways and at different moments in the reader's encounter with the text. What institutional or persuasive voices are expressed on other products?

The connotative potential of typography suggests that content and form are inextricably linked. Burt's study of the psychological impact of typography demonstrated that while many people had no formal knowledge of typography, and could not name individual fonts, they were generally sensitive to what they called 'the atmosphere' set up by the text (Burt, 1950). Memories of hated schoolbooks printed in certain typefaces were cited, proving that typeface can function as a strong intertextual device (it contains allusions to, or 'echoes' of, other texts). These days there are many websites dedicated to the discussion of typefaces, and extolling the virtues or otherwise of particular computer fonts.

We might accept, then, that typefaces can have a semantic function in texts in English. But what about such things as anagrams, alliteration and puns? To what extent can we talk about these occurring in visual English?

Visual anagrams and alliteration?

The repetition of consonants or vowels, often for dramatic effect – can sometimes be analogously seen in the visual as a repetition of graphic elements. Advertisements exhorting consumers to 'own it now', for example, are in part relying on the fact that 'own' and 'now' are anagrams and that the two words being so visually similar will work associatively and memorably. A slightly different technique of visual association is shown in Figure 4.8:

Figure 4.8

Figure 4.8 shows a shop logo, also used for the shop's print advertisements. Here we find recourse to a visual prototype (this shape represents a 'typical instance of' a fish, and stands for 'fish' in the collective imagination). There is the equivalent to alliteration (the repetition of letter sounds at the beginning of closely connected words) operating visually in these letters themselves, one in the icon represented by the text (the 'fish' shape), and one in the visual imagination, as 'fish' and 'fins' share three letters, are both four letters long, are semantically associated, etc.

Visual puns

Often it is possible to uncover intentional or unintentional visual puns in images. These may exist in the typography, or in parts of a drawing or photograph. Hammond and Hughes's study of puns in 1978 revealed that pictures can contain just as many different types of visual pun as we find in the verbal English language. These range from the entirely accidental, found in revered paintings in art galleries, to those found in children's drawings, satirical cartoons in newspapers and magazines (such as a line of rats to represent 'rat race'), through to lewd picture postcards. Some puns seem to be universal (there are visual puns on body parts and landscapes, for example, in most languages) – others are directly related to the language of the culture in which they appear.

Visual puns often rely on the interaction between visual and verbal elements to bring their meaning to the fore. The advertisement in Figure 4.9 appeared on British television, advertising a phone-in programme. It is aimed at an extraordinarily narrow audience: not only is it UK specific, it is also region specific – it plays on cockney rhyming slang associated with the East End of

London, substituting 'dog and bone' for 'telephone'. Visual puns can often highlight the cultural (and temporal) specificity of visual literacy – Geipel (1972, p. 30) notes that even within a single language they can be very hard to decipher out of context, or years later.

Figure 4.9

Popular newspapers, in particular, are apt to use visual puns as often as possible, and these often reinforce a point being made verbally. Figure 4.10 shows one that could only work in English. This headline employs visuals to reinforce an 'us and them' dichotomy, mocking bureaucracy in a range of public sector organisations, a common theme in UK popular newspapers. Gaddie (1989) notes the wide diversity of intentional and unintentional or latent puns in the alphabet itself. Names of rock groups such as U2 and INXS are examples, as are English nouns such as A-frame, U-turn, T-shirt, etc.

Figure 4.10

Where does all this leave us with regard to the boundaries between visual and verbal elements in English texts? Written English can be seen as having its own, often very complex, semantic codes, which are frequently expressed visually. We will now take a look at the idea of a visual English 'grammar', and consider to what extent it is appropriate (or possible) to speak of images in terms of a grammar.

4.4 Some elements of English visual ~~g~~

Many analysts of images and proponents of visual literacy cl
'grammar' inherent in images, just as there is in verbal langu
look at some visual elements that may be seen as containing
structures' in their own right, and consider their importance in the multimodal
text. Dondis (1973) and Arnheim (1988) both provide in-depth discussions of
'visual syntax' and principles of spatial composition. Others take a functional
approach and link the analysis of images to the functional theory of language
associated with the work of Michael Halliday (1978; 1985). In Halliday's words
(1978, p. 19), 'language is as it is because of what it has to do'. Following this view,
the choice of linguistic sign – the word – and the ways in which words are
combined in the clause, are related to the function(s) to which the language
is being put. This view takes language as being a 'map of the world' (a way
of representing things and events), rather than a 'window to the world'
(a way of looking straight out on to the world). The implication of this is
that there are alternative ways of representing the world – and that there
is, by extension, no such thing as objective 'truth'. The meanings we ascribe
to language are socially constructed and negotiated, or in Halliday's words
'The particular form taken by the grammatical system of language is closely
related to the social and personal needs that language is required to serve'
(Halliday, 1970, p. 142).

A Hallidayan framework is useful because it adds a semantic dimension to the
analysis of the text. It allows us to see differences in meaning between, for
example, different ways of addressing people (*Mr Smith* or *John*), or different
ways of describing events.

Any semiotic mode (words, pictures, sound) develops resources for fulfilling
three kinds of broad communicative function, or 'metafunction' in Halliday's
terminology: ideational, interpersonal and textual (see box overleaf).

For every act of communication in which a given semiotic mode is used,
a choice must be made from each of its systems. To form an English sentence,
for example, you must choose from the system of person (first, second or
third), the system of mood (statement, question or command), the system of
tense (past, present or future) and so on, and all these choices combine in the
sentence, each adding an element of meaning to the whole. Similarly, in
producing a picture, you must choose from the system of horizontal angle
(frontal, profile or somewhere in between), the system of vertical angle (from
above, at eye-level or from below), the system of distance (close shot,
medium shot or long shot) and so on, and again, all these choices combine in
the one picture, each adding an element of meaning.

[margin annotation:] we didn't choose the text or the pictures

[margin, rotated:] 124

Halliday's communicative metafunctions – a summary

1   *The ideational metafunction*
    Every semiotic mode will have resources for constructing
    representations of (aspects of) the world.

2   *The interpersonal metafunction*
    Every semiotic mode will have resources for constructing: (a)
    relations between the communicating parties (between writers and
    readers, painters and viewers, speakers and listeners); and (b)
    relations between these communicating parties and what they are
    representing, in other words, attitudes to the subject they are
    communicating about.

3   *The textual metafunction*
    Every semiotic mode will have resources for combining and
    integrating ideational and interpersonal meanings into the kinds of
    wholes we call 'texts' or 'communicative events' and recognise as
    news articles, paintings, jokes, conversations, lectures, and so on.

Some elements of visual English grammar can be directly related to verbal
English grammar, and it is often revealing to investigate the ways in which
different modes, such as words and pictures, may express the same things or
contradict each other. Pictures and words cannot both convey all the same
meanings, because not all meanings can be realised in every semiotic mode.
Some things can be expressed only verbally, some only visually, and some
both visually and verbally. Let's look at a few examples.

Direct and indirect address

Suppose we wanted to see whether the term 'direct address' can be used to
describe the way that certain images communicate. Verbal direct address can
be seen in:

> Hey, you there, what do you think you're doing?

Direct address in pictures, on the other hand, can be seen in Figure 4.11.

Both language and pictures can be used to address directly or indirectly, but
where language does it through the choice between second and third person
(and in other ways also, for example through vocatives, imperatives, etc.),
pictures do it by having people depicted in the image look at, and perhaps
also gesture at, the viewer of the picture. (It could also be, of course, that
depicted animals look at the viewer, or even things: in children's books, trains,
cars and other objects may have eyes and address the viewer directly.)

Many texts today, of course, contain both words and pictures. In a multimodal
text, then, we could ask:

- Does the verbal language address the listener or reader directly (e.g.
  through the use of the second person pronoun 'you')?

Figure 4.11

- Does the image address the viewer directly (which happens if a depicted person looks at the camera, and hence at the viewer)?

and if the text has both words and pictures we could ask:

- Is direct address chosen in both words and pictures? And if not, why?

The recruitment poster shown in Figure 4.11 has direct address in both visual and verbal modes, perhaps to reinforce the message in the strongest way possible. Other texts (often advertisements) may use direct address in the image and indirect address in the verbal text.

Given–new structures

Given–new structures are commonly found in verbal English. Given information refers to that which is stated but already known to the participants, and new information is that which is not already known (see Wales, 2001), for example:

> Besides being a well known literary critic (given), he also writes books on the history of aviation (new).

> (quoted in Wales, 2001, p. 179)

Given–new structures are often based on various types of opposition:

> Success is supposed to be an endangered species in this country.
> *Not any more.*

> (*Daily Mirror*, April 1994)

> Tense, nervous headache? Take Anadin.

> (advertisement)

In verbal English, such as in these examples, the given is what comes first in the clause and the new what comes last, and what, usually, has the greatest stress. In other words, given and new are realised sequentially (through 'before' and 'after'). These can be transcoded in images by use of the horizontal axis. In images, given and new are often represented spatially, through 'left' and 'right'. A vast number of advertisements in English use the visual axis in this way, positioning the taken-for-granted, 'already understood' information on the left and the new information on the right. The left side of the advertisement often outlines the problem, or given situation, while the right side shows the product (and the solution). Others go further and play with this convention, as shown in Figure 4.12.

H																	He
Li	Be											B	C	N	O	F	Ne
Na	Mg											Al	Si	P	S	Cl	Ar
K	Ca	Sc	Ti	V	Cr	Mn	Fe	Co	Ni	Cu	Zn	Ga	Ge	As	Se	Br	Kr
Rb	Sr	Y	Zr	Nb	Mo	Tc	Ru	Rh	Pd	Ag	Cd	In	Sn	Sb	Te	I	Xe
Cs	Ba	La	Hf	Ta	W	Re	Os	Ir	Pt	Au	Hg	Tl	Pb	Bi	Po	At	Rn
Fr	Ra	Ac	Rf	Db	Sg	Bh	Hs	Mt	Ds	Rg	VdT						

Figure 4.12   Audi advertisement

Figure 4.12 is a playful reworking of the periodic table of the elements, with the last 'element' shown as *VdT* in the 'new' position. *Vorsprung durch Technik* is the widely known slogan used by Audi in the UK for its television advertisements. The German phrase can be translated as 'progress through technology' and was used to associate Audi cars with the reputation that Germany has for high technical expertise and quality. The periodic table, which most readers will recognise, is itself expandable and if new elements are found, they are added to the table in that right-hand space.

The vertical axis can also be used as a structuring device, as shown in Figure 4.13. In this advertisement for Femigraine, we find visual representation of two opposing states (the 'before' and 'after' in relation to use of the product). Other advertisements use the top half as the space for the 'ideal' or the 'promise' – what you will become, or have, if you buy the product. The bottom half is reserved for the 'down to earth', the 'real' (often a product description in verbal English).

Figure 4.13

Vectors: visual transitivity?

Another grammatical element that can be seen in the visual is Halliday's theory of transitivity. Transitivity in Halliday's framework differs from the way in which the term is used in traditional grammar (where 'transitive' refers to verbs that normally require an object – *Sally cut the bread* – and 'intransitive' to verbs that do not require an object – *Sally ran*). For Halliday the system of transitivity provides a set of choices for representing 'what is going on in the world'. Put simply, it asks 'who does what to whom, and in what circumstances?' With what types of verb (processes, in his terms) are participants associated, and what does this tell us about social roles?

One of these choices is what Halliday (1985) has called the 'material process', the case in which 'what is going on' is represented as either an *action*, or a *transaction*, or an *event*. All three of these options are realised by grammatical structures. To understand this we first need to note that English requires us to analyse what is going on into two kinds of representational elements, *processes* (what is going on) and *participants* (the entities involved with what is going on). For example, in reality the flying of a bird may be a single, unanalysable whole, in which the bird can neither be separated from the flying nor the flying from the bird. But if we want to speak about it in English we must analyse the event into a participant (the bird) and a process (flying). Participants can be involved in material processes in one of two ways: as actor, 'the one who does the deed'; or as *goal*, 'the one to whom the deed is done' or 'to whom the event happens'. Three configurations are therefore possible (see box).

Outline of material processes

1   *Actions*
There is only one participant, an actor, so that the action is represented as though it is done 'in a void', for its own sake, without anyone or anything else being involved. An example:

Actor	Material process: action
The soldier	fired

2   *Transactions*
There are two participants, an actor and a goal, so that the deed is represented as having consequences for someone or something else. An example:

Actor	Material process: transaction	Goal
The soldier	killed	innocent villagers

3   *Event*
There is only one participant, a goal, so that whatever goes on is not explicitly represented as being done by someone or something. It is represented as 'just happening'. An example:

Goal	Material process: event
Innocent villagers	died

Clearly these examples constitute three different representations of the same event. Which option is chosen depends on the writer and on the context of writing. Writers with a technical interest in weaponry (in a specialist magazine, perhaps) might have an interest in obscuring the pain and destruction that weapons cause. Writers who are on the same side as the soldiers might also have an interest in obscuring their army's responsibility for the death of innocent civilians, and choose the 'event' option – usually adding a circumstantial element to flesh it out (e.g. *innocent villagers died in a large-scale military action yesterday*). A very clear example of the way such ideological choices are motivated by context can be found in Trew (1979a; 1979b).

Visual transitivity can be seen in the relationships between vectors. **Vectors** can be understood as 'lines which lead the eye' in an image. They may be formed by objects or parts of objects (arms, legs, guns, branches) or by angles set up in the image, or by such elements as the direction of a person's eye. Vectors can play an important part in portraying transitivity in images – about who is doing what to whom. If, in a photograph, a line is being sent out from one person or object towards another, then it is possible to say something about the relationship being depicted – who is acting, who is being acted upon.

It is possible to represent visually the English sentences in the preceding box, as shown in Figures 4.14 to 4.16.

Figure 4.14 *Action:* the soldier fired

Figure 4.15 *Transaction:* the soldier killed innocent villagers

Figure 4.16 *Event:* innocent villagers died

In film texts, there are different ways of combining these sorts of images to tell a story. Transactions in moving images can be realised in two ways.

They can connect actor and goal, as in Figure 4.17.

Actor and goal are *connected* spatially, shown together in the same shot.

Figure 4.17   The soldier killed innocent villagers

Alternatively, they can *disconnect* them, separating them through the editing process, as in Figure 4.18.

Here we see the same participants, but they are *disconnected*, shown in *separate* shots. The beginning of the process is shown in the first shot, and the continuation in the second — in the language of film and video editing this is called a 'matched action' cut.

Figure 4.18   The same participants disconnected

How is the second, 'disconnected' method different from the first one? Should we see the two shots as forming *one* unit of representation – the equivalent of a clause like *The soldier shoots the villagers*? Or as *two* units, whose transcoding in verbal English would be something like *The soldier fires. The villagers get shot*? It is not easy to decide which of the two views is best. On the one hand the editing brings about a disconnection between the action and its consequences which has no parallel in language. On the other hand disconnection *does* have parallels outside language – real-life parallels.

Vectors are also instrumental in constructing visual narratives – to show a chain of events unfolding, and to signpost the narrative path for the reader. We will look at examples of visual narratives later in this chapter.

Modality: visualising the 'real'

Modality is another important aspect of verbal English grammar. Modality in Halliday's social semiotic framework of language can be seen as, broadly, expressions of 'comment' or 'attitude' by the speaker towards a proposition, and is often realised by the use of modal auxiliary verbs, such as *should, could, ought, must* and so on. These indicate such things as obligation, permission, desirability and truth (for a fuller discussion of modality in a social semiotic framework, see Fowler, 1991, pp. 85–7). The expression of a speaker's attitude towards the truth value or reliability of a proposition can be particularly interesting to analyse. High modality (the expression of high truth value) occurs in *I know he is coming* – the speaker is expressing certainty about the other person's arrival. Low modality occurs in *He might come*, where the speaker is unsure that he will arrive.

Modality may also be realised by the use of distancing strategies: in statements such as *He says he is coming*, which may indicate the speaker's doubt about the likelihood of the other person's arrival; in hedges (*a bit, sort of*); and in tag questions (*doesn't he?*). Modality can be expressed visually too, in that some images are presented as 'more real' or 'more true' than others:

> Visuals can represent people, places and things as though they are real, as though they actually exist in this way, or as though they do not – as though they are imaginings, fantasies, caricatures, etc. And, here too, modality judgements are social, dependent on what is considered real (or true, or sacred) in the social group for which the representation is primarily intended.
>
> (Kress and van Leeuwen, 1996, p. 161)

A simple line drawing, for example, could be seen as having low modality – it may be seen as a simple sketch, or a rough outline, not intended to be accurate or proportioned. A sharply detailed, fine-grained photograph, on

remember that not some photographs are posed.

the other hand, could be ascribed high modality. For a start, people are accustomed to ascribing high truth value to photographs. Second, photographs often contain large amounts of detail, so seem to show more of the world 'as it is'. Diagrams, however, can also portray high modality because they purport to show more of what a photograph cannot, such as the inclusion of electrical circuits, or mental processes – what is actually 'there' and 'real'.

Diagrams can be used to portray what is normally only heard, or imagined. Consider a scientific diagram such as the one in Figure 4.19.

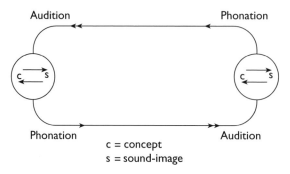

Figure 4.19   Saussure's schematised speech circuit, 1916

This drawing is about as abstract, as 'reduced' in every respect, as possible. There is no detail in the representation, no background, no colour, no representation of depth, or of light and shade – low modality, in other words. Yet scientists might not regard the diagram as unreal, because they might define reality not on the basis of surface resemblance – how much the image looks like what we would normally see – but on the basis of how accurately it represents a deeper, more abstract or general truth based on the essential characteristics of what is depicted. In this case then, although this appears to be a highly simplified drawing of what is a complex situation, Figure 4.19 might be ascribed high truth value, because it supposedly shows us more of spoken communication 'as it really is'.

Television news, textbooks and newspapers are filled with graphs and diagrams, whether they are for displaying economic indicators, to show a chemical reaction, or to depict the military strategy of an army. The purpose of diagrams and graphics is to simplify and explain complicated information. The creation of a diagram necessarily involves, however, taking decisions as to:

- what to include (i.e. what is considered significant and meaningful) and therefore what to exclude
- how to present information (colour, scales on graphs, symbols on maps).

Kress and van Leeuwen note that:

> Simplicity is ... always based on a particular cultural orientation and ideological stance, and the result of intensive training. It is only once this training is achieved that images (and the way of looking at the world expressed by their structure) can appear 'natural' and 'simple', and hence not in need of analysis.

(Kress and van Leeuwen, 1990, p. 15)

It is also important to recognise that there is more than one modality system, often dependent on the context in which the image appears. Just as we ascribe levels of modality to verbal English depending on the social context, the social context in which we ascribe levels of modality to images is an important factor. Colour, for instance, may have high modality in one context but low modality in another. Lynch and Edgerton's research (1988) into the visual presentation of scientific data, for example, revealed that while many scientists do not acknowledge that the aesthetic presentation of their work is important, many do in fact alter their images depending on the intended audience. The astronomers interviewed by Lynch and Edgerton all had examples of 'pretty pictures' which were produced specifically for certain readerships ('the public' or 'the scientists'). Images were digitally processed in different ways for the two audiences – in particular many images intended for a popular, non-scientific audience included false colours. Black and white images were used by the astronomers themselves for their work, as these are easier to interpret than colour which can confuse the eye. Colour, in this case, is associated with promotion and popularisation, but is a distraction from the scientific data.

ACTIVITY 4.5

Allow about 10 minutes

Actors and goals do not have to be human. They may be abstract shapes, for instance boxes in diagrams where concepts are related to each other, or triangles and circles in abstract art. Look at Figure 4.20, the book cover for *The Immigration Invasion*. You can decode a great deal of information from this one page. Some elements you should be looking at are:

Point of view	Whose point of view are we looking at, and how do we know?
Transitivity	Who, or what, is doing what to whom in this diagram?
Modality	What devices are used to convince us of the truth, or falsehood, of this scenario?

Figure 4.20

Comment

The Immigration Invasion laments the 'high number of immigrants' coming into the USA from South American countries. This point of view is reflected in the visuals as much as in the verbal English on the front cover – in fact you could say that it is not necessary to read the book in order to discover what the authors are advocating (which in this case is mass 'repatriation'). Most important of all here is the interaction of the visual and verbal elements – the way that the presence and positioning of individual elements affect and reinterpret the others.

The diagram in Figure 4.20 is a good example of the polysemous nature of visual representation – the way that images, like words and sentences, are open to more than one interpretation. What other valid interpretations of this diagram might there be? The viewer's point of view will affect how the diagram is 'read'. The producer's point of view also affects what is included in a diagram, and how it is presented – try to visualise how this diagram might have looked, told from the point of view of the 'invaders'.

4.5 Visual narratives

So far we have been looking at individual graphic elements and single images. To conclude, we take a brief look at longer texts such as cartoons and comic strips, and consider these in terms of narrative. We also look, in Reading B, at how a television advertisement combines words and images to get its message across to consumers.

Cartoons use most, if not all, of the devices outlined so far in this chapter. In addition, they employ specific devices to convey mood, movement and narrative structure. Print cartoons share some properties with photographs, as do animated cartoons with film. There are many genres: children's comics, teenage photo stories in magazines, adult comics, political satire in daily newspapers. Genre divisions are, as in literature, difficult to pin down, and they are breaking down further with the increasing availability of new multimedia technologies. Popular newspapers may use photo stories to portray a narrative on the problem page, and biting political satire may be achieved by using a visual style similar to that of comic books for the very young. Cartoons are also being increasingly used in traditionally non-pictorial contexts, such as job advertisements, so understanding the ways that visual and verbal codes communicate is becoming important in an increasing range of contexts.

Visual and verbal elements are so closely intertwined in cartoons that it can be difficult to separate them. Because of their visual format, cartoons provide rich resources for the representation of features common in face-to-face interaction that are unavailable to written English. These include paralinguistic features such as facial expression, gestures and posture. There are also proxemic indicators: how characters are positioned can reveal information about their relationships and attitudes to each other – closeness, distance, antipathy and so on.

In addition, cartoons contain vast amounts of graphic information used to represent verbal English. Some of these are directly related to English phrases: we say that we 'see stars' after a bump on the head, so stars or asterisks over a cartoon character's head are understood; we say we 'have a bright idea' or 'see the light' so the pictorial representation of a light bulb is also comprehensible; we know the shapes lightning can take in the sky, so can relate ➤ to concepts of danger, etc. There may also be recourse to the verbal, to emphasise the visual – even a nonsense word acquires semantic significance in a visual context (see Figure 4.21).

Punctuation is frequently used as a semantic device in cartoons. Exclamation marks can be added to a character's speech to indicate surprise or outrage, or punctuation marks can be used alone, indicating moments where feelings are running so high that verbal English is inadequate for expressing them, as in Figure 4.22.

Figure 4.21   **Figure 4.22**

Intonation may be expressed in a number of ways. Typefaces, in particular, can be used to show changes of pitch or stress – the size of the type and the use of emboldening, in particular, are common devices in this respect. Similarly, mixes of upper and lower case can suggest shouting and whispering respectively, as shown in Figure 4.6 (the headmaster and pupil poem) in Section 4.3.

Letters can be repeated to show st-st-stammering, and clues to a character's accent can be shown by using a semi-phonetic representation of speech, such as *wot* for *what*, or *'er* for *her*.

Creating a visual narrative

So how are narrative structures expressed visually? Movement can be conveyed as shown in Figure 4.23; or movement may be conveyed visually by repetitions or other devices, as shown in Figure 4.24 depicting a character's hand tossing a coin:

Figure 4.23   **Figure 4.24**

Cartoon narratives need to propel the reader forwards through the story, and this is often achieved through the use of vectors, as well as by utilising the conventional verbal reading path – in the case of English, left to right. In modern print cartoons the page will be divided into a number of frames, or vignettes. This is often standardised within a particular genre or for a particular artist. For example, languages which traditionally do not read left to right, such as Chinese, may use either a left-to-right progression, or top-to-bottom, as shown in Figure 4.25.

Here, the frames, as well as the speech, read downwards (although this does not always happen in Chinese). European and North American cartoons typically use the page format and reading paths shown in Figure 4.26, which follows the left-to-right pattern for the verbal language. In any case, it is not

Figure 4.25

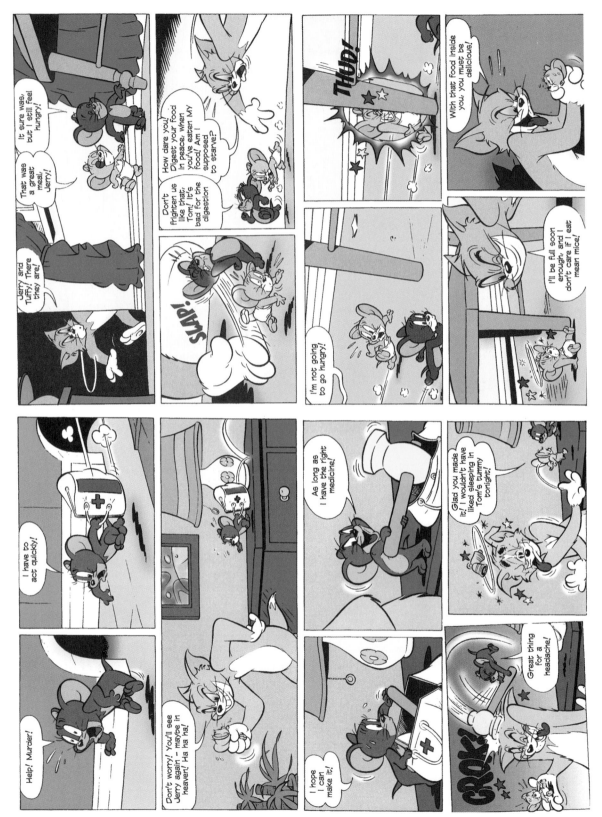

Figure 4.26 Tom & Jerry

possible to state definitively that different countries are associated with distinctive types or styles of cartoon – every country and language has a range of different styles, some of which will be influenced in turn by the styles of other countries. In addition, there is always a range of purposes to which visual depiction is put – cultural, religious and educational.

Indeed, the division of the page into frames is not the only way to create a visual narrative. McCloud (1994, pp. 12–13) notes that one can see the Bayeux tapestry (an enormous linear tapestry showing the Norman conquest in the eleventh century) as a type of cartoon – it reads left to right, leading the viewer onwards as the story of the battle unfolds in chronological order. He points out that although there are no distinct frames, changes of background and subject matter are used to create a coherent story.

The vectors of cartoon frames themselves may encode additional information about the next stage in the visual narrative, as illustrated in Figure 4.27. The shapes of these frames set up directional vectors. The character's arms and legs, too, are used to create vectors and thus convey directionality – the reader's eye is led from one frame to the next by literally following the central character, rather than by the conventional left-to-right direction in verbal English. We as readers follow Max's zig-zag path through the story – and until we get there, we are not quite sure where we are going next. And neither, of course, is Max; so here the vectors have an additional function – to create links between reader and character. In more traditional reading paths the reader knows the next step in advance (unlike the character) so is necessarily more of an observer. Here, Max and the reader share the unsettling experience.

The frame shapes can be semantically motivated: in the Mighty Max example the jagged and chaotic frames convey action and danger. Dondis argues that direction is one meaning-laden aspect of visual syntax: 'each visual direction has strong associative meaning and is a valuable tool in making visual messages' (Dondis, 1973, p. 46). He states that horizontal and vertical lines are associated with well-being and stability, whereas a diagonal line is unstable, provoking and even upsetting. Curves, on the other hand, are associated with encompassment, repetition and warmth.

Visual deixis?

Deixis, too, can be seen to operate in certain elements of visual English. For example, visual shapes can be used to show deictic expressions of time, such as 'then' or 'now'. Figure 4.28 (below), from the American comic artist Will Eisner, shows how the shapes of panel borders can be used to locate the reader in the past or the present.

Colour, too, can be used deictically. In particular, it can be used to indicate time and the passage of time (how do you know when it is dawn, or

Figure 4.27   Page from *The Adventures of Mighty Max* (December, 1994)

night-time?). Lack of colour is also significant, such as in the use of silhouettes. Black and white can often, as it can in film, convey past tense, and a transition to colour can indicate that the reader is now located in the present.

THE 'LANGUAGE' OF THE PANEL BORDER

In addition to its primary function as a frame in which to place objects and actions, the panel border itself can be used as part of the non-verbal 'language' of sequential art.

For example, rectangular panels with straight edged borders (A), unless the verbal portion of the narrative contradicts this, usually are meant to imply that the actions contained therein are set in the present tense. The flashback (a change in tense or shift in time) is often indicated by altering the line which makes up the frame. The wavy edged (B) or scalloped (C) panel border is the most common past time indicator. While there is no universally agreed upon convention for expressing tense through the outline of the frame, the 'character' of the line – as in the case of sound, emotion (D) or thought (C) – creates a hieroglyphic.

Figure 4.28

Portraying interpersonal relationships

One of the ways in which relationships (part of the interpersonal metafunction) may be represented in images is through the camera angle. Kress and van Leeuwen believe that the horizontal angle signifies involvement or distance, and that the vertical angle can represent power relationships between the viewer and those depicted:

> In many of the illustrations in school textbooks we look down rather steeply on people – workers in the hall; children in a school yard. In such books the social world lies at the feet of the viewer, so to speak: knowledge is power. The models in magazine advertisements and features, and newsworthy people and celebrities in magazine articles, on the other hand, generally look down on the viewer: these models are depicted as exercising symbolic power over us.

> (Kress and van Leeuwen, 1996, p. 146)

They also note that the size of the frame itself can be an indicator of social distance – realised by the choice between close-up, medium shot, long shot: 'The distances people keep ... depend on their social relation ... People are portrayed *as though* they are friends, or *as though* they are strangers' (Kress and van Leeuwen, 1996, pp. 131–2).

Angles in drawings can operate in similar ways to those in film or photographs – aerial shots can convey power, show more information and/or slow down the narrative. The (camera) angle therefore has an important effect on pace. Empathy with Max in Figure 4.27 is in part created through the use of 'camera' angles: in the third frame, where he is surrounded by enemies, the reader is placed on the same level with him – solidarity is created through equal positioning of reader and character. In the next frame we are looking down on the scene from a more distant position, where Max is in the visual centre, surrounded by an array of large threatening characters coming at him from all sides, and – importantly – from above. He is small in this frame, and looking up at the impending danger, which emphasises his vulnerability. Assuming we as readers are empathetically engaged with him, we feel powerless to intervene from this distance, and are further encouraged to read on by the last frame where Max is threatened with immediate death ...

As a further example, notice how, in Figure 4.29, the feeling of shock is heightened by the reader being placed on the balustrade with the security guard, watching the devastating explosion below.

Figure 4.29

ACTIVITY 4.6

Allow about
15 minutes

Find a print cartoon, and look closely at:
- devices for representing movement
- visual narrative paths: how is the reader moved on to the next frame?
- devices for creating empathy (and antipathy) with the characters: how is their effect achieved? with whom do the characters make eye contact?

It seems that culture and the influence of the verbal language also play an important role in the layout of the page. Different languages and cultures may express visual narrative structures in different ways. McCloud noted that traditional Japanese cartoons, for example, are far more cyclical in their layout than American ones. His analysis of the cartoon techniques and narrative paths used in different countries revealed that American artists used a far higher proportion of action-to-action frame transitions than Japanese artists. This held for other 'Western' countries (he studied Tintin, for example, and got similar results, in spite of other radical differences between French and American styles). In Japan, although artists did use action-to-action transitions between panels, they also used a striking number of subject-to-subject transitions, and moves from aspect to aspect. McCloud comments on this as follows: 'Most often used to establish a mood or a sense of place, time seems to stand still in these quiet, contemplative combinations ... Rather than acting as a bridge between separate moments, the reader here must assemble a single moment using scattered fragments' (McCloud, 1994, p. 79).

In considering the reasons for this difference, he notes that Japanese cartoons often appear in enormous anthologies, and that therefore 'dozens of panels can be devoted to portraying slow cinematic movement or to setting a mood' (McCloud, 1994, p. 80). But the fundamental reason, for him, is a difference between Eastern and Western cultural traditions (see Figure 4.30, overleaf).

Closure: making the viewer do the work

Many forms of visual information are now encountered in the context of verbal English. Newspaper photographs, corporate logos and graphic elements are often surrounded and intertwined with print. This then begs the question of how elements in visual and verbal modes interact on the page – a central issue in multimodal texts. How do the messages of words and pictures reinforce or undermine each other, and in what ways is the reader invited to see these meanings as connected or distinct?

Creating meaning from what we see in a multimodal text involves a complex interaction of visual elements and verbal English presented to the eye, as well as contextual and background knowledge. Arnheim has noted that 'the perception of a complex visual pattern may be modified by the presence of a second pattern' (Arnheim, 1970, p. 61). He was describing an experiment where observers were asked to give their impressions of two paintings of

Figure 4.30

quite different style shown next to each other – when one of the pair was replaced by another, the subjects' impressions of the paintings differed enormously from the first viewing. He terms this the 'privilege of observing everything in relation' (Arnheim, 1970, p. 62). What we see, then, depends not only upon the image itself, but also on the context and on the other images, or words, on the page.

You can see this at work in Figure 4.31. The large headline BLACKMAIL (with its negative connotations) is reflected by extension in the photograph of the footballer, a black male. This may be an entirely unintentional pun across semiotic modes, but it could also be argued that the negative connotations become entangled in the reader's or viewer's mind because of their positioning on the page. The juxtaposition of all the elements on the page – visual and verbal – produces a complex semantic cocktail.

Figure 4.31

We've seen in this chapter a range of ways in which images and words can be combined in meaningful ways in English language texts. We now come to a more detailed analysis of a longer text, this time we look at the semiotic elements of a television advertisement for the soft drink, Sprite.

ACTIVITY 4.7

Read 'Pictures, music, speech and writing' by Guy Cook (Reading B). As you read, note what Cook says about the possibilities for punning across semiotic modes in this text.

Comment

Cook is interested in how the semiotic modes of music, image and text are combined in this advertisement for Sprite. He breaks the advertisement down into its component parts (in as far as this is possible when trying to analyse moving images in writing) and shows how puns are created across modes using visual metaphors and equivalences. Commonly used phrases such as *when the heat is on* and *a twist of lemon* are reworked in the visual mode to increase the meanings available to the viewer in the advertisement. This is a more complex example of the kind of pun you met in the newspaper page shown in Figure 4.31.

4.6 Conclusion

In this chapter we have been considering some of the forms of visual information that are used to communicate in English texts. We've considered some of the ways images can represent semantic distinctions that in verbal English would be conveyed through grammatical structure. Different semiotic modes of communication convey all of the meanings that can be expressed individually, but there are often similarities between the two, and many texts make use of punning across modes to make these connections.

We have looked at how the meanings ascribed to visual information are to a large extent socially constructed and culturally dependent, rather than a natural or inherent characteristic of the visual form itself. Literacy in visual English, and in other visual languages, is affected by culture and also by the linguistic structure of the verbal language.

READING A: The semiotic construction of a wine label

David Graddol
(David Graddol is well known as a writer, broadcaster and lecturer on issues related to global English.)

Specially written by Graddol (1996, pp. 73–81).

The word 'text' carries with it, for many people, connotations of substantial content and seriousness of communicative purpose but the majority of texts which circulate in late modern times do not easily fit this description. For example, the packaging and labelling on food sold in supermarkets gives rise to a multitude of ephemeral texts which are in many ways typical of a consumer society. One might expect that the transient function of packaging would mean that limited resources would be expended on its design but, as all consumers are aware, this is not usually the case. A great deal of care goes into the creation of packaging and it routinely deploys a variety of semiotic resources – verbal, visual and sometimes tactile and olfactory.

One reason for this is that packaging serves several purposes, such as protecting the merchandise during distribution and storage, encouraging a shopper to buy the product, and informing the consumer of its content and potential use. It must accomplish all of these functions within a variety of constraints including legal (the law governs what must and may be said on labels), economic (such as the cost of packaging in relation to the cost of the goods, or a supermarket's requirements for display and merchandising), practical (such as the size and shape of the goods) and cultural (including the need to draw on discourses of consumer desire and to take account of social patterns of consumption). What might be perceived as its main function (that of persuading purchasers to buy) must be accomplished within a time constraint – the packaging must hail the potential purchaser from the shelves, draw attention to its presence among competitors' products, and communicate desirability both at a distance and on closer inspection.

The sophistication of packaging design thus reflects a complexity in communicative function. This point is well illustrated by the labels that can be found on the back of bottles of wine, such as that illustrated in Figure 1, taken from a Californian wine sold in California. I will examine the design of such labels more closely, showing how they address a multiple readership in complex and, at times, contradictory ways reflecting many of the ambiguities and contradictions associated with the consumer-subject in industrialised societies.

The multimodal nature of the label

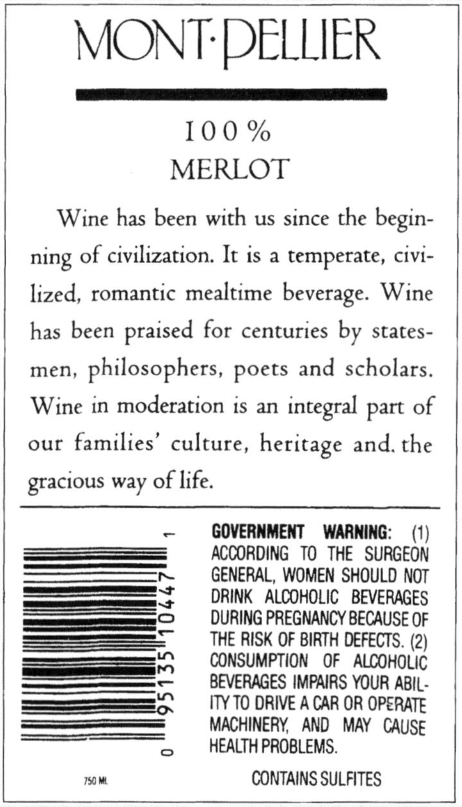

MONT·PELLIER

**100%
MERLOT**

Wine has been with us since the beginning of civilization. It is a temperate, civilized, romantic mealtime beverage. Wine has been praised for centuries by statesmen, philosophers, poets and scholars. Wine in moderation is an integral part of our families' culture, heritage and. the gracious way of life.

GOVERNMENT WARNING: (1) ACCORDING TO THE SURGEON GENERAL, WOMEN SHOULD NOT DRINK ALCOHOLIC BEVERAGES DURING PREGNANCY BECAUSE OF THE RISK OF BIRTH DEFECTS. (2) CONSUMPTION OF ALCOHOLIC BEVERAGES IMPAIRS YOUR ABILITY TO DRIVE A CAR OR OPERATE MACHINERY, AND MAY CAUSE HEALTH PROBLEMS.

0 95135 10447 1

750 ML   CONTAINS SULFITES

Figure 1

The label shown in Figure 1 communicates its complex message by means of a variety of codes and devices in addition to the verbal channel. These semiotic modalities include:

- a code of numbers: 100%, 750 ML, numerical value of the bar code
- the bar code
- nibbles around the label indicating the batch and time of bottling (not shown)
- graphic design features such as rules
- words, which are organised in space
- typography – a visual coding of language.

The label is thus a multimodal text. As a consequence the meanings conveyed by the label are potentially complex: different messages may be conveyed through each mode, and these may reinforce each other or give rise to tensions and even contradictions – not necessarily in the basic information conveyed but in the way the reader is addressed.

The complexity of audience address

Before it reaches the supermarket shelves the bottle will be handled by many intermediaries such as shippers, wholesalers, buyers for the supermarket, store managers and shelf fillers. At each stage the labelling must present the product in a way that ensures the best treatment so that it eventually achieves a prominent place in the store. In the supermarket it must speak to purchasers, persuading them that the product is attractive and worth the price being asked. There is thus no sole occasion on which the label serves its communicative function nor only one kind of person who will read it.

The different semiotic resources of the text are employed to address this multiple audience in a way that recognises the different social and economic relations the text producer wishes to construct with each. For example, the bar code addresses the retailer, or rather the machines and computer systems used for stock control and pricing; the bar code also impinges on the relation between retailer and customer, since it records details of the particular transaction (location, time, quantity) in order to build profiles of consumer activity for marketing purposes. Bar codes are thus difficult things to integrate into a label design. If they are too prominent they may highlight the retailer's convenience and interest more than that of the consumer, drawing attention to the goods as revenue potential rather than as a satisfier of consumer need or desire. Unfortunately, in order to be read by automated check-out tills (and thus minimise staff costs) such bar codes need to be of a minimum size and standard placement. Practical label design must thus compromise between the two potentially competing requirements. In Figure 1 the bar code is located in the lower portion of the label, marked off from the main text by a rule.

It is not clear who is intended to read the batch information that is communicated by nibbles on the label edge. It addresses, however, some of the legal and institutional relations that govern the exchange of goods between manufacturer, distributor, retailer, customer and consumer. It is a part of the text that is not ordinarily read, but may become a focus of interest if these economic, legal and social relations are called into question – such as in the case of damaged or contaminated goods. The fact that this code is not transparent to the consumer, of course, is a part of that social relation.

The contradictory nature of the consumer-subject

The most prominent part of the text of the label is clearly addressed to the consumer. But food buying is a complex social as well as economic activity which is highly structured according to region, ethnicity, social class and gender. A retailer's market research, for example, may show that wine in their supermarkets is bought mainly by women but drunk largely by men, or that higher price wines are bought mainly for meals to which guests are invited.

This means that the label will, at the very least, have to address the consumer-purchaser, the consumer-host and the consumer-guest. And how does such a wine label speak to guests at the dinner table, and what does it say about the host's taste, judgement, wealth and hospitality? This will depend to large measure on the cultural practices with which the consumption of wine is associated. What, for example, is the significance of serving wine at the dinner table (in different countries, among different social and ethnic groups)? What little rituals of opening and serving are associated with it? In the UK, a supermarket brand name on the label may, for example, reassure the consumer-purchaser that a particular wine is of reliable quality and good value, but the consumer-guest may regard it as more suitable for family consumption than for a special occasion.

Heteroglossia in the text

There is a further contradiction in the way the consumer is addressed which arises from the legislation governing label design.

The text in Figure 1, for example, contains two paragraphs: the upper one addresses the consumer as one with desires, appetites and choices. The lower text, however, addresses the reader as a consumer who has certain rights and to whom the manufacturer has certain duties of care. The result is that consumers are simultaneously told that this wine will enhance their life, and that it will damage it. This particular contradiction arises from the law governing wine labelling in California, but the words and descriptions that can be placed on wine labels are, in most countries, highly regulated. By regulating the ways in which the reader can be addressed by the text, they regulate also the kinds of social relation that can be established with a reader. There is thus a contradiction which arises from the competing 'interests' established by consumer law and the manufacturer/retailer and which results in different voices being represented in the text.

The contradictions are clearly signalled by the language genres in which the two fragments are written. The persuasive text is highly evaluative, using words such as *civilized* and *gracious*. It incorporates the reader in this evaluation by the use of the first person: *wine has been with **us**, **our** culture*. The Surgeon General's warning, in contrast, draws on language genres of information giving and objective authority. It uses modal constructions such as *should not*, terms from a formal scientific register, *alcoholic beverages*, employs a discourse of medical cause and effect, *because of the risk of birth defects*, uses impersonal address in the third person, *women should not*, or in the second person, *impairs your ability*, and includes enumerated paragraphs.

These two text fragments thus not only give contradictory messages at the surface level ('drink and enjoy' versus 'drink and die'), they also position the reader in quite different ways and attempt to construct different ideas about what it is to be a consumer. In the remainder of this reading I want to examine this heteroglossia more closely, showing how the tension between promotion and regulation affects other parts of the text and how the perception of contradiction is minimised by visual design.

The legal restrictions

There is certain information which must by law be given on labels carried by the wine sold in the European Union (EU), such as the alcoholic strength, volume, country of origin and category of wine. There are also various kinds of optional information, such as recommendations to the consumer about:

- dishes with which the wine might be served
- manner of serving
- appropriate handling of the wine
- proper storage of the wine
- the history of the particular wine or of the bottler
- the natural and technical conditions under which the wine was made.

If information is neither required nor optional, then it cannot be given on the label. The purpose of the legislation is to ensure that consumers know exactly what they are getting and are not misled about the quality of the wine. For example, EU law states that compulsory information, including the country of origin and category of wine, shall be given in one or more official languages of the community so that the consumer can easily understand it. EU law establishes different classes of wine, of which 'Table Wine' is one of the lowest, but in many cases this can be stated in the national language of origin. Hence a phrase such as *vin de table* is acceptable on a bottle of French wine sold in the UK and *vino da tavola* would be accepted on a bottle of Italian wine. By printing the classification in the national language, the label designers may feel that the perceived quality of the wine will be indirectly enhanced. But only standard, familiar non-English phrases can be used on wine sold in Britain. If the wine is the produce of more than one country, this description must be in English, because the regulators fear that the majority of British consumers would fail to understand if it were given in French or Italian. Indeed, it may give a false impression of quality if consumers recognised the language as being the national language of a traditional wine-producing country, but did not actually understand what it meant.

Such 'language display' in advertising is more usually associated with the English language worldwide: the perceived value of many consumer products is enhanced by being associated with a piece of English language text. In Europe, however, the use of English in connection with wine does not usually enhance the perceived quality of the product, since England is not a traditional wine-producing country.

The regulatory structure which governs label design has a wider effect on the discourse of back labels. Since quality and desirability cannot be stated explicitly, labels typically communicate indirectly through conventional discourses which have grown up around the marketing and consumption of wine in different countries. The label on a red wine bottle from France may state that the wine is an excellent accompaniment to red meat and cheese. A label from an Italian wine might add that it will be ideal with pasta or pizza. These descriptions are not directly informative: they are the conventional terms in which good red wine is described. More importantly, they allow a word like 'excellent' (which cannot be used to describe the wine itself) to be used in connection with the wine's suitability to accompany conventional foods.

...

The importance of visual design

The strict regulation of what must and can be said on wine labels may be one reason why visual design is so important. There are fewer legal restrictions on appearance than on words. In fact, European regulations have very little to say about visual design other than that lettering must be clear and legible, with minimum heights specified for key information, and that key information should be visible within one 'field of view' (i.e. either all on the front or all on the back).

This limited prescription does nevertheless explain one major feature of the visual design. Since basic information, such as the name, must be displayed clearly on the front label so that it is visible on a supermarket shelf, this means that *all* the key information is usually placed on the front label and the optional information located on the back.

Between the front label and the back label there is the bottle itself, containing the main contents, which has a colour and shape which conventionally indicates the style of wine. The bottle as a whole, then, can be regarded as a single text with an internal structure of front, body and back. ... The front label shows the title and other 'headline' information about the wine. The bottle provides the main contents, and the back label includes textual apparatus not dissimilar to the index at the back of a book, providing detailed data about contents and use.

Visual design is used extensively to resolve some of the contradictions which arise from regulations which govern the verbal. For example, the contradiction between upper and lower text fragments in Figure 1 means that the label speaks with at least two distinct voices but the priority between these voices is clearly signalled by the placing of the promotional text at the start of the reading path. The Surgeon General's warning is marked off by a horizontal rule and relegated 'below stairs' with the other 'housekeeping' text fragments such as the bar code.

The status of the two parts of the text, promotional and warning, is also clearly signalled typographically. The persuasive, upper text is in a serif typeface called Centaur. The Surgeon General's warning is set in a sans serif face called Helvetica. Few readers will recognise the typefaces employed, but they will intuitively make very different associations with each.

...

Conclusion

I have tried to show the importance of visual design in the construction of labels, in addressing the different audiences and meeting contradictory needs, and in disciplining the heteroglossia which necessarily arises in such texts.

Labelling is no different from other, more conventional texts, in the way it attempts to position readers within particular social and economic relationships and in the way it speaks with several, at times contradictory, voices. Visual communication is still poorly understood, despite the fact that visual design is becoming a more prominent feature of texts in mass circulation. Packaging has been given less scholarly attention, perhaps, than its impact on people's everyday lives warrants.

READING B: Pictures, music, speech and writing

Guy Cook
(Guy Cook is Professor of Language and Education at The Open University and co-editor of the journal Applied Linguistics.*)*

Source: Cook, G. (2001) *The Discourse of Advertising*, London, Routledge, pp. 43–50.

This reading examines the effect of the selection and combination of the different modes in ads, and of three sub-modes of language: song, speech and writing.

Any analysis of the language of ads immediately encounters the paradox that it both must and cannot take the musical and pictorial modes into account as well. It must do this because there are many ads in which picture and music are the essence of the communication: creating mood, imparting information, persuading and making claims so strongly that, if language features at all – and there are many ads in which it does not – it is often only in a peripheral or auxiliary way. Even in those ads where language is the dominant mode of communication (perhaps a minority), it is still deceptive to look at it in isolation, because it rebounds against both picture and music, gaining and giving new meanings and connections. Yet analysis cannot adequately cope with music and pictures, because they are different from the mode of the analysis itself, which is language. While the words of this book can put the words of an ad on the page, they can only hint at the nature of its music and pictures, for these cannot be written down 'as themselves' but only as something else – words or frozen stills. This problem is more serious with television ads than with printed ones. On television, pictures move, music plays, and language comes in changing combinations of speech, song and writing; on paper, pictures stand still (and can even be reproduced), and there is no sound. Yet even in analyses of printed ads the problems are legion. Reproduction is unlikely to do justice to such factors as size and colour, and the relation of the ad to its accompanying discourse.

...

Advertising, unlike analysis, operates in all modes and media at once, and must be treated accordingly. Therefore, though the focus [here] is on language, it also considers the effect on language of the other modes. Music and pictures are part of the discourse of ads, and to ignore or downplay them is a serious distortion.

An example: *The Perfect Combination*

These problems and pitfalls are best illustrated by an example. Let us take a fairly ordinary television ad, firstly as words only, and secondly as words in interaction with music and pictures. The example raises two quite separate problems: how to transcribe music and pictures on the page; and how to analyse their interaction with each other and with language. The ad is a television commercial for the soft drink Sprite[1] (screened in Britain in 1990, but representative of a type of ad which has persisted from the 1970s to the present). The words of the song are:

> When the heat is on,
> And the pace is slow,
> There's a cool fresh world
> Where you can go:
> Clear, crisp and light,
> It tastes of Sprite.
>
> A twist of lemon
> For a taste sensation;
> A squeeze of lime
> Is the perfect combination:
> Clear, crisp and light,
> Sheer taste of Sprite;
> Clear, crisp and light,
> Sheer taste of Sprite.

During the course of the ad two small written texts appear briefly at the bottom of the screen. The first says:

> Sprite and Diet Sprite are registered trademarks of the Coca-Cola company.

and the second:

> Diet Sprite can help slimming or weight control only as part of a calorie controlled diet.

In addition the words 'Sprite' and 'Diet Sprite' are visible on the product itself. The jingle, the small print, and the brand names are the only language. Along with these words go eighteen camera shots of four separate locations; and the words are sung – rather than spoken – by a man's voice (with inevitable cheerfulness!).

The music and singing pass through four phases, distinguished by marked changes in speed and beat. The first phase conveys a sense of urgency building to a climax; the second phase releases the tension of the first with a bouncy and regular rhythm; in the third phase this rhythm disappears, and the beat is replaced by sound effects creating an air of magic and mystery; finally, the fourth phase repeats the second, confident and animated as before.

The relation of the words to accompanying pictures and to these phases of the music is set out, approximately, below. ... [three of the locations are shown in Figure 1.]

Song words		Pictures
SCENE ONE: THE TRAFFIC JAM **MUSIC BUILDING TO A CLIMAX**		
When the heat is on,	1	Couple in an open car in a traffic jam at the entrance to a coastal road tunnel. The driver of the lorry behind has left his cab to try to see the cause of the jam. Everyone is hot and frustrated.
And the pace is slow,		
There's a cool, fresh world	2	Close up of hands reaching into a cool-box containing ice, Sprite and Diet Sprite.
Where you can go:	3	Close-up of couple in the car. The man (the driver) looks at the woman.
	4	Both swig from their cans.
	5	The camera takes us through the opening in the top of the can, and into the Sprite inside!

SCENE TWO: THE TOBOGGAN RUN
MUSIC INTENSIFIES, SPEEDS UP, LOOSENS

Clear, crisp and light,	6	A professional toboggan run as seen from a high-speed toboggan emerging from a tunnel.
It tastes of Sprite.	7	Close-up of yellow helmet of the tobogganer.
	8	Toboggan run as seen by tobogganer.
A twist of lemon	9	The track is blocked by a giant slice of lemon.
For a taste sensation;	10	We see the lemon reflected in the visor of the approaching tobogganer.
	11	Close up of the slice of lemon: drops of juice are oozing out of it.
	12	We now see there are two riders on the toboggan, the pillion rider is holding on tightly. The toboggan smashes through the lemon and enters a tunnel.

SCENE THREE: IN THE TUNNEL
MUSIC SLOWS, LOSES BEAT, GROWS WHIMSICAL

	13	An underwater shot inside the can of Sprite. We are moving through ice cubes towards the surface.
A squeeze of lime	14	On the toboggan run, the camera comes to a slice of lime at the other end of the tunnel, and breaks through.
Is the perfect combination:	15	The two tobogganers are out in the open again. Their toboggan is approaching another tunnel.

SCENE FOUR: MOVING TRAFFIC
MUSIC RETURNS TO REGULAR CONFIDENT BEAT

Clear, crisp and light,	16	The toboggan enters the tunnel.
Sheer taste of Sprite;	17	Close-up of couple back in the car, moving fast.
Clear, crisp and light,		The woman is drinking from a can of Sprite.
Sheer taste of Sprite.	18	The car emerges from a tunnel on a coastal road. The man and woman are cool, happy and relaxed.

Figure 1 'The Perfect Combination': advertisement for Sprite. (*Sprite* is a registered trade mark of the Coca-Cola Company, *Sprite light* is a trade mark of the Coca-Cola Company and are reproduced with kind permission of the Coca-Cola Company.)

Taken together with the pictures in these four scenes, and the four corresponding phases of the music, the words of the jingle, which are so one-dimensional in isolation, take on new meaning, and contribute to a complex set of visual metaphors and parallels. A number of words, phrases and clauses become puns. Thus

When the heat is on

no longer has only its dead metaphorical sense of 'when life is difficult'. It also refers literally to the uncomfortable heat experienced in the waiting vehicles. By the same process

And the pace is slow

refers literally to the traffic jam, as well as, idiomatically, to a dull period of life. The pictures reinstate the lost force of the dead metaphor from which its idiomatic sense derives. In the line

There's a cool, fresh world

'world' in the context of Scene Two refers to the fantasy world of the toboggan run which is apparently inside the can; the words

Where you can go

accompany the transition shot in which we see the can from the point of view of the person drinking from it, who then appears to shrink and enter into it. In this fantasy world, inside the Sprite, all the undesirable qualities of the world in the opening scenes are reversed. There is cool snow and fast movement. In the lines of the bouncy chorus which accompanies these new pictures, 'it' refers both to this fantasy world, and to the Sprite itself:

Clear, crisp and light,
It tastes of Sprite.

The visually created puns continue.

A twist of lemon

is also a twist in the toboggan run, and a twist in the tale – for who would expect to find either a toboggan run inside a soft-drink can, or a giant slice of lemon on a toboggan run? The lemon, appearing on the track, is both a fantasy within a fantasy (and thus at even further remove) but also, because Sprite tastes of lemon, the beginning of a transition back to the opening scene, for on the other side of the lemon we are back in the can, and as we emerge from it, the car emerges from the tunnel in Scene Four. Perhaps it is far-fetched to say that

A squeeze of lime

refers punningly to the squeezing of the front rider by the pillion rider, but it does seem reasonable to say that the words

is the perfect combination

occurring with the picture of the two tobogganers, refers simultaneously to their athletic teamwork, to the relationship of the couple in the car (who are presumably also the tobogganers), to the combination of cold Sprite with hot weather, and to the combination of lemon and lime flavours in the Sprite itself.

These complex relations between the three worlds (road, toboggan run, Sprite can) are all aided by the image of the tunnel, which occurs in each one, and whose darkness effects the transition from one world to the next. Connections between the worlds are reinforced by the puns, but separated in mood by changes in the music, allowing the ad to make two suggestions – both frequent in ads. The first is that the product is a solution to a problem, the second that the product will bring people together. In this ad, the couple (good-looking, young, affluent, happy, heterosexual) have a problem. They are stuck in a traffic jam on a hot day. Perhaps this symbolises a rather dull or stressful period in their life ('The heat is on ... the pace is slow'). They drink Sprite and enter its magic world. Within that world, the problems of heat and inertia do not exist; but when they return from that world these problems have ceased to exist in the everyday world too. We do not see what started the traffic moving, but we feel it was Sprite.

The young man and the young woman are, like the flavours in Sprite, 'the perfect combination'. They are also dressed in the Sprite colours of yellow and green – both in the car, and on the toboggan. As they drink, they look at each other. The product appears to contribute to their perfect compatibility!

What I have tried to show by this analysis is that the effect of the ad is not to be found in any of the three major modes alone, but only in their combination. Each mode gains from the other. In this ad, the message is distributed fairly evenly between music, pictures and (sung) language. The least powerful sub-mode of language in this ad is writing, used in the reminder of trademark registration and the caveat imposed by the Independent Television Commission[2] (ITC) code of advertising practice neither of which is part of the story, and both of which are emasculated by their small print and brief duration.

[1] 'Sprite' is a registered trademark of the Coca-Cola Company

[2] This body replaced the Independent Broadcasting Authority in January 1991.

English manuscripts: the emergence of a visual identity

David Graddol

5.1 Introduction

Chapter 4 focused on the increasingly visual nature of English, and the growing interest in developing analytical frameworks for analysing visual and multimodal texts. While there is evidence that new technologies are creating greater opportunities for multimodal text design and production, it is important to recognise that written English has always had a multimodal dimension: most obviously, written English is visual in that it has a particular set of letters or characters but is also multimodal in nature in that it is often produced alongside other types of visual representation, such as decorative illustration, and involves a range of materials in terms of its production. In this chapter, I take a historical look at the development of written English and explore how written English developed from early Anglo-Saxon inscriptions on bone and stone, to a wide diversity of manuscripts from the eighth century onwards. I will illustrate how changing technologies influenced the kinds of writing and texts produced and consider an issue that continues to generate debates, notably the standardisation of spelling and the question of spelling reforms.

5.2 The origins of written English

No one is very sure what the 'original' language of Britain was, or even if it is sensible to ask such a question. The early history of Britain is one of successive invasions, of the arrival of new populations who spoke new languages which displaced or mixed with existing ones. In this section, I consider the emergence of the earliest writing systems in this changing social linguistic and cultural context.

The Anglo-Saxon futhorc

When did written English emerge? What did the first words look like? The oldest known piece of writing in English (see Figure 5.1) is a carving on a roe deer's ankle bone found in a cemetery site at Caistor-by-Norwich, Norfolk. It dates from circa AD 400 and appears to read raïhan ('roe deer'). This is only a single word, so it may be disputed that it represents English rather than some other, closely related, Germanic dialect. Nevertheless, it demonstrates the **runic script** in which the earliest English was written. This is known as the 'futhorc' after the first few letters of its alphabet (see Figure 5.2). The letters are based on simple lines that can be cut easily with a blade. The origins of the runic writing system are obscure – it appears to be modelled loosely on the Latin or Greek alphabet, but exactly where and when it was devised is unclear. It is known, however, that runes were used in various Germanic languages from the third century AD, and that they were brought to England by people from mainland Europe.

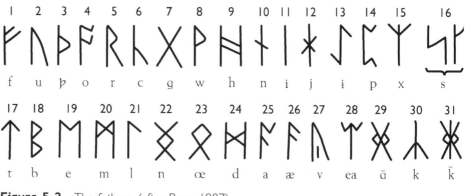

Figure 5.1   Runic inscriptions from Caistor-by-Norwich, circa AD 400. This is the oldest known text in English.

1	2	3	4	5	6	7	8	9	10	11	12	13	14	15	16
f	u	þ	o	r	c	g	w	h	n	i	j	ï	p	x	s

17	18	19	20	21	22	23	24	25	26	27	28	29	30	31
t	b	e	m	l	n	œ	d	a	æ	y	ea	ā	k	k̄

Figure 5.2   The futhorc (after Page, 1987)

Figure 5.3 illustrates a panel from a carved box known as the Franks Casket that was carved in whalebone in the early eighth century in northern England. Around the perimeter of the panel is a runic text which describes the story of Romulus and Remus, the mythical founders of Rome who were, according to legend, suckled by a she-wolf.

Figure 5.3   The Franks Casket was carved in whalebone in Northumbria in the early eighth century. (British Museum)

ACTIVITY 5.1

Allow about 15 minutes

Using the key to the futhorc shown in Figure 5.2, transliterate the first part of the inscription carved on the Franks Casket (shown in Figure 5.4) into Old English. Use the exercise to look more closely at the shape of runic letters. How many runic characters seem to be related to the modern English alphabet?

ᚱᚩᛗᚹᚪᛚᚢᛋᚪᚾᛞᚱᛖᚢᛗᚹᚪᛚᚢᛋᛏᚹᛟᚷᛖᚾ

Figure 5.4

COMMENT

In modern English, the full inscription reads: 'Romulus and Remus, two brothers, a she-wolf nourished them in Rome, far from their native land'.

Runic inscriptions are interesting to the historian of English for several reasons:

- *The range of letters contained in the futhorc*
  The Old English futhorc contained, at various times, between twenty-four and thirty-one letters, several of which have no equivalent in the modern English alphabet or in the Graeco-Latin alphabet from which the futhorc was descended. Runic inscriptions in Britain thus show the development of a set of letters found only in English.
- *The order in which the letters were conventionally given*
  The futhorc takes its name from the first six letters of the series, but the reason for this order is not known. The order was used for learning and memorising the futhorc itself. The use of a fixed 'alphabetical order' for the purpose of ordering items in a list or for arranging books in libraries did not occur until some centuries later.
- *The shape of the letters*
  The angular form of runes was particularly suited to inscription on hard surfaces, such as wood or stone, as opposed to writing with ink on parchment. The shape of the letters thus reflects the technology used to create them. We will see how changes in the implements used for writing in later times have led to changes in the shape of letters.
- *The direction of writing*
  The writing on the Franks Casket is read in a circle, so that the text on the lower edge is upside down. The text on the Ruthwell Cross (Figure 5.5) runs vertically. Wherever writing is used as decoration (runes figure frequently on jewellery because writing had magical associations) it will, like the panel of the Franks Casket, follow the shape of the design. Writing in early English was not as rigidly left to right, top to bottom, as in later times.
- *The evidence it provides about pronunciation*
  The form of the runic alphabet used in Scandinavia was reduced to sixteen letters. In England it expanded to thirty-one. The additional letters give clues as to how the pronunciation of English was developing. For example,

ᚠᚨᚠ   ᛁᚳ   ᚱᛁᛁᚳᚾᚨ   ᚷᚾᛏᛁᚾᚷ
ahof   ic   riicnæ   kyniŋc
lifted up   I   a great   king

ᚺᛏᚠᚾᛏᛋ   ᚺᛚᚠᚠᚱᚺ
heafunæs   hlafard
heaven's   lord

ᚺᚠᚳᚺᚠ   ᛁᚳ   ᛏᛁ   ᚺᚠᚱᛋᛏᚠ
hælda   ic   ni   dorstæ
bow   I   not   did dare

ᛒᛁᛋᚠᚱᚠᚳᚢ   ᚾᛟᚷᛏ   ᛗᛗᛏ
bismærædu   uŋket   men
mocked   us two   men

ᛒᚠ   ᚠᛏᚷᚠᚺᚱᚠ   ᛁᚳ   ᚹᚠᛋ   ᛗᛁᚦ
ba   ætgadræ   ic   wæs   miþ
both   together   I   was   with

ᛒᛚᚠᚺᚠ   ᛒᛁᛋᛏᛗᛖᛁᚺ
blodæ   bistemid
blood   bedewed

Figure 5.5   The Ruthwell Cross in Northumbria was inscribed circa AD 700 in Latin and in runes with a religious Anglo-Saxon poem, *The Dream of the Rood*.

a general sound change occurred in Old English, causing *k* to be pronounced differently when it occurred before certain vowel sounds. Anglo-Saxon rune masters created a new rune (number thirty in the list in Figure 5.2) to enable them to distinguish between these sounds. The original rune six came to be used for the new, softer *ch* sound, and the new rune for the original hard *k*.

In England runic inscriptions on rocks and large monuments also give evidence of developing dialect differences: unlike small portable items, they were probably constructed close to where they still stand, and so their form of language presumably reflects local usage (see Figure 5.5).

Other writing systems used in early Britain

The runes were not the only writing system used in the British Isles at this early time. The 'ogham' script (Figure 5.6) was used for some Celtic inscriptions, mainly in Ireland and Wales. Like the futhorc, it was based on angular forms suited to carving in hard materials, but unlike the futhorc the characters appear unrelated to the Greek or Latin script. Inscriptions in ogham often read from bottom to top, or left to right. The ogham script seems not to have influenced the development of English writing.

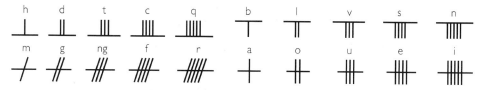

Figure 5.6 The ogham script used for early inscriptions in the Celtic languages

The most widespread writing system in England before the Anglo-Saxon invasion was that used for Latin. Even though the Romans themselves had departed from Britain, Latin continued to be used for many centuries as the main language of writing for religious texts, legal documents and science. This reflected the importance of the church, for whom Latin was the lingua franca and official language. Runic inscriptions in Old English often appeared alongside Latin inscriptions. Both the Franks Casket and the Ruthwell Cross (see Figures 5.3 and 5.5), for example, are bilingual – the Latin is inscribed in Roman script and the Old English in runes.

By the eighth century the church, rather than the rune masters, effectively controlled the skills of writing and it is not surprising that the first books in English employed the Latin model of writing, with one or two additions to the alphabet to represent sounds not found in Latin. These additional letters, as discussed in the next section, were taken from the futhorc. The runes remained in use for some centuries as magical devices or for secret writing.

Two rather different forms of lettering were used for Latin – an incised form of capital letters used for engraved plaques and monuments, and a handwritten style which we look at more closely in the next section. The form of monumental lettering was remarkably standard throughout the Roman empire. The inscription shown in Figure 5.7, for example, is very similar to inscriptions made at that time in Rome. This form of lettering looks very 'modern' because in later centuries it greatly influenced the form of printed type. Figure 5.8 shows an unusual runic inscription found in the north-east of England which has obviously been cut by a mason who was familiar with the Roman style.

Figure 5.7   A typical incised inscription in Latin from a Roman site in the north-east of England

Figure 5.8   A grave slab for Hildithryth, found in an Anglo-Saxon cemetery at Hartlepool, north-east England

5.3 Medieval manuscripts and books

Old and Middle English were largely spoken, rather than written, languages but the only evidence we have of what they were like comes from the relatively few documents and books that have survived to modern times. This, then, is one reason for studying medieval English texts – they represent our only (and unfortunately incomplete) evidence of earlier stages of English. But medieval texts are full of other kinds of interest. Many are beautiful works of art, demonstrating contemporary artistic and cultural values. Their changing character and content provide evidence of the changing institutional and political influences that have helped shape the English language. Lastly, the form of early handwritten texts has influenced the appearance of English texts, including printed texts, up to the present day. Many of the conventions of layout, spelling and punctuation, for example, were first worked out in connection with hand-produced manuscripts.

Book production in medieval Britain was an international business. The knowledge of how to create books was acquired by Anglo-Saxon scribes from Irish (Celtic) missionaries, who in turn had learnt from Rome. Furthermore, many books were made in England for customers in continental Europe. Hence English books have always been influenced by writing practices in other countries and other languages, and English books and scribal practices have affected practice elsewhere. In this section, I focus particularly on those contributions to book and manuscript style that were distinctively English, especially those scribal practices that reflected the special needs of the English language or that in some way influenced its development.

You should bear in mind while reading this chapter that the vast majority of books and manuscripts produced in England before the invention of printing were written in Latin or (in later times) French. Administrative documents were not written in English in any number until the fourteenth century. The story of early written English is one of a local vernacular language struggling to achieve a distinct visual identity and written usage.

Techniques of manuscript production

Early manuscripts were valuable and expensive commodities. Not only was there a scarcity of the skills and knowledge necessary to produce them, but the materials themselves – parchment, ink, tools – were all expensive and their manufacture required skilled labour. This is why book production in medieval times was located almost entirely in monasteries, for whom it was an important industry that helped maintain status and economy. Before labour in England became organised around guilds and it became possible for independent scriveners' (i.e. secular scribes') shops to be set up, manuscript copying and production required the resources of an institution – for the training of scribes, the provision of access to original works and the supply of appropriate working conditions and materials.

Books were copied in the scriptorium (Figure 5.9) – usually sited near the monastery library and often the only heated room in the building. Copyists typically had their own seats at double-sided lectern desks – perhaps with a higher, smaller lectern (like a modern secretarial copyholder) to hold the original. Much of the work was carried out in a standing position and a

Figure 5.9 A scribe at work in the scriptorium (Bibliothèque Nationale)

copyist might be expected to copy about four leaves per day – the speed of production was notably poorer in winter and in northern centres of production, when the daylight hours were fewer and the weather much colder. Some of the copyists speak to us directly in 'colophons' – footnotes added to manuscripts in which copyists identified themselves and perhaps illustrated themselves at work. Both nuns and monks worked as scribes.

The creation of a book involved many people. Several copyists might work on the same book, each responsible for different pages. An assistant might read the original aloud, working from the other side of the desk. When the scribe had finished, the manuscript would be passed to the 'rubricator', who added any headings and initials in red colour. The word 'rubricator' comes from the Latin *rubrica*, literally 'red earth', which produced the red pigment used to write laws and other important parts of texts. Finally, an artist – the illuminator – would create the elaborate miniature paintings which adorn the finer manuscripts.

As I said earlier, manuscripts provide us with incomplete and indirect evidence of the spoken language. In order to interpret the historical linguistic data they give us, we need to understand the division of labour and working conditions involved. The fact that an original was nearly always recited in spoken form during the copying process, for example, is one reason why the spelling in manuscripts often reflected the accent of the copyist instead of maintaining faith with an original. Each copy of a medieval book was slightly different from others, and some copies were made in a different century and country from the original. For example, the page from Bede's *Ecclesiastical History of the English People* shown in Figure 5.10 was produced nearly a century after Bede's original manuscript.

Many of the earliest English manuscripts were created in the north-east of England. Lindisfarne – a small island off the north-east coast, close to the modern border with Scotland – was the centre of the Northumbrian school of scribes and illuminators. This was where Anglo-Saxon scholars were first introduced to the Roman alphabet, through the medium of Latin. Other key libraries and copying centres were established about seventy kilometres away at Monkwearmouth and Jarrow.

The Lindisfarne Gospels, written in Latin by Eadrith, bishop of Lindisfarne circa AD 700, is perhaps the greatest work from the northern scriptoria to have survived from the eighth century. Figure 5.11 shows one of the large decorated initials which begin each of the four gospels after two full pages of decoration. The first words are *In principio erat verbum et verbum erat apud d(eu)m et d(eu)s [erat verbum]* ('In the beginning was the word, and the word was with God and God [was the word]').

This page illustrates several characteristics of early manuscripts produced in England, notably the extent to which writing had become a form of art. Letters are entwined with animal figures and multicoloured tracery, and set out in a way which creates a larger design on the page. The *ci* of *principio* is, like *et*,

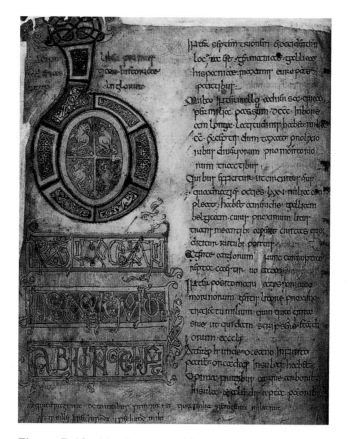

Figure 5.10 The first page of Bede's *Ecclesiastical History of the English People*. This is a copy made circa AD 820 of the Latin original completed in AD 731. (British Library)

in the form of a monogram (entwined to create a single graphical device) and a small human face appears within it. A number of tricks are used to ensure that each line fits the space. For example, the penultimate line, *et verbum erat*, demonstrates three kinds of shortening: the *et* is monogrammed (a forerunner of the printer's ampersand – *&*); the *u* and *m* of *verbum* are run together so that they share an upright pen stroke; the *a* of *erat* is placed above the *t*. In the final line the vowels of *deum* and *deus* are omitted, and this is marked by a short line above the words. This last practice was one of many conventions available to the scribe for contracting and abbreviating words.

The lack of gaps between words was common in Latin texts – the inscriptions on neither the Franks Casket nor the Ruthwell Cross, for example, show word spacing. Latin possessed an easily recognisable pattern of word endings which made spaces less important. Writing in English, however, needed spaces since, even in Old English, word endings were less predictable. Word spacing soon became the norm in English scriptoria even when writing in Latin, and word spacing is used in the main text of the Lindisfarne Gospels.

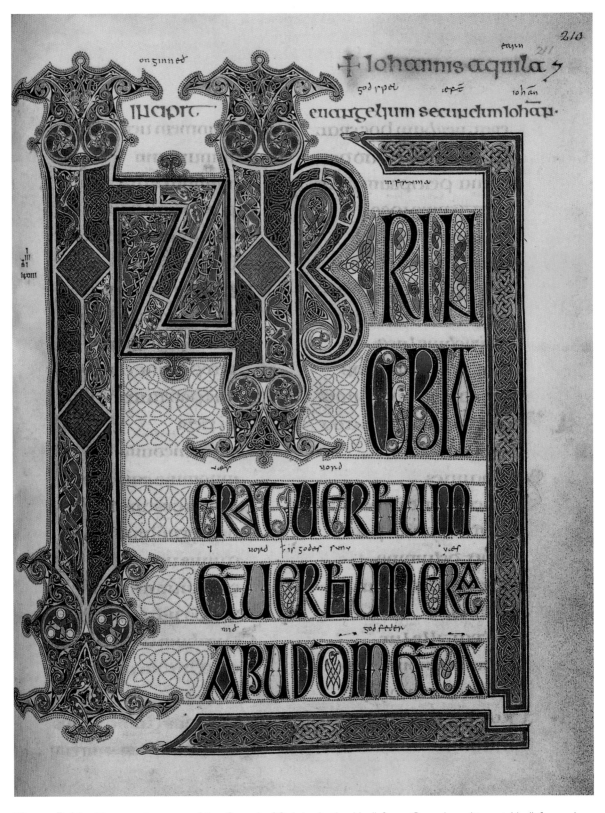

Figure 5.11 The opening page of the Gospel of St John in the Lindisfarne Gospels, written at Lindisfarne circa AD 700 (British Library)

Figure 5.12 (overleaf) shows one of the lesser initials in this manuscript and illustrates the script used for the text. (I'll return to the smaller writing visible between the main lines later.) The handwriting is in a form that has come to be called 'insular majuscule', a large **book hand** first developed by the Christian scribes in Ireland. This script is a development of 'uncial' – the standard book hand used throughout the Roman empire in the fourth century AD and for some centuries after. Uncial was the Roman square capital (see Figure 5.7) modified to suit the action of a pen on parchment, as opposed to a chisel on stone. It is what is sometimes called a two-line script – all letters have the same height. When the Roman empire broke up, the different parts of Europe each developed their own 'national hands', and insular majuscule can be regarded as the first distinctively British script.

Although some letters (such as *b*) have extensions which rise above the height of other letters (ascenders) and some (such as *p*) have extensions which fall below (descenders), these extensions tend to be truncated, so that the script maintains a two-line character (Figure 5.13). Insular majuscule was the script used in the Lindisfarne scriptorium for prestigious, ceremonial books.

There was another hand used in ancient Northumbria that was a more cursive and less formal development of the insular majuscule. This hand was called 'insular minuscule', and was a true four-line script (Figure 5.13). The term 'minuscule' is used for any script formed from 'little' letters, many of which have ascenders and descenders. A 'cursive' script is one in which the letters tend to 'run' into one another. Insular minuscule began as a documentary hand and was used first for less important items, working drafts, business and legal texts. It was made into an acceptable book hand by the Northumbrian scriptoria, probably because it was quicker, and therefore cheaper, to copy books in it. For example, the scriptoria at Wearmouth-Jarrow were in the habit of using uncial as their main display script (as opposed to the insular majuscule of the Lindisfarne Gospels), but Parkes (1982) has argued that they changed their handwriting to meet the demand from the continent for copies of works by their best-selling author, the Venerable Bede. In other words, they developed the insular minuscule into a fast but more presentable hand and began to use it instead of uncial.

Even when insular minuscule had been adopted as the main book hand, uncial might be used for headings and other important sections. In this way, different scripts acquired conventional meanings and the importance of different parts of texts could be signalled by a switch of script (see Figure 5.14). The distinction between a 'display' script for headings and a smaller, less decorative script for the main text anticipates modern typographic practice. The manuscript shown in Figure 5.14 also shows one of the earliest forms of punctuation: the hedera or ivy-leaf which separates the proverb from the commentary. (See Chapter 6 for the way in which digitisation is revolutionising access to valuable documents.)

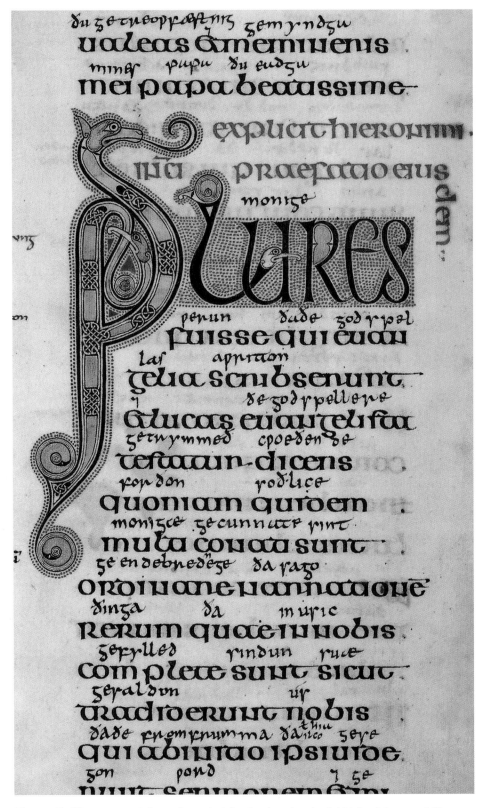

Figure 5.12   The Lindisfarne Gospels folio 5v, showing the initial *P* of the word *Plures* at the start of St Jerome's Preface to the four gospels (British Library)

A TWO-LINE SCRIPT

a four-line script bdgh

Figure 5.13   Two-line and four-line scripts

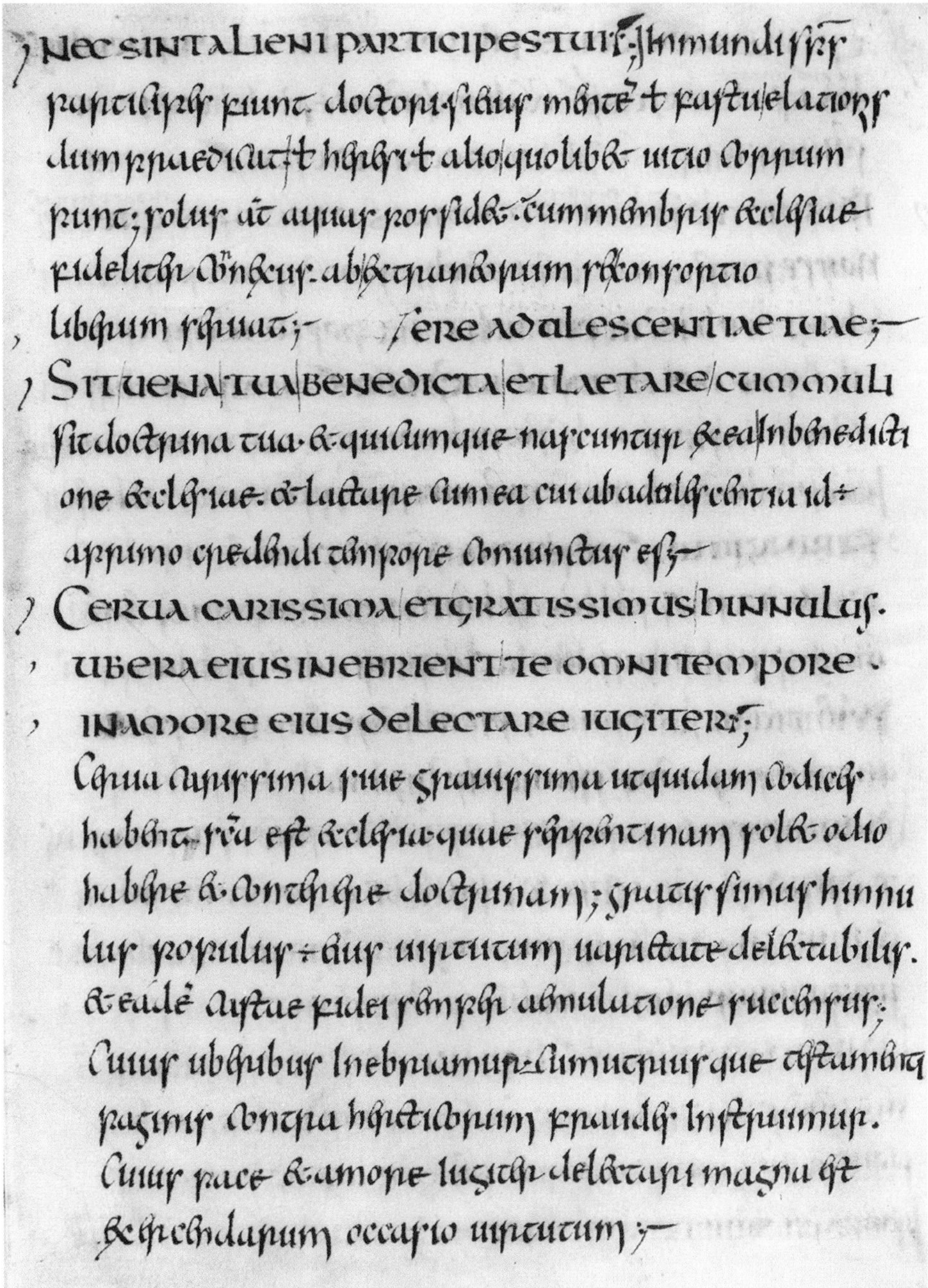

Figure 5.14   Bede's commentary on the Book of Proverbs, in a copy made in the second half of the eighth century at Wearmouth-Jarrow. The proverbs are in uncial and the commentary by Bede is in insular minuscule. Conservation requirements prevent new colour photographs being taken of this manuscript. (Bodleian Library)

Within this hierarchy of scripts it was insular minuscule – the most humble of book hands – which became adopted for Old English. This is demonstrated within the Lindisfarne Gospels manuscript itself. An 'interlinear gloss', which provides a word-by-word translation into Old English between the lines of the original, was added by Aldred the priest in the tenth century (see Figure 5.12). The text thus bears witness to the bilingual nature of learning and literacy at that period: the importance of Latin as the European lingua franca of Christian religion, science and scholarship, and the developing (but later) recognition of English vernacular as a vehicle of learning. Aldred's vernacular translation is written in a variety of insular minuscule.

Insular minuscule had to be adapted before it could be used for Old English. The Roman alphabet was augmented with extra letters, each with a special name, used to denote some sounds of Old English not found in Latin. The *thorn* (þ), used for the sound *th* in words such as **thick**, and *wyn* (ƿ) used for the sound *w*, were taken from the futhorc. Also added was the letter *eth* (ð) used for the sound *th* in words like **the** and a new vowel, *ash* (æ). The letter *g* came to be shaped as ȝ and was called *yogh*. Old English did not use the *j, v, w* of the modern English alphabet, and only rarely *q* and *z*. The Old English alphabet thus included the letters shown in Figure 5.15.

a	æ	b	c	d	e	t	ȝ	h	i	k	l	m
n	o	p	r	s	t	þ	ð	u	ƿ	x	y	

Figure 5.15   The Old English alphabet

The earliest Old English writing appeared alongside Latin, and the relative statuses of the languages were signalled through use of script. Figure 5.16, for example, shows a later manuscript detailing the marvels of the east. Distant lands were conventionally described in exotic terms – the far-off isles of Britannia had themselves once been described by the Roman author Tacitus as containing such mythical creatures. Illustrated is a page from this manuscript, written at Winchester or Canterbury circa AD 1040. *The Marvels of the East* is bilingual by design. The (upper) Latin paragraphs are in a 'carolingian' script, whereas the Old English is in an insular minuscule.

The carolingian (sometimes called 'caroline') script was adopted by a decree of Charlemagne in AD 789. This was in part a 'back-to-basics' policy – to reassert earlier cultural values and forms of Roman writing among scripts that had 'degenerated' into a diversity of 'national' hands. The word 'national' is placed in quotation marks here because at this time there were no nation states in the modern sense of the term. These emerged during the Renaissance (after circa 1500). It was also politically motivated – an attempt to reintroduce a common book hand throughout western Europe. As it happened, the job of establishing this standard hand fell to Alcuin of York, an English scholar-priest who was then abbot at Tours. Carolingian script was a small, very legible and modern-looking writing which, because of Alcuin's involvement, drew in part on the Anglo-Saxon tradition. Like the insular hands, it made no differentiation

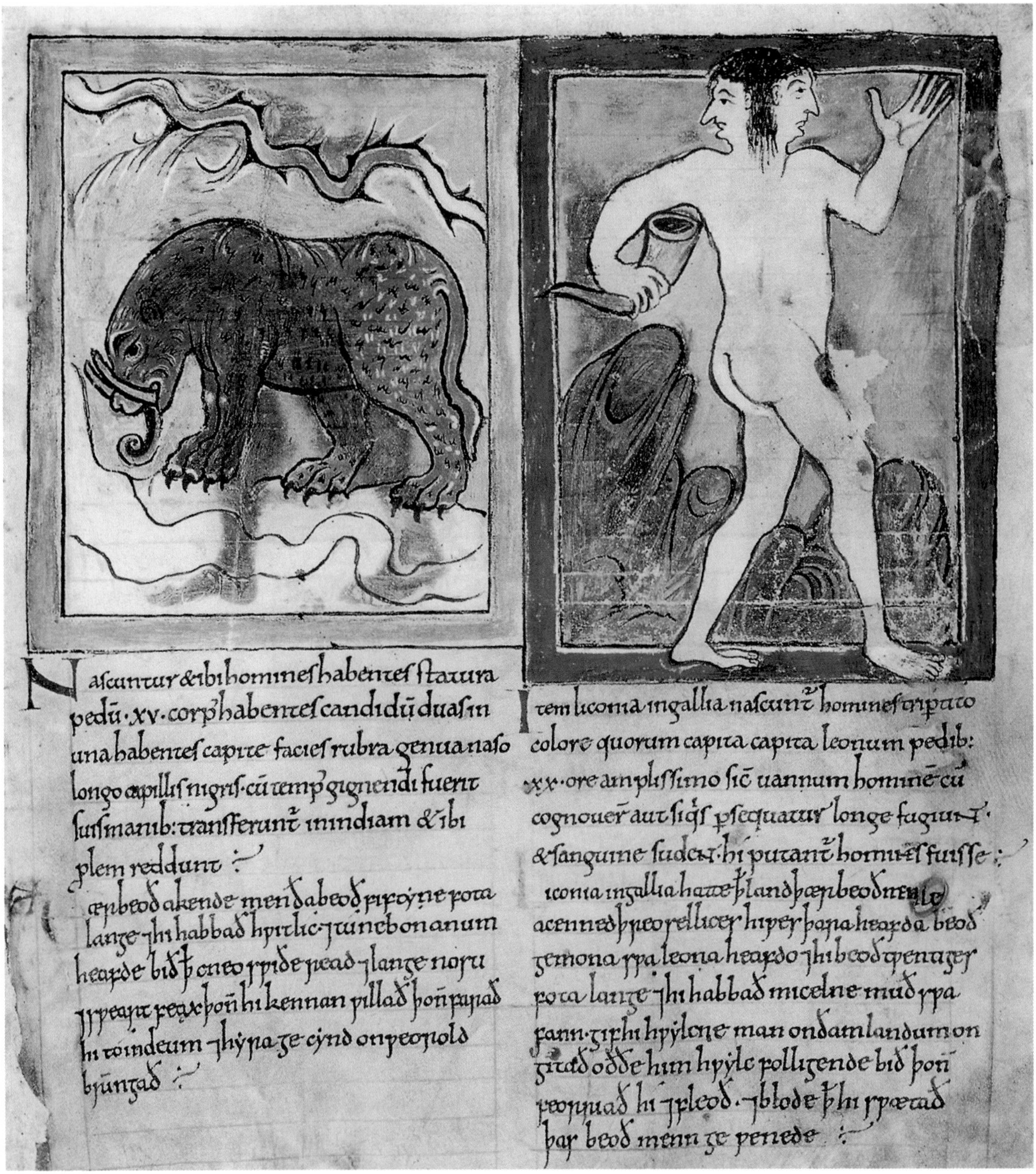

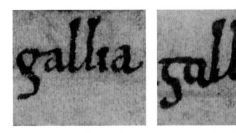

Figure 5.16 (above) The Marvels of the East, written circa AD 1040 at Winchester or Canterbury. The text is bilingual – with the Old English below the Latin. The Latin is written in an English carolingian, the Old English in an insular minuscule. (British Library)

Figure 5.17 The word *gallia* in Latin (far left) and Old English (left). Note the different shape of *g* and *a* in the carolingian and insular scripts (British Library)

between capital and lower-case letters: initials were still marked by size and decoration rather than by different shape. Figure 5.17 contrasts the word *gallia* in the two scripts used in the manuscript. Note that the letter *a* in the new carolingian hand (as in the earlier uncial) has the form a, whereas in insular hands (both majuscule and minuscule) it has the form ɑ. In the carolingian script *g* has its modern form, while in the insular minuscule it retains the open (yogh) form (ȝ). Both scripts used the long *s* (ʃ). A huge number of religious and classical works were copied into the new carolingian hand, and it became the respectful hand for religious and Latin texts in the ninth and tenth centuries.

ACTIVITY 5.2

Allow about
30 minutes

The manuscripts in Figures 5.12, 5.14 and 5.16 illustrate four styles of lettering: insular majuscule, insular minuscule, uncial and carolingian. Try to write out the four alphabets for yourself. You may find it helpful to prepare a sheet of paper with six columns. In the first two columns on the left write out the modern English alphabet in your own hand, in both capital letters and lower case. Leave space for the extra letters of Old English. Now try to find as many of the letters as possible in each manuscript hand and copy each letter into a column on your sheet of paper. This activity will take some time, but it is a good way of looking closely at the differences between the letter shapes of different hands.

The growth of learning in Old English

The emergence of books written in English was unusual. In no other part of Europe, with the exception of Ireland, did a tradition of vernacular literature emerge so early. Written Old English thus grew up in intimate contact with Latin, with the two languages acquiring a differentiated visual identity which reflected their different statuses and functions. In the ninth century, when northern monasteries had been attacked and destroyed – by Viking raiders from Scandinavia, according to many accounts – the focus of book production and learning shifted further south. By the end of the ninth century, King Alfred had apparently become concerned about what he perceived as falling standards of literacy and learning, and in circa AD 890 he issued a document known as the Preface to the *Pastoral Care*. The *Pastoral Care* itself was a work composed some 300 years earlier by Pope Gregory the Great, and which Alfred translated into Old English. In his Preface he appeals to his bishops to assist in the renewal of learning by translating more works into the vernacular (see Figure 5.18).

From this time on a great many manuscripts and books were written in Old English, and by no means only religious texts. Perhaps the most famous of all Old English literary texts is *Beowulf* (see Figure 5.19), an epic poem concerning the origins of the first English settlers – the Germanic people described by Bede.

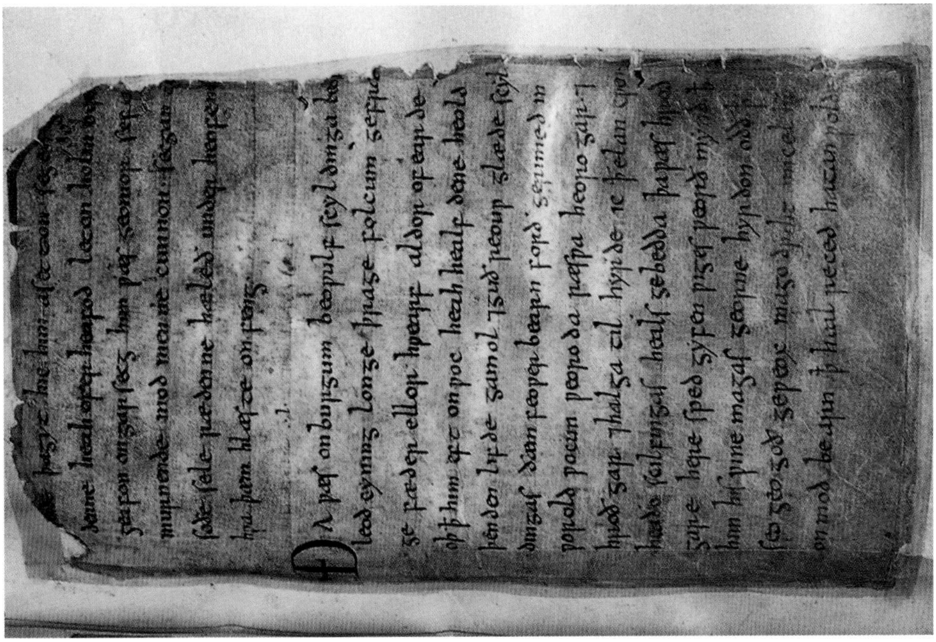

Figure 5.19   A page from the epic Old English poem *Beowulf* (British Library)

Figure 5.18   Alfred's Preface to his Old English translation of Pope Gregory the Great's *Pastoral Care*, written circa AD 890, probably at Winchester (Bodleian Library)

The poem is known only through a single tenth-century manuscript, but it was probably originally composed in the seventh century.

5.4 The Middle English period

The eleventh century was a key period in the history of the English language, marking the transition between Old English and Middle English. One of the historical events traditionally regarded as triggering major changes in the English language is the so-called Norman conquest, following which some documents were written in French. However, it is striking that even though French became the fashionable language of the court, Latin regained its position as the language of record. One historian of this period remarks:

> On the whole, Norman administrators probably had less experience than Anglo-Saxon ones of written records, and the Normans before 1066 had not shown such a consistent interest as the Anglo-Saxons in recording their history and institutions in literate forms ...

> In the eyes of contemporaries on the European continent Latin was the only language of record; a person unfamiliar with it was illiterate.

(Clanchy, 1993, pp. 26–7)

Although manuscripts continued to be made using more or less the same methods as before, there was less use of illustration and more emphasis on the text. Since fewer texts were in English, the carolingian hand became more widely used. One of the best-known texts from this period, written in Latin in the carolingian script, is shown in Figure 5.20. This is the Domesday Book, the great survey of English estates and inhabitants made for William the Conqueror and completed in AD 1086.

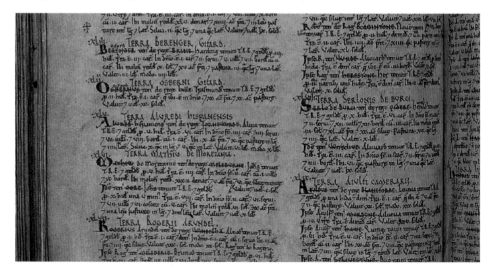

Figure 5.20 An extract from the Domesday Book, written in the carolingian hand, completed in 1086 (Record Office)

The carolingian book hand evolved during the twelfth century into a narrower form in which round strokes became straightened and squared. This script was called 'gothic' or black letter (Figure 5.21) and evolved partly from an increasing need in ceremonial manuscripts for an ornate script that was more economical of space. It also reflected the use of a reed rather than a quill pen and, in large measure, changing aesthetic ideas in which a trend towards tall perpendicular, ornamented forms was apparent in architecture as well as writing. This was the era in which many of the great European cathedrals were built, such as Canterbury and York Minster in England. Frederic Goudy, an American calligrapher and typographer, describes the emergence of gothic lettering as follows:

> Gothic letters are essentially written forms made with one stroke of the slanted pen, and while the Caroline letters written in the same way kept an open, round appearance, in the Gothic, for the sake of greater economy of space, the curves were reduced to straight lines (at first of scarcely varying thickness), making the letters narrower, more angular, and stiffer, until the written page was made up of rows of perpendicular thick strokes connected at the top & bottom by oblique hairlines.

(Goudy, 1963 [1942], p. 66)

gothic minuscule

Figure 5.21 Gothic handwriting as reconstructed by Goudy (1963 [1942], p. 66)

Commercial manuscript production

Towards the end of the twelfth century the church lost its near-monopoly over the making of manuscripts. Monasteries had for a long time employed secular scribes in order to maintain production, and these scriveners began to form their own guilds (which were an early form of trade union) and workshops. Secular books expanded in number and scribal workshops diversified (for an example of the different scripts they offered, see Figure 5.22). The need for such secular workshops arose from the emergence of a merchant class who required official documents to be drawn up. These middle classes also began to demand books – on philosophy, science, logic, mathematics and astronomy.

More authors began to write in the vernacular, though Latin was still the dominant language for scientific writing throughout Europe. They produced works in English on cookery, educational matters and literature, and medical manuals. A client who wished to commission, for example, a copy of *The Song of Roland*, might visit a stationer who would act as an agent (a role not dissimilar to that of the modern publisher), and commission a copy with the client's preferred calligraphic style and type of illustration.

The European universities had appeared in the twelfth and thirteenth centuries, and with them a new demand from students. Students could not

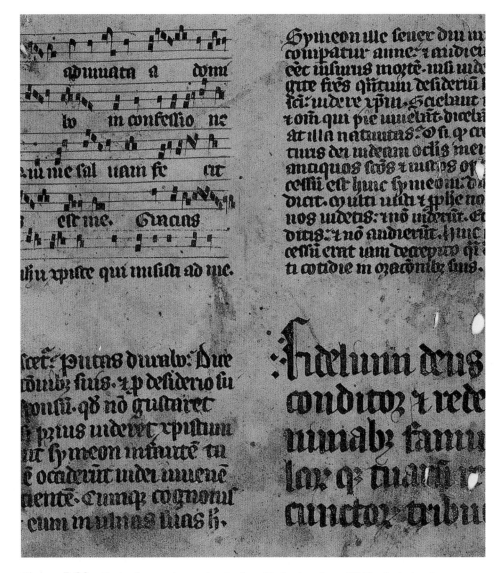

Figure 5.22   Part of a specimen sheet of an Oxford scribe c.1340, displaying to customers of a scrivener's shop the range of gothic scripts in which manuscripts could be commissioned (Bodleian Library)

afford to commission copies, but might hire a book from a workshop and make notes. Increasingly, then, individuals needed to learn the skills of writing in order to create documents for their personal, trade and business use.

A typical literary manuscript from the late Middle English period is John Lydgate's *The Siege of Thebes*, shown in Figure 5.23. The writing is in a gothic hand typical of this period. The miniature painting, contrary to common practice during the Old English period, illustrates the content of the work rather than acting as decoration to the text. The third figure from the left is probably Lydgate himself, and the other figures are characters from Chaucer's Prologue to *The Canterbury Tales* (the second from the left may be Chaucer). This section of Lydgate's text is also a prologue – to a proposed 'additional' tale.

Figure 5.23   A page from *The Siege of Thebes* written by John Lydgate c.1421. This manuscript was commissioned c.1460 as a gift for Henry VI or Edward IV and is written in a gothic hand. (British Library)

Other features of the manuscript show continuity with earlier traditions: the manuscript divides the page into two columns; there is a rubric which provides a caption to the picture; and the initial letter at the beginning of a section is decorated. Some of the special letters used in the Old English manuscript have now been dropped – yogh (ʒ) now appears as *gh, eth* (ð) has been dropped in favour of *th*, but thorn (þ) is still also occasionally used. There is still no punctuation except for a mid point (like a full stop but placed at mid height) marking each half-line. The long *s* (ʃ) is occasionally used, but not at the end of words.

Punctuation in English

Early manuscripts employed very little in the way of punctuation marks. Scribes used space and decoration to divide texts into structural units, though they sometimes adopted the Latin convention of using points, or stops, to mark breaks within the text. Various kinds of point existed – raised, mid and low – and these typically marked anything from word breaks to paragraphs. The carolingian writing reforms introduced some new marks, thought to have come from musical notation, which helped the reader to adopt an appropriate intonation. Such marks included what became exclamation and question marks. But the majority of modern punctuation marks were introduced into English after the invention of printing.

Until about 1700 such punctuation as existed was designed to help someone reading aloud: marks indicated suitable places for pausing or breathing, or guided the inflection of the voice. Gradually, the practice emerged of using punctuation to mark grammatical structure – such as clauses and sentences – and to guide a reader's interpretation of a text. By the eighteenth century, punctuation in English looked much as it does today. There remains an ambiguity in modern English as to whether punctuation should reflect grammatical boundaries or potential reading behaviour.

In the fourteenth century, English again began to replace Norman French and Latin as a language of record. Latin, however, continued to be used for many formal legal documents until the eighteenth century, despite various attempts to promote the use of English.

By the fifteenth century, economic growth had led to the writing of many more business documents. A clear distinction emerged between the slow, 'print' lettering of the book hands and the faster, more cursive business hands. These business hands were known collectively as 'court hands', and the style of writing as 'bastard' (that is, a cross between a formal book hand and the kind of fast cursive used for personal writing).

5.5 Handwriting after the invention of printing

The Lydgate manuscript dates from a significant period in English book production, since the earliest printed books had already been made in Germany and the first book to be printed in English was soon to appear, in 1473. The coming of printing had a profound effect on the look of English books and on the status of handwriting. The need for a book hand, for example, all but disappeared, and after the fifteenth century handwriting was used almost exclusively for commercial, legal and personal purposes. By the sixteenth century, in the period of English known as 'early modern English', there was a diversity of hands for such needs, of which two were in common use.

The first was the italic hand (see the lower example in Figure 5.24). Italic writing became popular in England after about 1550 and was often used for documents in Latin and as a display script in manuscripts written in English – for headings, titles and occasionally for emphasis. It was used especially by women, for whom the alternative hands were thought too closely associated with the male preserve of business. Martin Billingsley, author of *The Pens Excellencie* (1618), commented:

> ... it is conceiued to be easiest hand that is written with Pen, and to be taught in the shortest time: Therefore it is vsually taught to women, for as much as they (hauing not the patience to take any great paines, besides phantasticall and humorsome) must be taught that which they may instantly learne?
>
> (quoted in Dawson and Kennedy-Skipton, 1968, p. 10)

The usual business hand in the Elizabethan era was a development of what was called the 'secretary' (see the upper example in Figure 5.24). This was used not only in England but also in the American colonies, where business and legal interests were fast developing. However, after about 1700 use of the secretary hand everywhere declined in favour of the italic.

The Latin documents produced in various governmental departments had by this time each developed their own more ornamented and distinctive styles. This maintained the tradition of using different scripts for different languages or, rather, for the different functions that different languages served. Hector remarks:

> The departmental set hands were all the products of a more or less self-conscious search for distinctiveness. This fact alone would have prevented them, or any one of them, from setting standards of utility and legibility; and their use for the most formal purposes was bound to result in their being written almost exclusively by a relatively small, and relatively humble, class of specialist clerks and copyists. Their highly mannered style was completely divorced from the circumstances of everyday life, and ... by the middle of the 17th century they had come to be regarded as part of the apparatus of professional mystification.
>
> (Hector, 1966, p. 66)

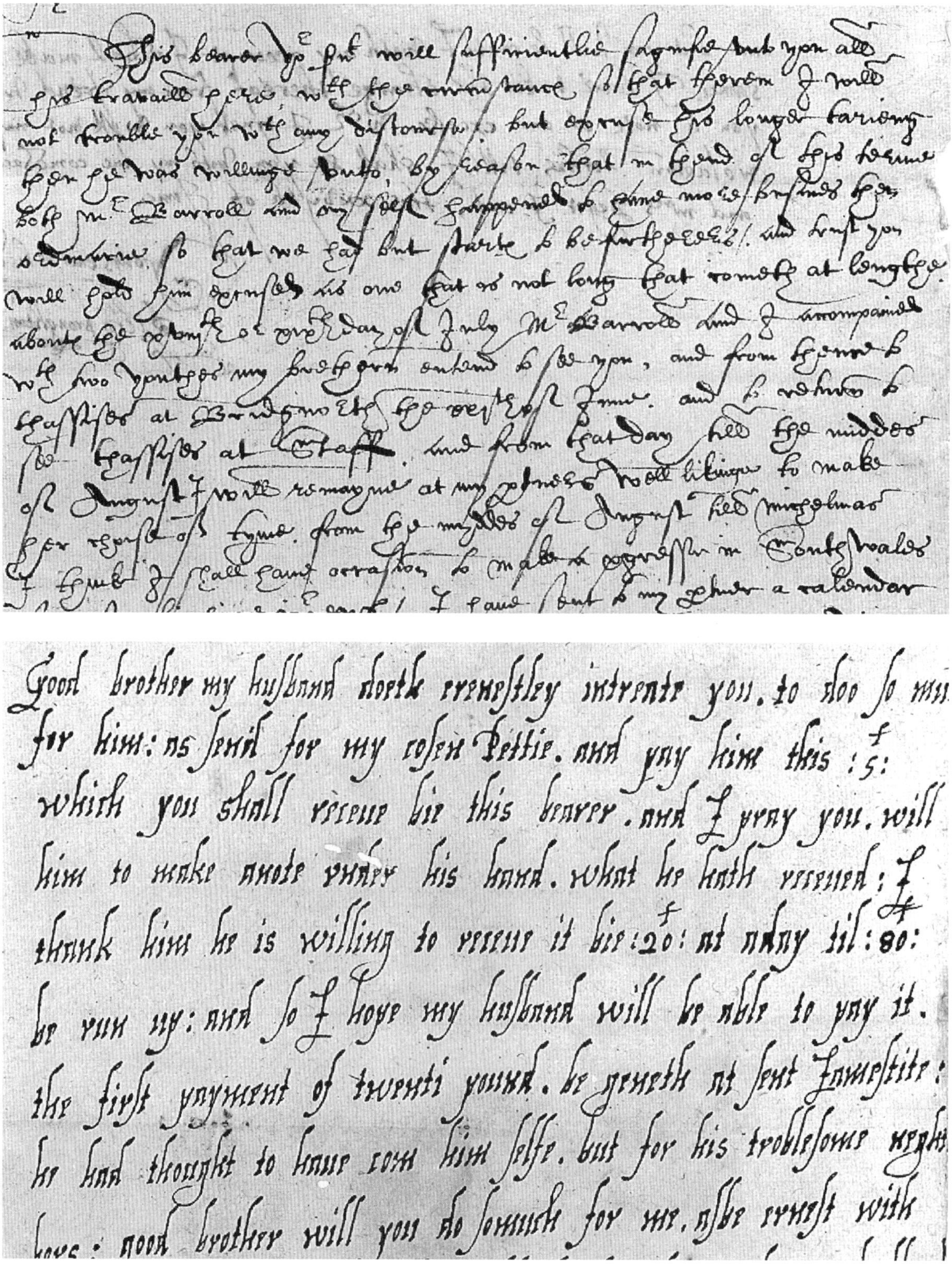

Figure 5.24 Two examples of Elizabethan handwriting: secretary hand as used by Richard Broughton, 1597; italic as used by Lady Lettice Kynnersley, c.1615 (Folger Shakespeare Library)

As handwriting grew in importance as both a business and educational accomplishment, so manuals and handbooks for the teaching of writing proliferated. Such books showed examples of writing by means of copperplate engravings, but this meant that the model scripts they presented reflected the behaviour of an engraving tool rather than a pen; the width of the lines, for example, depended on pressure on the pen rather than the angle at which it was held. People started to use pointed, rather than edged, pens to achieve this effect in handwriting: under pressure on the downward stroke the points of the pen splayed out and so gave extra width. One of the most popular works on writing in the eighteenth century, illustrating this copperplate italic style, was George Bickham's *The Universal Penman* (Figure 5.25). 'Writing is the first step, and essential in furnishing out the Man of Business ... In order to write well, there must be Rules given, and much Practice to put 'em into Execution' (Bickham, 1941 [1741])

Figure 5.25 The engraved frontispiece for Bickham's *The Universal Penman*, 1741, with title in ornamented gothic letters and text in copperplate italic

Copperplate was a more open, rounded version of the italic favoured by women, but was originally developed by the writing masters of the eighteenth century as a more 'robust and manly' hand suited to English commercial purposes. It became known, indeed, as the 'English round hand' and was used throughout the English-speaking world for over a century. This, then, was the main hand of British colonial administration.

Although the shift to copperplate italic was not strictly a change of script, it marked a radical change in writing behaviour. A quill pen, such as that used by medieval monks, needed to be held vertically so that the ink flowed smoothly. It was held in such a way that it could easily be pulled laterally but very little vertical pressure could be applied. It was more difficult to make upward movements than sideways or downwards ones because the quill nib was more easily pulled than pushed, hence the tendency to create a rounded letter such as *o* with two downward strokes, lifting the pen from the page. A downward stroke used the full width of the pen nib, whereas a sideways stroke made a thin line. The modulation between thin and thick lines thus arose from the direction of movement, and from the slope of the pen. With copperplate, however, modulation of thickness arose from pressure on the pen, hence both a different kind of pen and a different way of holding it were required.

ACTIVITY 5.3

Allow about
10 minutes

To do this exercise you might like to use tracing paper. Figure 5.26 gives examples of various styles of writing. Copy each line of text as closely as you can. If possible use a variety of pens such as a traditional-edged fountain pen, a fountain pen with a pointed nib which splays under pressure, and a modern ballpoint or felt-tip pen. Experiment with different pens, and with holding them different ways (in both the medieval manner described above, using directional movement to alter line thickness, and in the modern manner, using pressure on the pen to change line thickness). Observe what happens to the script when you change pen or method. Which scripts can be produced with a modern ballpoint pen?

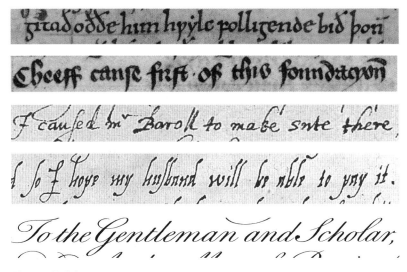

Figure 5.26

Writing in the English colonies tended to follow the European models. In America in the eighteenth century, writing masters would boast that they could write in 'all the known hands of Great Britain'. One such master was Abiah Holbrook, who died in Boston in 1769. Figure 5.27 shows a reproduction of his writing as it appeared in a book published a century later and reprinted as recently as 1957. It is clear that the 'known hands of Great Britain' included both gothic lettering and copperplate.

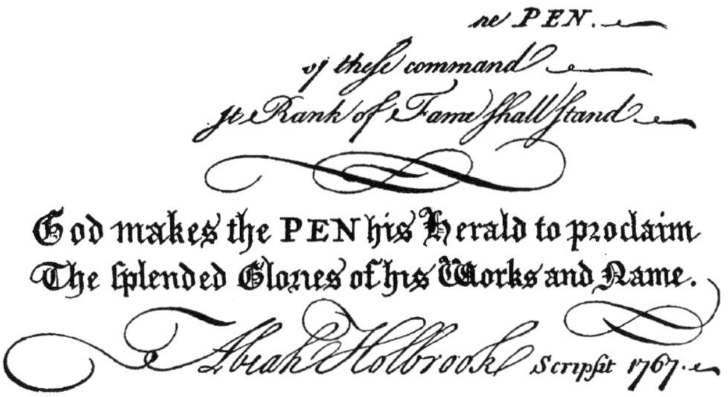

Figure 5.27 The handwriting of Abiah Holbrook, an eighteenth-century writing master from Boston (Earle, 1899, p. 155)

Handwriting in the nineteenth century

When elementary education became widely available in the nineteenth century, young children from all social classes needed to be taught how to write. For the first time, writing became a matter for the ordinary citizen, and many made use of it in their later lives for private correspondence and leisure activities. Indeed, schools today remain one of the few institutional locations where extended handwritten documents are to be found.

In the early nineteenth century there was considerable uncertainty as to the form of script that should be taught to children. All subjects in the elementary school had to be taught in ways that maintained both the social order of the classroom and the wider social order based on stable social class relations. For the Victorians, teaching children to write raised a number of moral, economic and political issues: teaching working-class boys a business hand might encourage them to aspire to jobs that were not open to them, yet the teaching of different styles to different children was costly and divisive.

Crellin (1989) suggests that the English educational establishment was reluctant to implement a single, standard script in schools. The reasons for this were partly a political dislike of monopolies – a single script would require the adoption of a standard copybook – and partly a belief in England that writing, like other aspects of education, was an essential aspect of personal development and expression, and should not be regarded as a narrow vocational matter. There was a continuing debate about what style of writing to teach, and whether a single, general purpose style could be envisaged which was suitable for both middle and working classes, and for both boys and girls. One of the most influential styles was created by an Irish philanthropist, Vere Foster. After using his wealth for some time to help young women from poor Irish families to emigrate to America, Foster turned his attention to schools and to the problem of how to improve children's handwriting (Figure 5.28). As one school inspector remarked of handwriting: 'it enters more largely than any other literary attainment into the qualification of a boy for clerkships and kindred situations; and furthermore, it is the chief test by which the parents judge of their children's progress at school' (quoted in McNeill, 1971, p. 129).

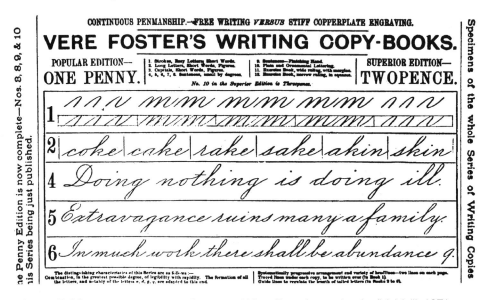

Figure 5.28   An advertisement for one of Vere Foster's copybooks (McNeill, 1971, p. 131)

Vere Foster had once worked under the British prime minister, Lord Palmerston, and remembered his insistence on the importance of legible handwriting among government officials.

> As early as 1854, Lord Palmerston had written to Committee of Council asking them to improve the writing taught in schools, Copperplate was becoming narrower and more slanting; its ascenders and descenders had grown even longer until they crossed with lines above and below. It was less legible than the styles of the 18th century, and its fine hairstrokes could not be picked up by the duplicating systems then in use. It was slow. But recruits to the civil service who had come from the classical schools had a style of writing which, though different, was equally unsuitable. It was casually illegible. Palmerston recommended that pupils should be taught 'rather to imitate broad printing than fine Copperplate engraving'. Ten years later there had been no improvement; and the civil

service commissioners were obliged to say that in their examinations 'we
do not demand or desire that the writing should be of any particular style,
provided that it possesses the main characteristics of legibility'.

Palmerston invited Vere-Foster to visit him. He criticised and altered some
of the copy lines, and allowed the resulting copybooks to come out in
1865 under the title 'Palmerston Series'. Within three years Vere-Foster was
encouraged to carry the reform even further, and the Civil Service Hand
had arrived.

Vere-Foster's ... upright, squat and simple style buried Copperplate and
The Ladies' Angular Hand in one go ...

Until the enthusiasm for Italic writing in the 1950s, Britain had one
common cursive hand. It was a style without the exactness or the beauty
of Copperplate. In the hands of different people, it developed all sorts of
personal idiosyncracies [*sic*] of slope or shape.

(Crellin, 1989, pp. 6–7)

Crellin argues that Vere Foster was responsible for the disuse of the 'English
round hand' and the creation of a general purpose style of writing – one used
by men and women yet showing considerable individual variation. But Vere
Foster's solution was not universally accepted; even where it was, the hand
taught was still rounded and open. It was, as a result of its roundness,
regarded as being more suitable for vocational than for personal use, and this
of course meant a hand suited to boys who might expect to gain employment
as clerks. There was a resistance to the round hand from girls' schools:
'Female pupils, especially those whose parents are in comfortable
circumstances, object to the roundness of style which characterizes the
advanced or 'finishing' headlines ... headlines of angular hand ... would render
those copy-books more popular in Girls' schools than they are at present'
(quoted in McNeill, 1971, p. 136).

We see here how habits of handwriting continued to be stratified by social
class and gender. Roundness, as with the earlier secretary hand, was a signifier
of trade – a spikier hand was regarded as more fitting for young ladies'
personal letter writing.

The quotation from Crellin (above) ends with a reference to a revival of italic
handwriting in Britain in the 1950s. In 1952 Alfred Fairbank founded the
Society for Italic Handwriting, but this was probably the last high point of the
arts and crafts movement, which had started at the beginning of the century
among a group of artists and calligraphers who shared a commitment to the
maintenance of traditional craft skills in an age of increasing mechanisation.
An example of Fairbank's model italic is shown in Figure 5.29.

In the seventeenth century it used to be said that from the handwriting,
one could tell the department of the government in which a document had
been produced. In other words, slight differences in style were to be

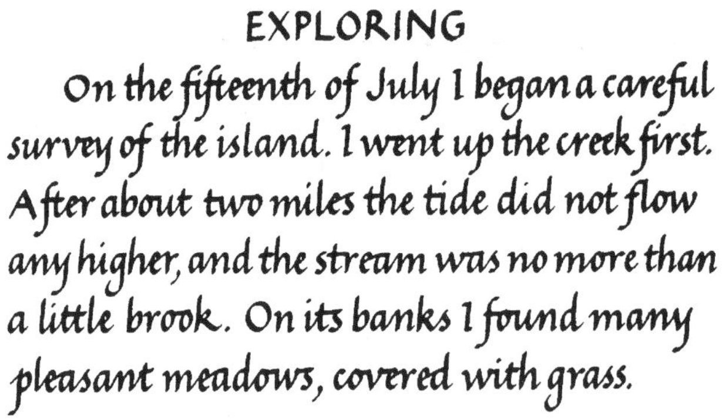

EXPLORING

On the fifteenth of July I began a careful survey of the island. I went up the creek first. After about two miles the tide did not flow any higher, and the stream was no more than a little brook. On its banks I found many pleasant meadows, covered with grass.

Figure 5.29   Fairbank italic (Fairbank, 1968, plate 80)

explained by the rigorous way in which house styles of different institutions were imposed on individual clerks. The reality, of course, was that the everyday writing of most people showed considerable individual style. Although some consistency in copperplate business hands emerged during the eighteenth century, the legacy of the Victorian education system has been a lack of a single, standard style of handwriting in English schools. School systems in some areas of the USA, Canada and Australia have been more vigorous in demanding a particular form of script. Nevertheless, there is a widespread idea in the English-speaking world that handwritten documents can (and should) betray the identity of an individual more readily than that of the institution within which the writer was trained.

Related to this shift in the perception of handwriting has been a decline in the importance of handwritten English in public communication. By the turn of the twentieth century, typewriters were increasingly being used for business correspondence, and handwriting gradually lost even its commercial function in the developed countries. Handwriting in the modern era has thus moved almost completely from the public to the private sphere and is now used primarily for personal writing – notes, drafts of material to be made public in other forms, private letters and diaries. Perhaps the main residual public use of handwriting is for filling in the forms and questionnaires that structure an individual citizen's interactions with the state (e.g. tax forms) and other bureaucratic organisations (such as banks and educational institutions). In these documents the writer is often instructed to use 'block capitals', showing how capital lettering has largely become the modern 'print' style of writing.

ACTIVITY 5.4

Allow about
5 minutes

Can you remember how you were taught to write in school? Do any of the descriptions of technique or style of script given above remind you of your schooling? To what extent were you encouraged to develop your own style?

Try asking these questions of friends and family members. Do any differences emerge which might relate to age, or to the geographical area in which individuals were taught, or to the kinds of school they attended?

5.6 Orthographies of English: tradition and reform

The appearance of words in English reflects the inventory of letters used (the Roman alphabet), the way these letters are shaped in a particular style of handwriting or typeface in printed texts and the way these letter shapes are used in particular words (the spelling). The term **orthography** (literally 'correct writing') embraces all these things. In this section, I discuss changes in attitude towards standard spelling, and the surprising number of attempts that have occurred to reform English orthography, not just by reforming spelling but by making radical changes in the alphabet itself.

Spelling in Old and Middle English

There is a mistaken view that in early times the spelling of English reflected the capricious whims of individual scribes. In fact, spelling in Old English manuscripts was based largely on practice in Latin, with modifications required to accommodate the different sound systems of English. I have already described, for example, how Old English manuscripts adopted some runic characters to represent the sounds which, in modern English, are spelt *th*. Although the spelling of words tended to reflect local dialect features and differed to some extent from one region to another, there was within each dialect area a certain consistency of approach. But it is only from the time of King Alfred that a sufficient number of contemporary Old English texts exist to permit a clear analysis of spelling. At that time spelling seems to have been fairly standardised, and Old English spelling provided a more accurate representation of current pronunciation than present-day orthography does. One reason why a strong standard emerged was because books at that period were being produced from a relatively small area in which there was both little dialect variation and effective institutional control.

The Norman invasion led to the collapse of this standard, and to increasing regionalism of spelling. Such regionalism had at least two causes. The first was that English developed striking dialect differences: northern parts of the country continued to be influenced by Scandinavian languages while parts of the south were affected by intimate contact with French. Figure 5.30 (overleaf) shows some of the variation in the Middle English spelling of *such* in southern England. McIntosh (1969) has suggested that certain differences in spelling, for example the variant spellings of *such – swilk, swich, soch* – indicated differences in pronunciation, even though it is not possible to tell with any precision exactly *what* each pronunciation might have been.

There were, however, some differences in spelling that did not imply differences in pronunciation; they simply reflected different habits of spelling. This kind of variation was common in Middle English times because English scribal practices were influenced by the practices of French, leading to a confusion of the principles for representing sounds. For example, words such as *cwene* ('queen') came to be spelt, according to the Norman French

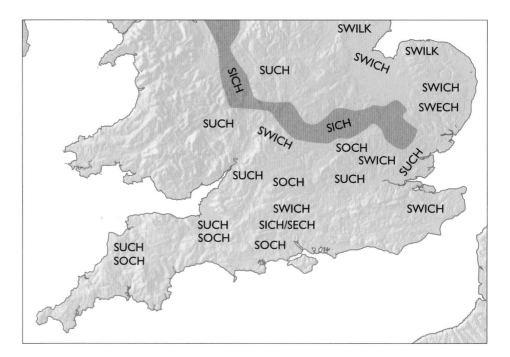

Figure 5.30 Distribution of different spellings of *such* in Middle English, according to Samuels (Samuels, 1969, p. 408)

convention, as *quene*, thus introducing *qu* into the spelling repertoire of English. Words spelt with the Old English thorn (þ) were usually respelt by Norman scribes with *th*, and so on. McIntosh (1969) has argued that such differences in spelling should be carefully studied as they can yield valuable information that can help to identify the source of a manuscript.

There is no doubt that the arrival of printing helped consolidate and establish fixed patterns in English spelling, but the process got off to an uncertain start. Caxton, the first person to print books in English, is sometimes credited with standardising English spelling but this had already been accomplished to some extent by the scriveners' guilds. Printing did, however, have a major standardising effect in so far as every reader now possessed identical copies of a work.

By the eighteenth century, English spelling had reached more or less the state in which we find it today. Unfortunately, the fixing of spellings rather than conventions to indicate pronunciation has led to a situation in which English spelling better reflects the pronunciation of several centuries ago than that of the present day. English spelling thus provides a witness to history: to changes in pronunciation; to the changing economics of manuscript production; and to the standardising effects of printing. It also reflects a number of minor reforms to spelling that have taken place over the last three centuries or so.

The reformers

There have been many campaigns to reform English spelling and indeed the whole orthographic system; a significant number of influential people, including well-known writers, linguists and publishers, have long argued the cause. Many proposals have sought to make English orthography more **phonetic** – that is, to make spelling reflect more closely the pronunciation of modern English, letter by letter.

Identifying phonemes

A phonemic transcription is one that represents all the significant contrasts between the vowels and consonants of a language. Linguists often use the technique of 'minimal pairs' to identify phonemes. The English words *tin* and *din* are a minimal pair: they are identical apart from their initial sound. Switching these sounds – changing *t* to *d* – produces a different English word. On the other hand, even though the vowel in *tin* is usually longer than the one in *tick* (try saying *tin* and *tick* to yourself, listening carefully to how you pronounce the vowel in each), this is not a phonemic difference because we can't find a minimal pair of words in which switching these shorter and longer variants of *i* creates a different word. Strictly speaking, most so-called phonetic spelling reforms attempt to be phonemic, rather than phonetic. That is, they usually represent significant contrasts rather than minor details of pronunciation and accent.

John Hart, author of several early books on English spelling, argued in his *Orthographie* of 1569 that 'writing should have so many letters as the pronunciation neadeth voices and no more or less'. The orthography of modern English falls a long way short of such an 'ideal' for several reasons:

1   There are far more distinctive sounds (or **phonemes**, see box) in spoken English than there are letters in the Roman alphabet. In the accents of many British speakers, for example, there are about forty-five phonemes which need to be represented.

2   Because there are insufficient letters they are not used in a simple way to represent particular sounds: one of the commonest techniques in English orthography is the use of 'digraphs' – two letters together which represent a single sound such as *ch, sh, ee*.

3   Even taking the need for digraphs into account, there is no systematic correspondence between letters and sounds in English. For example, the *c* in *medicine* and *medical* are pronounced in different ways. On the other hand, a *k* sound might sometimes be represented by *k* (as in *kiss*), sometimes by *c* (as in *medical*), sometimes by *ch* (as in *Christian*), and so on.

4   In an ideal phonemic orthography the representation of pronunciation
     should operate in a linear fashion, but in English spelling you sometimes
     have to look to the end of a word to work out how an earlier vowel
     should be pronounced. The most common example is the final 'silent' *e* in
     words like *pine* (as opposed to *pin*) or *tape* (as opposed to *tap*).

Spelling reform faces a number of technical problems, as described by David
Abercrombie:

> One apparently obvious solution would seemingly be to extend the
> number of characters so that all sounds can be represented. However,
> reforming spelling through extension has been unsuccessfully attempted
> for some three hundred years demonstrating how reforming spelling is far
> from straightforward. The possibilities in sheer invention of new letters are
> more limited than one might suppose: an apparently satisfactory new
> character will often turn out, in use, to be ill-suited to mixture with the
> rest of the alphabet, or to be too like letters which already exist.

(Abercrombie, 1981, p. 210)

And there is a further problem inherent in any phonetic writing system: how
to cater for variation in pronunciation. English is pronounced in diverse
ways – both regionally within Britain (which of all English-speaking countries
probably contains the greatest variation of accent) and globally between
countries. For example, some English speakers make a distinction between
father and *farther* by pronouncing an *r* sound in the second word, while
others (including speakers of the British accent known as Received
Pronunciation) do not make a distinction. So a phonetic spelling system is
faced with a difficult choice – does it spell a word like *farther* in a standard
way, or does it allow different speakers to spell in accordance with their own
accent? If it elects to do the former, then one accent is privileged over others,
and people who speak with other accents will either find themselves no better
off than before (because for them the spelling system is not phonetic) or be
expected to change the way they speak – to adopt the pronunciations
represented by the standard writing. If the latter option is followed (as
happened to a certain extent with spelling reform in Norway in 1957), then
there is no single standard spelling for words, and books may have to be
published in a variety of editions.

Of course, even more intractable than the more technical problems associated
with spelling reforms are issues connected to culture, politics and economics.
There have always been vested interests (in publishing and education, for
example) which would be put to enormous inconvenience, discomfort and
cost by the introduction of a new orthography. The American dictionary
maker Noah Webster tried to turn these problems to advantage in the late
eighteenth century. He argued that American spelling should be reformed in

order to create a new visual identity for American English suitable for the newly independent state. Present-day differences in American and British spelling derive largely from Webster's work (1991 [1789]), although they are a great deal less radical than his original proposal.

ACTIVITY 5.5

Read the extract from Noah Webster's 'An essay on the necessity, advantages and practicability of reforming the mode of spelling, and of rendering the orthography of words correspondent to the pronunciation' (Reading A). Note the various political, cultural and economic arguments that Webster makes for orthographic reform.

Phonetic spelling reform acquired little institutional support or financial backing in Britain until the middle of the nineteenth century when the publisher Sir Isaac Pitman introduced a system of shorthand writing that he called 'phonography'. The system was intended to facilitate rapid transcription of spoken language, whether for the dictation of business correspondence or for journalists' verbatim notes of interviews. There have been many shorthand systems devised for English (Crystal, 1987, p. 206, suggests there have been more than 400), but Pitman based his on a careful analysis of spoken English. His system was commercially very successful and by the end of the century he claimed that:

> In Great Britain, Pitman's Shorthand is every year more extensively taught and practised; it is used by 95 per cent of newspaper reporters and 98 per cent of shorthand clerks. In the United States, where a number of publishers have issued the system with slight alterations, 97 per cent of the shorthand writers use either Pitman's Phonography or an American presentation of it. The percentage of phonographers in Australia is 96.

> (Pitman, undated, p. iii)

Pitman was perhaps being a little touchy here about rival systems, but it is nevertheless clear that phonography was far from being a minority, cranky interest. Rather, it had become a writing system for English with international currency and considerable commercial interest.

Pitman's work on phonography stimulated an interest in spelling reform and he began to use the associations and networks that had been established to promote shorthand as a basis for his new campaign. He recognised that a new, phonemically-based orthography required extensive research and he collaborated with a phonetician, Alexander Ellis, in devising and refining dozens of alphabets that were phonetically well-founded and practical from the points of view of both writing and printing. Its printing practicability was achieved by a series of publishing ventures, including the *Phonographic Journal* and the *Phonotypic Journal*. By the end of the century Pitman was able to launch the more popular journal *The Speler* (see Figure 5.31).

THE SPELER,

Devoated (1) tu the Wŭrship and Lŭv ov the Lord God and Saivier Jesus Christ, az "The Aulmeiti" (Matt. 28. 18-20 ; Rev. 1. 8) ; (2) The Kŭltiur ov the Relijŭs Leif, and thairbei the Ekstenshon ov the Kingdom ov God, or the Chŭrch, konsisting ov aul hu wŭrship the Lord and keep Hiz Komandments ; (3) The Investigashon ov Spiritiual Tru'th ; (4) Speling Reform ; (5) Short'hand ; (6) Pees on Er'th.

KOND'UKTED BEI SER EIZAK PITMAN, BATH.

Preis ½d. ; Poast Paid, 1d. Tú or moar kopiz, Poast Free.

London : Sir Isaac Pitman and Sons.   Bath : Ser Eizak Pitman.   New York : Clarence Pitman, 33, Union Square.

No. 1.   JANIUERI, 1895.   VOL. 1.

SPELING.

A "spel" iz ŭpon the nashon az tu speling. Korekt speling iz sed tu be a mark ov an ediukaited person. Whot iz speling? It iz the plaising tugether ov the leterz that maik a wŭrd. Everi leter haz a naim. The naim ekspresez its sound, if a vouel or vois ; and indikaits the akshon ov sŭm part ov the mou'th that produiez it, if it iz a konsonant. Az a konsonant iz not a sound, bŭt meerli the kontakt ov tú parts ov the mou'th, either cheking or propeling a sound, the naimz ov the konsonants ar formd bei meenz ov a vouel preseeding or folo'ing the kontakt ; az f, *ef* ; v, *vee* ; m, *em* ; b, *bee*. The vouel or sound reprezented by "o" haz for its naim the sound which "o" reprezents, az herd in *no*, *so* ; and the konsonant "p," which iz prodiust bei a preshur ov the lips, seeing that ther iz no sound in the preshur, reseevz a naim bei meenz ov the vouel "ee," and iz kauld *pee*.

The moar efektiuali tu distingwish the "bre'th konsonants" from thair koresponding "vokalz," the vouel yuzd in naiming a non-vokal, or bre'th leter, iz plaist BEFOAR it ; and it iz plaist AFTER the vokal ; as f, *ef* ; v, *vee* ; th (in *thin*), *ith* ; th (in *then*), *thee* ; s, *es* ; z, *zee* ; sh, *ish* ; zh, *zhee*. In naiming the eksplosiv konsonants the vouel iz ŭterd AFTER the kontakt in boa'th keindz ov leterz, vokal and non-vokal ; az, p, *pee* ; b, *bee* ; t, *tee* ; d, *dee* ; and, for eez ov pronŭnsiashon, *ee* iz chainjd to *ai* in ch, *chay* ; j, *jay* : k, *kay* ; g, *gay*. The vouel PRESEEDZ the kontakt in naiming the tú likwidz l, *el*, r, *ar* ; and the 'three nazalz, m, *em* ; n, *en* ; ng, *ing* (*ing* iz moar eezili spoaken than *eng.*) W and y hav the vouel that maiks them audibel, az leterz, plaist AFTER, and ar kauld *way, yay.* (In the old alfabet w iz "dŭbel-yu," and y is "wei.") The aspirait iz konveenientli naimd "aich." The meer ekspŭlshon ov bre'th wud not be herd in speeking ov the leter ; and "haa," or "hay," wud not streik the eer so redili as "aich."

The siks long vouelz, which hav no singel-leter reprezentativz in the komon alfabet, are *aa, ai, ee ; au, oa, oo*. (At the END ov a wŭrd, *ai, au,* ar riten *ay, aw.*) The short vouel in *bŭt,* az distinkt from "u" in *put*, iz not reprezented in the komon alfabet. Ther ar aulso siks konsonants that hav no singel

RULES of the SPELLING REFORM.

First Stage.—Reject *c* (= *k* or *s*), *q* (= *k, qu* = *kw*), *x* (= *ks* or *kz*). Use the other 23 letters thus :—*Consonants* as usual ; and *a, e, i, o, u,* SHORT, as in *pat, pet, pit, pot, put.* For the remaining 13 sounds, *Italicized* in the following words, use the letters below :

cheap ;	thin, then ;	wish, vision ;	sing.
ch ;	'th, th ;	sh, zh ;	ng.
ch ;	*th, th ;*	*sh, zh ;*	*ng.*
palm, pale, peel ;	pall, pole, pool ;	but.
aa, ai, ee ;	au, oa, oo :	ŭ.
aa, ai, ee ;	*au, oa, oo :*	*ŭ.*

For brevity write *a, e, o, u,* for *ai, ee, oa, oo,* at the end of an *accented* syllable, as in *fa-vor, fe-ver, ho-li, tru-li,* (not *fai-vor, fee-ver,* etc.) When "ŭ" iz not in stock, print "u."

Write the 5 Diphthongs thus : *ei* (by), *ou* (out), *iu* (new), *ăi* [*ai* in the Second Stage], (Kaiser), *oi* (toil). When the letters of a digraph represent separate values, interpose a "turned point" (·), as "be·ing" (not *bei-ng*), "short·hand" (not *shor-thand*).

Second Stage.—Each letter has but one sound : Consonants and Diphthongs as above ; *a, e, i, o, u,* SHORT, as in *pat, pet, pit, pot, put.* For the 13 sounds above, use the following 13 new letters (whose names are below them) : thus making a complete *Phonetic Alphabet* of 24 consonants and 12 vowels, or 36 letters in all.

Ꞔ ꞓ;	Ꜧ ꜩ,	ꝺ ꝺ;	Σ ʃ;	Ȝ ȝ;	Ꞃ ꞃ.
(chay)	(ith)	(thee)	(ish)	(zhee)	(ing)

Ꜳ ꜳ,	Ɛ ɛ,	Ƒ ɿ;	ꝏ ꝏ,	Ꝍ ꝍ,	Ꝥ ꝩ :	Ƽ ƽ.
(ah)	(eh)	(ee)	(aw)	(oh)	(oo)	(ut)

NOTE : FIRST STAGE.—Write, *if preferred* -At the END of a word, *ay, aw, ow, oy,* for *ai, au, ou, oi,* as in *may, law, now, boy* ; use *u* for *oo* in *truth,* etc. ; *I* (the pronoun) for *ei* ; *yu* for *iu* when initial, as "yus" (*use*) ; *n* for *ng,* when followed by *k* or *g,* as *bank* (bangk), *anger* (ang-ger) ; *father, old,* etc., for *faather, oald,* etc. Use caution, and avoid giving offence. Proper names and addresses should not be altered at present. It is best to adopt phonetic spelling for one's own name if it does not need a new letter. In teaching reading, use the Second Stage.

Tu prodiŭs a Fonetik, or tru reprezentashon ov the Englisǝ

Figure 5.31   The first issue of Isaac Pitman's journal devoted to spelling reform (*The Speler*, 1895, vol. 1, no. 1)

In the early twentieth century, enthusiasm for phonetic spelling was becoming sufficiently great to disturb more conservative minds. The poet Robert Bridges, for example, worried that the fashion for spelling words as they were pronounced would result in 'degraded conversational forms' of southern English being fixed in English orthography. He devised his own proposal, which was to provide a more aesthetically pleasing script suitable for works of literature. Bridges decided to adopt the insular majuscule – the script of the Lindisfarne Gospels – as a model, but in the end made do with 'an old Anglo-Saxon fount, which was lying disused at the Clarendon Press' (Bridges, 1913, p. 19). An example is shown in Figure 5.32.

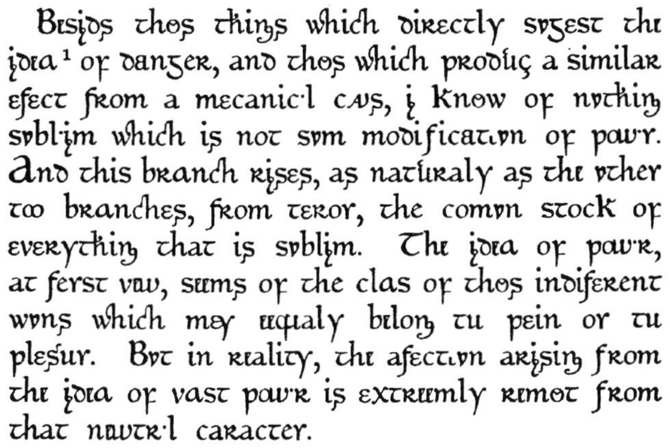

Figure 5.32   An example of Robert Bridges' simplified spelling from 1913 (Bridges, 1913, pp. 32–3)

Yet another literary proposal was facilitated by the playwright Bernard Shaw, an ardent supporter of spelling reform. When he died in 1950 it was found that his will directed a public trustee to seek and publish a new 'Proposed Alphabet' and:

> ... employ a phonetic expert to transliterate my play entitled *Androcles and the Lion* into the proposed British Alphabet assuming the pronunciation to resemble that recorded of His Majesty our late King George V and sometimes described as Northern English; to employ an artist calligrapher to copy the transliteration for reproduction by lithography, photography or any other method that may serve in the absence of printers' types; to advertise and publish the transliteration with the original Doctor Johnson's lettering opposite the transliteration page by page and a glossary of the two alphabets at the end and to present copies to public libraries in the British Isles, the British Commonwealth, the American States North and South and to national libraries everywhere in that order.

> (Shaw, 1962, p. 9)

An international competition was duly put in hand, resulting in about 450 designs. The winning one is illustrated in Figure 5.33, taken from the edition of *Androcles and the Lion* that was published by Penguin in 1962.

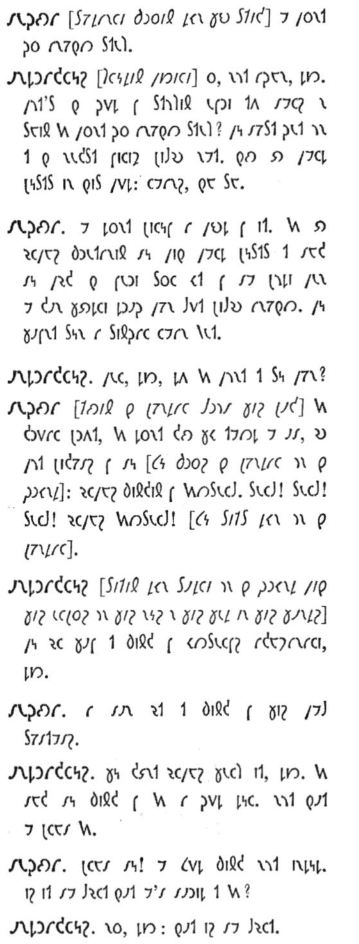

MEGAERA [*suddenly throwing down her stick*] I wont go another step.

ANDROCLES [*pleading wearily*] Oh, not again, dear. Whats the good of stopping every two miles and saying you wont go another step? We must get on to the next village before night. There are wild beasts in this wood: lions, they say.

MEGAERA. I dont believe a word of it. You are always threatening me with wild beasts to make me walk the very soul out of my body when I can hardly drag one foot before another. We havnt seen a single lion yet.

ANDROCLES. Well, dear, do you want to see one?

MEGAERA [*tearing the bundle from his back*] You cruel brute, you dont care how tired I am, or what becomes of me [*she throws the bundle on the ground*]: always thinking of yourself. Self! self! self! always yourself! [*She sits down on the bundle*].

ANDROCLES [*sitting down sadly on the ground with his elbows on his knees and his head in his hands*] We all have to think of ourselves occasionally, dear.

MEGAERA. A man ought to think of his wife sometimes.

ANDROCLES. He cant always help it, dear. You make me think of you a good deal. Not that I blame you.

MEGAERA. Blame me! I should think not indeed. Is it my fault that I'm married to you?

ANDROCLES. No, dear: that is my fault.

Figure 5.33 An extract from *Androcles and the Lion* printed in Shaw's alphabet (Shaw, 1962, pp. 22–3)

The work by Sir Isaac Pitman and Alexander Ellis in designing a more phonetically transparent orthography led to another quite different project in the 1960s, when Pitman's grandson Sir James Pitman played a key role in implementing a new orthography called the 'initial teaching alphabet', or 'i t a', for use in schools. For a while the scheme gained popularity in several English-speaking countries and was supported by both publishers and education ministries. In an endorsement to one book in the scheme (Downing, 1964), the British minister of education, Sir Edward Boyle, described the introduction of i t a as an 'exciting and important' experiment – 'It is a subject on which there is the possibility of a really dramatic break-through'. No capital letters were used in the i t a – initial letters were indicated in the medieval manner with an enlarged letter. It was intended as an orthography for children's writing as well as for reading, but despite some institutional support the fashion did not last longer than about a decade.

Glossic was a phonetic transcription system invented by Alexander Ellis and used by several writers for the English Dialect Society in the late nineteenth century. Unlike a general purpose orthography which needs to ignore minor, insignificant differences in pronunciation, glossic was created in order to represent fine nuances of accent. Ellis himself used it in his *English Dialects: Their Sounds and Homes* (Ellis, 1890), one of the earliest systematic surveys of British accents (see Figure 5.34). Ellis's glossic fell into disuse but a number of similar phonetic alphabets, many based on the research carried out by Ellis and Pitman, have been used by linguists for similar purposes. In Britain and Australia the International Phonetic Alphabet (IPA) is now the commonest system for making transcriptions of pronunciations in phonetic detail. (See Crystal, 1987, p.159).

RECEIVED EDUCATED LONDON dt.

1. *Soa· (soa·w) ei sai· (sai·y), mai·ts, you see· nou, dhŭt ei ŭm reit ŭbou·t dhat lit·l gyu·l kum·ing from dhŭ skoo·l yon·dŭr.*
2. *Shee· iz goa·ing doun dhŭ roa·d dhe·r throo· dhŭ red gai·t on dhŭ left hand seid ŭv dhŭ wai·y.*
3. *Shoo·ŭr inuf· dhŭ cheild hŭz gon strai·t up tŭ dhŭ doa·ŭr (dau·ŭr, dau·r) ŭv dhŭ rong hous,*
4. *whe·r shee· wil chaan·s tŭ feind dhat drung·kn, def, shriv·ŭld fel·oa (fel·ŭ) ŭu dhŭ nai·m ŭv Tom·us.·*
5. *Wee· au·l noa· (noa·w) him ver·i wel.*
6. *Woa·nt dhi oa·ld chap soo·n tee·ch hŭr not tŭ doo· it ŭgen· (ŭgai·n), puo·ŭ thing!*
7. *Luok·! iz·nt it troo·?*

Figure 5.34 A.J. Ellis's glossic alphabet from 1890 (Ellis, 1890)

5.7 Conclusion

The visual nature of English

This chapter has focused on the materiality of English texts. There is a long tradition in linguistic study that is concerned with the outward forms of speech (phonetics), but for some reason *visual* manifestations of language were regarded for a long time as somehow less central to linguistic study than *audible* ones. Both this and the previous chapter indicate the importance of focusing on the visual nature of language.

The historical location of texts

We tend to think of language as something which allows *individuals* to communicate with each other. The language and design of a medieval manuscript (as with the newspaper articles discussed in Chapter 3), however, is the product of many people. Hence each text can be said to speak with several voices – those of the composer, the copyist(s), the illustrators and rubricators, the later editors and publishers, and sometimes readers who add marginal comments. In any account of the English language we need to recognise that not only the language in a larger sense but also individual texts represent the work of many people. For this reason we need to understand a great deal about the historical, political, cultural and economic context in which texts were created in order that we might understand their historical significance, the meaning they might have had for readers, and the evidence they provide of how and why the English language changed.

Trends towards standardisation and divergence

Another important theme in this chapter is the idea that homogeneity – in handwriting, in spelling, in book production – represents an institutional achievement. It can be brought about only when many people work to explicit agreed house rules, or when a single person has been trained to follow standard conventions. In the history of English texts we can perceive two divergent tendencies. One is for texts to become less uniform, written in hands which are more idiosyncratic, and designed and spelt in ways which reflect local practices. We can see this in the development of 'national hands' at various times, in the local spelling practices of Middle English scribes, and in the increase in idiosyncrasies. There is, however, a competing trend towards standardisation and uniformity – for instance by the imposition of a house style by the institutions which control the production and circulation of texts. The role of the church was apparent in Old English times, and again with the carolingian revival, but printing and schools also had a major standardising effect on spelling and punctuation in later times. The history of English suggests, however, that there is no inevitable progress towards standardisation and uniformity – the two tendencies seem always to be in uneasy competition, as other chapters in this book show.

READING A: An essay on the necessity, advantages and practicability of reforming the mode of spelling, and of rendering the orthography of words correspondent to the pronunciation

Noah Webster
(Noah Webster (1758–1843) was an American lexicographer, textbook
author, Bible translator, spelling reformer, writer and editor.)

Source: Webster, N. (1991 [1789]) 'An essay on the necessity, advantages and
practicability of reforming the mode of spelling, and of rendering the
orthography of words correspondent to the pronunciation' [extracts from the
appendix to *Dissertations on the English Language*, 1789], in Crowley, T. (ed.)
Proper English: Readings in Language, History and Cultural Identity,
London, Routledge, pp. 83–93.

It has been observed by all writers on the English language, that the
orthography or spelling of words is very irregular; the same letters often
representing different sounds, and the same sounds often expressed by
different letters. For this irregularity, two principal causes may be assigned:

1   The changes to which the pronunciation of a language is liable, from the
    progress of science and civilisation.

2   The mixture of different languages, occasioned by revolutions in England,
    or by a predilection of the learned, for words of foreign growth and
    ancient origin.

But such is the state of our language. The pronunciation of the words which
are strictly *English*, has gradually been changing for ages, and since the revival
of science in Europe, the language has received a vast accession of words
from other languages, many of which retain an orthography very ill-suited to
exhibit the true pronunciation.

The question now occurs; ought the Americans to retain these faults which
produce innumerable inconveniences in the acquisition and use of the
language, or ought they at once to reform these abuses, and introduce order
and regularity into the orthography of the AMERICAN TONGUE?

Let us consider this subject with some attention.

Several attempts were formerly made in England to rectify the orthography of
the language. But I apprehend their schemes failed of success, rather on
account of their intrinsic difficulties, than on account of any necessary
impracticability of a reform. It was proposed in most of these schemes, not
merely to throw out superfluous and silent letters, but to introduce a number

of new characters. Any attempt on such a plan must undoubtedly prove unsuccessful. It is not to be expected that an orthography, perfectly regular and simple, such as would be formed by a 'Synod of Grammarians on principles of science', will ever be substituted for that confused mode of spelling which is now established. But it is apprehended that great improvements may be made, and an orthography almost regular, or such as shall obviate most of the present difficulties which occur in learning our language, may be introduced and established with little trouble and opposition.

The principal alterations, necessary to render our orthography sufficiently regular and easy, are these:

1   The omission of all superfluous or silent letters; as *a* in *bread*. Thus *bread, head, give, breast, built, meant, realm, friend,* would be *spelt, bred, hed, giv, brest, bilt, ment, relm, frend.* Would this alteration produce any inconvenience, any embarrassment or expense? By no means. On the other hand, it would lessen the trouble of writing, and much more, of learning the language; it would reduce the true pronunciation to a certainty; and while it would assist foreigners and our own children in acquiring the language, it would render the pronunciation uniform, in different parts of the country, and almost prevent the possibility of changes.

2   A substitution of a character that has a certain definite sound for one that is more vague and indeterminate. Thus by putting *ee* instead of *ea* or *ie*, the words *mean, near, speak, grieve, zeal*, would become *meen, neer, speek, greev, zeel*. This alteration could not occasion a moment's trouble; at the same time it would prevent a doubt respecting the pronunciation; whereas the *ea* and *ie* having different sounds, may give a learner much difficulty ...

3   A trifling alteration in a character, or the addition of a point would distinguish different sounds, without the substitution of a new character. Thus a very small stroke across *th* would distinguish its two sounds. A point over a vowel, in this manner *ȧ*, or *ȯ*, or *ī*, might answer all the purposes of different letters. And for the diphthong *ow*, let the two letters be united by a small stroke, or both engraven on the same piece of metal, with the left hand line of the *w* united to the *o*.

These, with a few other inconsiderable alterations, would answer every purpose, and render the orthography sufficiently correct and regular.

The advantages to be derived from alterations are numerous, great and permanent.

1   The simplicity of the orthography would facilitate the learning of the language. It is now the work of years for children to learn to spell; and after all, the business is rarely accomplished. A few men, who are bred to some business that requires constant exercise in writing, finally learn to

spell most words without hesitation; but most people remain, all their lives, imperfect masters of spelling, and liable to make mistakes, whenever they take up a pen to write a short note. Nay, many people, even of education and fashion, never attempt to write a letter, without frequently consulting a dictionary.

But with the proposed orthography, a child would learn to spell, without trouble, in a very short time, and the orthography being very regular, he would ever afterwards find it difficult to make a mistake. It would, in that case, be as difficult to spell *wrong*, as it is now to spell *right*.

Besides this advantage, foreigners would be able to acquire the pronunciation of English, which is now so difficult and embarrassing, that they are either wholly discouraged on the first attempt, or obliged, after many years labor, to rest contented with an imperfect knowledge of the subject.

2 A correct orthography would render the pronunciation of the language, as uniform as in the spelling books. A general uniformity thro the United States, would be the event of such a reformation as I am here recommending. All persons, of every rank, would speak with some degree of precision and uniformity. Such a uniformity in these states is very desirable; it would remove prejudice, and conciliate mutual affection and respect.

3 Such a reform would diminish the number of letters about one sixteenth or eighteenth; this would save a page in eighteen; and a saving of an eighteenth in the expense of books, is an advantage that should not be overlooked.

4 But a capital advantage of this reform in these states would be, that it would make a difference between the English orthography and the American. This will startle those who have not attended to the subject; but I am confident that such an event is an object of vast political consequence. For, [*sic*]

The alteration, however small, would encourage the publication of books in our own country. It would render it, in some measure, necessary that all books should be printed in America. The English would never copy our orthography for their own use; and consequently the same impressions of books would not answer for both countries. The inhabitants of the present generation would read the English impressions; but posterity, being taught a different spelling, would prefer the American orthography.

Besides this, a *national language* is a band of *national union*. Every engine should be employed to make the people of this country *national*; to call their attachments home to their own country; and to inspire them with the pride of national character. However they may boast of Independence, and the freedom of their government, yet their *opinions* are not sufficiently independent; an astonishing respect for the arts and literature of their parent country, and a blind imitation of its manners, are still prevalent among the Americans. Thus an habitual respect for another country, deserved indeed and once laudable, turns their attention from their own interests, and prevents their respecting themselves ...

But America is in a situation most favourable for great reformations; and the present time is, in a singular degree, auspicious. The minds of men in this country have been awakened. New scenes have been, for many years, presenting new occasions for exertion; unexpected distresses have called forth the powers of invention; and the application of new expedients has demanded every possible exercise of wisdom and talents. Attention is roused; the mind expanded; and the intellectual faculties invigorated. Here men are prepared to receive improvements, which would be rejected by nations, whose habits have not been shaken by similar events.

Now is the time, and *this* is the country, in which we may expect success, in attempting changes favourable to language, science and government. Delay, in the plan here proposed, may be fatal; under the tranquil general government, the minds of men may again sink into indolence; a national acquiescence in error will follow; and posterity will be doomed to struggle with difficulties, which time and accident will perpetually multiply.

Let us then seize the present moment, and establish a *national language* as well as a national government. Let us remember that there is a certain respect due to the opinions of other nations. As an independent people, our reputation abroad demands that, in all things, we should be federal; be *national*; for if we do not respect *ourselves*, we may be assured that other nations will not respect us. In short, let it be impressed upon the mind of every American, that to neglect the means of commanding respect abroad, is treason against the character and dignity of a brave independent people.

English and new media

Colin Gardner

6.1 Introduction

In this chapter I will explore some key aspects of the relationship between new media and the use of English in a global context. I will focus on how various aspects of new media have changed the kind of English used, changed how people do things with texts in English and facilitated new ways of analysing English texts. By 'new' I mean media that are essentially the products of computer technology. I begin by considering the extent to which English is the dominant language of the internet and the contexts in which it serves as a lingua franca, that is, the language used for communication among speakers of many languages. Next, I briefly consider whether new media technology is affecting the nature of English itself, including the possible emergence of new 'varieties' of English used on the internet. I move on to consider new practices and procedures resulting from the use of new media, including the digitisation of English artefacts, such as the electronic book. I then look at how the technology of hypertext permits new forms of creativity by looking at **hyperfiction**, an emergent form of new writing that combines the traditional aspects of the novel with hyperlinks. Finally, I consider the artificial production of English through *chatbots* and consider some of the issues raised by this form of English.

6.2 The place of English on the internet

'Internet' and 'Web' are often used interchangeably. In fact, there is a distinction between the internet and the Web, and it is a simple one. The internet is the network of computers and the physical connections between them, stretching across continents and, in the case of satellite links, into space. The Web is a system based on electronic files (web pages) transmitted between computers connected to the internet.

How do the technologies of the internet seem to be affecting the status of English as a global medium of communication? There are two current positions on this question. The first, and most common up to the time of writing, is that English is and will continue to be the dominant language of communication via the internet. This is a position outlined by many sociolinguistic commentators who have argued, often from a critical perspective, that the dominance of English as the global lingua franca is a linguistic phenomenon with an economic imperative (Phillipson, 1992; Skutnabb-Kangas, 2000). This process, sometimes referred to as **Englishisation**, is outlined by Daniel Dor, 'the process of Englishization is equated with the process of economic globalization (however conceptualized); the driving forces behind the spread of English are equated with those pushing economic globalization; and the "interests" of English (and English speakers) are equated with those of the beneficiaries of economic globalization' (Dor, 2004, p. 102).

New technologies are key resources for globalisation and they seem to have assured a dominant position for English. This is evident in the central place of English in the development and labelling of much computer technology (as you find later from Table 6.2). More fundamentally, the speed and spread of communication via the internet seems to have generated a greater demand for a global lingua franca and English seems to have met such a demand. Given the dominance of English on the internet, 'local' languages (languages other than English) and cultural diversity are seen to be directly threatened (Chapter 7 gives a more detailed discussion of this view).

Globalisation

[T]he term is often used in vague or ambiguous ways. There are several key dimensions to globalisation which have been explored within sociolinguistics.

Economic – this refers to the way in which processes of production and consumption operate increasingly on a global rather than 'local' or national levels ...

Technological – rapid changes in information technology have profoundly affected the ways in which people communicate across the globe, not least in terms of speed ...

Cultural – cultural practices no longer remain tied to one particular location but are rather dispersed across the world, predominantly through the possibilities afforded by information technology ...

(Swann et al., 2004, pp. 125–6)

However, a second position is currently gaining more ground: the same economic imperative that has pushed English to a position of dominance, is now pushing multilingualism to the fore. Dor considers the use of

English alongside other languages but through the lens of globalisation. In 'From Englishization to imposed multilingualism', Dor (2004) argues that commerce is changing the nature of language proliferation on the Web by seeking to provide goods and services in the languages of its potential customers. One example of this might be the BBC World Service which broadcasts in thirty-three different languages, combining elements both of a broadening of cultural concerns to a widening audience and of commercial interest in promoting the goods and services of the corporation. Providing web content in many different languages as the BBC does is one way in which multilingualism may thrive. Another is the way in which search engines provide translation services. For example, by selecting the 'Translate this page' option in a search engine such as Google, users are provided with a rudimentary word-for-word translation of the page being viewed. This works, of course, only for those languages that the search engine can handle and the results, as with many machine-based translations, are often quite comical.

I will be returning to Dor's argument, but first I want to consider the statistical evidence for English dominance versus growth in multilingualism on the internet.

ACTIVITY 6.1

Allow about
10 minutes

In Figure 6.1 (overleaf) you can see how the proportion of internet users for whom English is a first language has changed between 2000 and 2005. Before reading the comment below, consider the information in Figure 6.1 with the following questions in mind.

- What do you notice about the percentage of internet use by speakers of English as a first language?
- What do you notice about the percentage of internet use by speakers of other languages?
- Which languages seem to have increased their presence?

Comment

While it is often claimed that English dominates the internet, Figure 6.1 shows clearly that the proportion of internet users for whom English is a first language has actually been decreasing: from 51.3 per cent in 2000 to 32 per cent in 2005. The total for populations who are users of first languages other than English has increased with some – notably Chinese – showing a marked increase. The proportion of 'other languages' has also increased, indicating that the total number of languages being used on the internet is growing.

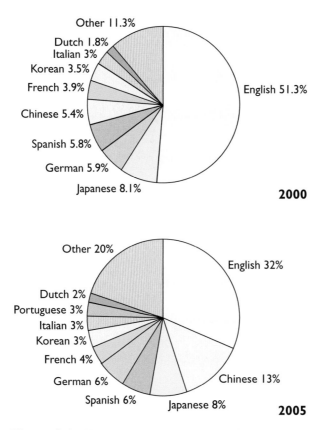

Figure 6.1 The changing demography of internet users by first language (Graddol, 2005)

ACTIVITY 6.2

Allow about 15 minutes

Now, again before reading the comment below, consider the following questions in relation to Table 6.1.

- To what extent are the figures for percentage of internet use by language (see column third from left) similar to or different from those in Figure 6.1?
- What additional information does Table 6.1 tell you about changing patterns of internet use by language groups?

Comment

The first thing to note is that the figures for 2005 in Table 6.1 differ slightly from those in Figure 6.1: notably, the percentage of language users by language differs somewhat (for example, 30.6 per cent is the figure given for all internet users who are speakers of English as a first language in Table 6.1, as compared with 32 per cent in Figure 6.1). Estimating internet use by language is a

Table 6.1 The top ten languages used in the Web

Top ten languages in the internet	Internet users by language	% of all internet users	World population 2005 estimate for language	% internet penetration by language	% internet growth for language (2000–05)
English	311,241,881	30.6	1,125,664,397	27.6	126.9
Chinese	132,301,513	13.0	1,340,767,863	9.9	309.6
Japanese	86,300,000	8.5	128,389,000	67.2	83.3
Spanish	63,971,898	6.3	392,053,192	16.3	163.8
German	56,853,162	5.6	95,982,043	59.2	106.0
French	40,974,005	4.0	381,193,149	10.7	235.9
Korean	33,900,000	3.3	73,945,860	45.8	78.0
Portuguese	32,372,000	3.2	230,846,275	14.0	327.3
Italian	28,870,000	2.8	59,115,261	48.8	118.7
Russian	23,700,000	2.3	143,682,757	16.5	664.5
Top ten languages	810,484,459	79.6	3,971,639,798	20.4	150.5
Rest of the world languages	207,572,930	20.4	2,528,057,262	8.2	453.9
World total	1,018,057,389	100.0	6,499,697,060	15.7	182.0

Internet top ten language usage statistics were updated on December 31, 2005.

Internet penetration is the ratio between the sum of internet users speaking a language and the total population estimate that speaks that specific language.

(Internet World Stats, 2006)

complex activity. One reason for the different percentages is that all percentages are estimates based on extrapolations from a range of data, often using different calculation techniques. A second reason for difference is that use on the internet is rapidly changing. However, although there is a difference in the figures given, the general trend shown in Table 6.1 is similar to that in Figure 6.1. Web users who are speakers of English as a first language currently account for almost one third of all web users, which roughly agrees with Figure 6.1. The top six languages are also the same. What should be noted in Table 6.1, however, is that additional information is provided about the rate of growth (see last column on the right). In the top four languages in this column, English lags behind both Chinese (by a considerable margin) and Spanish, whereas English has grown half as much again as the rate of Japanese. Within this group of four languages, the ratio of user level to population appears to be the inverse of growth between 2000 and 2005 (see the last two columns on the right in Table 6.1). That is, those with the highest growth rate have the lowest user level. I don't think this is coincidental. To me it suggests that growth in online linguistic populations is reaching saturation, most noticeably for those languages where usage is already high.

It seems clear that while English is a powerful language on the internet, there is a growing use and presence of other languages. Dor argues that this kind of multilingualism is not 'negotiated' by which he means subject to local control, but rather *imposed,* that is imposed or driven by economic interests often outside the control of 'local' language users:

> ... the very same global economic pressures that are traditionally assumed to push the global expansion of English may actually be working to strengthen a significant set of other languages – at the expense of English. The potential result of this process is neither imposed Englishization nor negotiated multilingualism but a specific pattern of *imposed multilingualism*: local linguistic variability imposed and controlled by the economic center.

> (Dor, 2004, p. 98)

The extent to which control over economic, cultural and linguistic resources can be sustained in local contexts is an ongoing point of debate (Chapter 7 provides an example of shifting control over language policy in Papua New Guinea). What seems clear, however, is that multilingualism alongside English is a significant feature of language use on the internet.

One example of such multilingualism is illustrated in Reading A by Mercedes Durham. Thus far I have been considering the use of English on the internet by focusing on users of English *as a first language*. But of course, many more people use English as a second, third or even fourth language, which means that the use of English may continue to grow, even as other languages are also increasing their presence on the internet.

ACTIVITY 6.3

Now read the article 'Language choice on a Swiss mailing list' by Mercedes Durham (Reading A), which is part of a wider project that aims to chart the evolving use of English in Switzerland. Here, Durham looks at the online discussion list of a Swiss medical association and describes a change in the language used by a community of multilingual participants. All of the students in the association are either Swiss, German or Italian, but Durham notes that, at some point over a period of three years, English becomes the main language of communication for the group. Read this shortened version of Durham's original article with the following questions in mind.

- What prompted the change to English?
- What role do you think the specific mode of communication – email – played in the decision to switch to English?
- What does this article tell us about the way that English is being used in multilingual contents?

Comment

The decision to switch codes is taken first by one student 'to get [things] clear in this meeting story'. Durham explains how the President of the Association had informed students of a limit on numbers who could attend a conference. The confusion centred on whether those who had already registered, but who had exceeded the quota for their group, would be allowed to go. In the absence of the President, emails were exchanged in French and German. However, the confusion continued, suggesting that some of the users felt that they were not successfully communicating with each other in these languages. The switch to English suggests that the group initially used it to clarify a point of information which was unclear in the multilingual exchange.

The discussion list played a role in this switch, partly because the speed of the exchange created a greater sense of urgency among the participants and partly because many participants were contributing to the discussion simultaneously. In an offline situation, the process of communication would have been much slower, presumably giving time for the position to be clarified at the outset.

English in this instance was used for a purpose. It had a specific function in the community: first, as a method of clarification and feedback; and, eventually, as a lingua franca for the group. However, the use of English clearly relies on its existing status as a second language for many of the users. As Durham notes, English is promoted in this Association, because it gives access to conferences and journal literature, which are predominantly in the English language.

Although a small case study, Durham's is an interesting account of the specific way in which English comes to be used as a lingua franca in a particular multilingual context. It may be that Switzerland is a special case, having three official languages. The study is part of a wider project, and it will be interesting to see how the situation develops.

Having considered the extent to which English dominates internet usage, I will now turn to consider whether internet and new media technology are affecting the nature of English itself.

6.3 Is new media technology changing English?

It is understandable that we should ask what effect, if any, new media technology is having on the English language. Can we tell, for example, if English is changing? What evidence should we look for, and where? If there are changes, are they significant, lasting? How can we go about exploring these changes in English?

The most obvious indication of change is the introduction of new words or word forms, many of which are used internationally, to refer to new media and new media practices. Some examples of these are listed in Table 6.2 (n. = noun; v. = verb).

Table 6.2 New words and word forms referring to new media practices

blog	(n.) Shortened form of *web log*; 1 a personal, web-based, online journal 2 also *blogger*, one who performs such an activity. (v.) To keep a journal of this kind.
elearning	(n.) Educational provision that makes use of computer-based connectivity.
multicast/ narrowcast/ podcast, netcast/webcast	(n. and v.) These terms emphasise different aspects of the way material is distributed (hence 'cast') to users: *to multicast/narrowcast/podcast* is to transmit data to subscribers in a group. *Netcasting* and *webcasting* are more akin to traditional broadcasting in that data is transmitted to a general audience rather than specified subscribers. *Podcasting* is becoming increasingly common, since listeners are able to subscribe to a service and download content at their own convenience rather than at scheduled times.
P2P networking	(n.) 'Peer-to-peer' networking. Traditional networks operate on the principle that documents to be shared over the internet by individual users are sent to a central computer (a server). When other users access these documents, they are sent from the server, not the original user's machine. In *P2P* networking, there is no central computer; machines connected to the *P2P* network (peers) are accessed directly by other machines on the network.
spam	(n. and v.) Also called *junk mail*. *Spam* is invariably unsolicited, and usually involves some form of advertising, marketing or money-making scheme. Although increasingly subject to regulatory control, *spam* is notoriously difficult to eradicate.
splog	(n.) Combines 'spam' and 'blog' (see above). *Splogs* are fake blog articles where the sole intention of the splogger is to direct viewers towards spam-related content.
tele-conference/ video-conference	(n.) A *teleconference* is a popular way of connecting users using audio telephone conferencing. *Videoconferencing* uses video and audio.
typo-squatting	(n.) Users can access a website by inputting its address (known as a URL – uniform resource locator) into the web browser and then hitting the 'Go' button. However, a user may mistype the address. If commonly mistyped URLs are owned and purposely used by advertisers, for example, this would be a form of *typosquatting*.
webinar	(n.) 'Web' and 'seminar'. A *webinar* is an online workshop that contains video, audio and some form of interactive whiteboard to enable real-time, synchronous feedback, such as questions and answers, between participants.
wi-fi	(n.) 'Wireless' and 'fidelity' (compare 'hi-fi'). *Wi-fi* refers to a form of wireless connectivity that permits mobile phone and laptop users, for example, to make a connection to the internet while on the move. City spaces, bars and cafes may contain *wi-fi* hotspots – areas where it is possible to make such a connection.
wiki	(n.) A multi-authored web space in which users are able to add content simply by submitting an online form. The ease with which contributions can be made, and the freedom from editorial controls and restrictions makes *wikis* a very popular feedback forum (see *Wikipedia*, an online encyclopedia).

Indications of language change are evident from several studies (e.g. Paolillo, 1999; Crystal, 2001). Key changes include variations of existing words using some of the following linguistic processes: existing words are given a new context, as in *camping*, 'hovering in one place in an online game'; abbreviated forms are introduced, such as *thnx* for 'thanks', and acronyms, such as *TTFN* for 'ta-ta for now'; and greater use is made of visual symbols, for example, the use of @, numbers and punctuation marks for emoticons; and greater use of stylistic changes, for example, the use of archaic words and constructions, and non-standard syntax. Word creation is often achieved in the following ways: compounding, affixation, blends, conversions and other creative forms (Crystal, 2003, p. 429). Examples of these linguistic formations are listed in Table 6.3 (and some are also found in Table 6.2).

Table 6.3 Word formation

compounding	Two words added together to form a single unit, e.g. *mouse* + *click* forms *mouseclick*.
affixation: prefix suffix	This category is divided into prefix and suffix: the prefix *hyper-* added to *fiction* becomes *hyperfiction* the suffix *-bot* added to *chat* becomes *chatbot*.
blends	Two words are welded, e.g.: *cybernetic* + *astronaut* becomes *cybernaut*; *spam* + *indexing* becomes *spamdexing*; *Web* + *broadcast* = *webcast*.
conversion	Word class change so that *Caps Lock* (keyboard key, noun) becomes a verb, e.g. *Don't 'CAPS lock' someone if you're looking for help.*
substitution	Substitution of similar sounding elements, e.g. *ecruit* for *recruit*.
punctuation	Infix the dot in *net.art*.

(based on Crystal, 2001, pp. 82–5)

Although some of the new linguistic and semiotic forms may be used by many people, much of the innovation I have been talking about so far may be attributable to small communities of language users. One such community is that of online gamers. These individuals are typically young, technically adroit, with time and energy to invest in hours of online activity. Gamers participate in 'game worlds', websites where individuals can meet online, communicate and play in a mutual environment. The kind of game world I am thinking about here is a text-based one, meaning that participants enter a virtual space, where communication is through text input from a keyboard. Users can assume identities (known as 'avatars'), and they can employ a set of verbal commands to navigate their way around the space.

ACTIVITY 6.4

Read 'L33t-sp34k' by Erin McKean (Reading B) and as you do so, consider to what extent suggestions that new technologies are revolutionising language use may be justified. Focus on the kinds of words that are created and the ways in which visual elements are used.

Comment

You probably noticed quite a number of different innovations. The first and most visually striking method described by McKean is that of substitution, where letters are replaced by similarly formed numbers, such as *3* (a reversed uppercase 'E') and *4* (visually similar to uppercase 'A'). Random capitalisation adds further visual impact. A distinctive rhetoric exists, for example, in the archaic constructions often used in commands such as *ph33r my l33t 5kill5* ('fear my elite skills'). Finally, words such as *camping* are simply adapted to a new situation or context, while others, such as *warph4x* and *warpz0r* seem unique to this specific context. You may think that these uses confirm a commonly held impression of disregard for authority and rules. Yet clearly rules exist: the rebukes are made to those who flout the rules or are inexperienced enough to stand out.

What also strikes me is the visual nature of the forms used. Claims are often made that this kind of interaction is more like spoken than written language, yet there is clearly considerable attention being paid to the graphical features of the language, thus indicating that in some ways the interaction is conceptualised as a written text (visual aspects of communication are discussed in Chapter 4).

It is difficult to predict whether specific uses of language emerging from one small community will be taken up more widely. Search engines can be used to give a rough idea of the take-up of language items represented on the Web as they evolve over time. The following *Wikipedia* entry claims that the term *podcast* has developed as follows:

> The word about podcasting rapidly spread through the already-popular weblogs of Curry, Winer and other early podcasters and podcast-listeners. Fellow blogger and technology columnist Doc Searls began keeping track of how many 'hits' Google found for the word 'podcasts' on September 28, 2004. On that day, the result was 24 hits ... There were 526 hits on September 30, then 2,750 three days later. The number doubled every few days, passing 100,000 by October 18. A year later, Google found more than 100,000,000 hits on the word 'podcasts'.

(*Wikipedia*, 2006)

You may like to try this yourself for some of the terms in McKean's article. At the time of writing, entering *warph4x* in Google results in only one hit, while *warpz0r* has 2,840 hits. This seems rather a small number in any event. Perhaps we should not expect to find many hits for these words since, as McKean suggests, the function of l33t-sp34k is to be exclusive, accessible to only a small number of enthusiastic followers.

6.4 Digitisation and ebooks

Crystal argues that '[a]ll areas of English language study have been profoundly affected by technological developments' (Crystal, 2003, p. 446). First, the speed with which operations can be carried out is unprecedented. Second, the ways in which information can be processed and analysed has changed. Third, digital artefacts are open to a wider community. For example, at the touch of a button, digital copies of historical manuscripts stored in the geographically distinct museums can be brought together on demand, and the reader, while perusing these documents can have an email exchange with the curator; references can be made to other documents which, again, can be immediately brought to the virtual desktop. Aspects of this way of working have much in common with traditional scholarly practice but, according to some commentators, immediacy introduces new perspectives on interrelationships between hitherto disparate fields of enquiry. In this section, I will therefore focus on new practices involving the use of technology applied to the production, mediation and provision of English language texts. I will begin by looking at digitisation.

Digitisation

Digitisation is a term applied to the transfer of physical artefacts, either by scanning, camera, or any other digital recording device, into a form that can be processed by a computer. The process can be lengthy: it took a team of fourteen staff from Keio University, Tokyo, ten days to photograph the British Library's two editions of the *Canterbury Tales* (British Library, 2006a). These documents may be stored optically on CD-ROM, DVD, etc., or may be stored magnetically on a hard disk drive and made available online through **digital repositories** – projects or organisations dedicated to the storage and distribution of digitised texts. Through the website of The Joint Information Systems Committee (JISC) and using the projects link, you would find listed the many digitised texts of projects in the UK related to further and higher education. Such documents exist in what is said to be a 'virtual space', the point being that they can be accessed from anywhere with an internet connection. Although access to such connections are not equally available around the world as indicated by population usage figures (see Table 6.4, the third and fifth columns from the left), the storage of documents in a virtual space means that documents in English are potentially more easily available to those in less prosperous regions. Digital Imaging South Africa (2006), for example, makes available a fully searchable database of a rare and otherwise inaccessible body of South African journal literature.

Table 6.4 Internet usage statistics – the big picture

World regions	Population (2005 est.)	% population of the world	Internet usage, latest data	% population (penetration)	% usage of world	% usage growth 2000–2005
Africa	896,721,874	14.0	23,917,500	2.7	2.5	429.8
Asia	3,622,994,130	56.4	332,590,713	9.2	34.2	191.0
Europe	804,574,696	12.5	285,408,118	35.5	29.3	171.6
Middle East	187,258,006	2.9	16,163,500	8.6	1.7	392.1
North America	328,387,059	5.1	224,103,811	68.2	23.0	107.3
Latin America/Caribbean	546,723,509	8.5	72,953,597	13.3	7.5	303.8
Oceania/Australia	33,443,448	0.5	17,690,762	52.9	1.8	132.2
World total	6,420,102,722	100.0	972,828,001	15.2	100.0	169.5

Internet usage and world population statistics were updated on November 21, 2005. (Internet World Stats, 2005)

In the UK, there is considerable access to the internet: in February 2006, it was estimated that 33,521,621 people in the UK had access to an internet connection (Nielson/NetRatings, 2006). This means that hundreds of projects and programmes designed to bring collections online are available to many users. The British Library (2006b) is one such repository; its *Treasures in Full* includes online editions of Shakespeare, Chaucer, Gutenberg Bible, Magna Carta and a selection of Renaissance festival books.

The reader can do many things with the British Library editions of these manuscripts: compare various editions side by side; browse the digital documents (that is, search page by page); jump to a specific place in the text by entering a page or line number; magnify images up to double the original size. These are all interesting ways of manipulating views of the images. However, probably the most significant feature is the way that these texts open to public scrutiny the raw data of textual scholarship. The British Library website states:

> Not only can we give more people access to them. In many ways we provide better access too, remembering that for some purposes nothing can replace the originals ... The careful examination of [Caxton's] type has also allowed the creation of a chronological order of his works.

> This type of examination is now open to everybody, and it is possible to detect more detailed information about individual pieces of type from the digital images to help us further in understanding how Caxton and his contemporaries worked.

(British Library, 2006c, p. 1)

ACTIVITY 6.5

Allow about
20 minutes

When a manuscript has been copied in the form of an image and combined with a transcription, more detailed word searches are possible. Figure 6.2 is a page from an online edition of the British Library's Caxton manuscripts. Identify what functions this edition has by looking at the options fields (list and text entry boxes). Then, before reading the comment below, look at the results of a word search for *weren* (Figure 6.3, overleaf). What do you think may be some of the advantages of making documents available in this way?

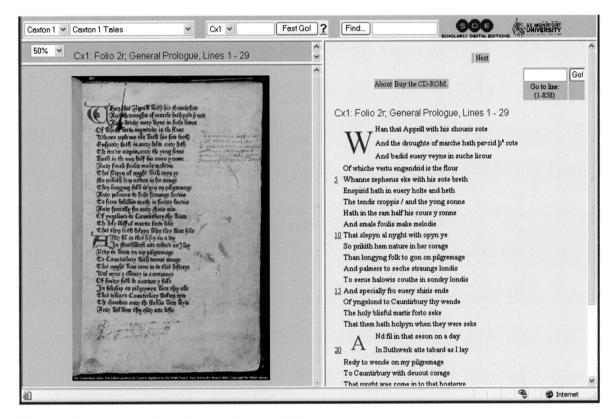

Figure 6.2 An extract from Caxton's Chaucer (British Library)

Comment

First of all, in Figure 6.2 there are a number of options made available to the user, such as allowing the reader to select one of two versions of the *Canterbury Tales* (Caxton 1 or Caxton 2), as indicated in the drop-down box in the upper left-hand corner. In the top right of the page is the 'Find' feature, to search for a sample word of the *Canterbury Tales*. This is a concordancing feature: as you may recall from Chapter 1, a **concordance** is a computer software tool which enables analysts to find out which words occur alongside, or near other words.

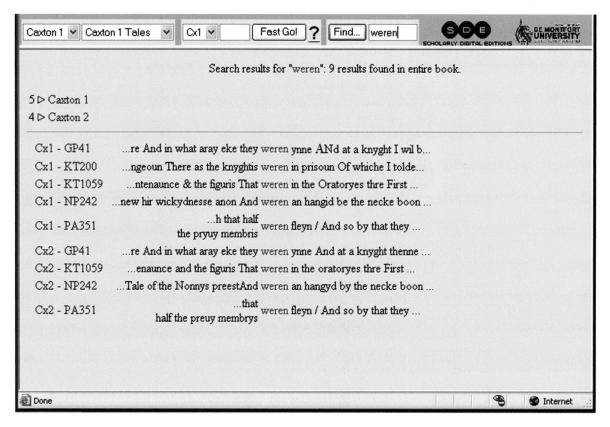

Figure 6.3   Search results for *weren*

From Figure 6.3, you can see that there are only nine occurences of *weren*: five in Caxton I and four in Caxton 2. If you searched for *were* for example, there would be considerably more instances found – at the time of writing, I was given 484 results for the form *were* in Caxton I and 487 in Caxton 2. You can see that it is also possible to magnify the document, and to jump to specific locations within the text.

There are a number of obvious benefits to digitising texts. Digitised collections help preservation by reducing the physical disturbance to texts caused by frequent use and consultation. A digitised text, magnified many times, can reveal more information than the manuscript in its physical setting. Caxton's *Canterbury Tales* are made available to many more people than the physical artefact ever could, thus widening access to a previously 'hidden' resource. In terms of consequences for English, the main point is that an object of special interest is potentially transformed into an object of general interest, accessible to anyone with the physical means to access it. The history of the language, in this case, and linguistic resources generally, become more widely available.

The ebook

The ebook (electronic book) is a form closely approximating that of the traditional book. Quite often, as with the Caxton digitised manuscripts, the page is formatted as a book page, with margins and page numbers, and may be displayed either at a PC terminal, using reading software, or on a hand-held computer with the necessary software. The images may be digitised, rather than textual information, although most are text scanned and optically recognised, thus permitting search functions.

Ebooks can be divided into two types: the kinds of digital repositories associated with manuscript archives or rare books, and those available from online publishers. In the first type, a relatively small number of Web-based electronic book sites can be found on the internet. Two well-known examples are The Million Books Project and Project Gutenberg. Both have the intention of committing as many books as possible out of copyright to electronic form, to be made freely available to anyone with the means to access and download them. Project Gutenberg contains many English language books, although it is not devoted exclusively to English language texts. It contains over 15,000 books in English and about 2,000 in other languages. The number and range of books, considering that the digitisation is carried out by enthusiasts, is impressive by any standards.

Online publishing is rather different. Most major publishers have some Web presence, in the sense of a website advertising their catalogues, editorial policies, information for authors, and so on. Although they have a Web presence, these publishers are traditionally in the business of publishing works to be printed and bound. But there are publishers, such as US publishers, Random House and Eastgate Systems, Inc., that commission works published exclusively in electronic form. Random House publish in both media and have a separate ebook category, further divided into subjects and genre.

On the other hand, Eastgate Systems almost exclusively publishes electronic, hypertext material based on its proprietary authoring system 'Storyspace'. The significance of Eastgate is that the publishing is centred on **hypertext** – the linking mechanism that permits users to bring different pages to the desktop via an electronic button known as a **hyperlink**. Publication of fiction in this form is still certainly not widespread, but it is growing. In the next section, I will look at hypertext fiction and consider, in particular, how the dynamics of reading are altered in a hypertextual environment.

6.5 Hypertext fiction and new reading practices

Thus far, I have considered some aspects of the relationship between computer technology and English in the context of more conventional approaches to reading. I would now like to consider new practices in English applied to 'creative' texts. Here, I am going to focus on web-based writing such as the hypertext novel, the collaborative story and multimedia art forms.

The central feature of web-based writing is the inclusion of hypertext, the electronic links which, when activated, bring another associated portion of the text immediately into view. These links have the potential to create new opportunities for artistic expression and new contexts for the language of computer-based literary texts. According to George Landow, they do this primarily by altering the relationships between the reader and the author, and the reader and the text (Landow, 1997). For example, the reader must choose which way to go at every page, and for this reason is sometimes thought of as having more control over the production of the text than a conventional reader. This notion of 'choosing' a path raises the foremost issue in hypertext-based literature (the term I use hereafter is 'hyperfiction'), which is that of **linearity**. Traditionally, the print-based novel is presented in an order that is meant to be read linearly, that is, page by page from front to back (experimental and avant-garde writing notwithstanding). This does not mean, of course, that events in the story are related only chronologically. What it does mean, however, is that a tacit understanding exists between the author and reader that the narrative will be read in one order. Various plot effects, such as suspense and resolution, for example, rely on this understanding. Theories of literature, unsurprisingly, generally make an assumption that this is the case.

Hyperfiction, in contrast, is said to be non-linear. Non-linearity in this context means that there are multiple possible pathways through the work, pathways defined by the author but navigated variously by different readers. This situation may make hypertext fiction presented on a computer more interesting – if more challenging – from a reader's perspective. Readers have to 'work' at the text, making choices at every turn, in a process that can be both exhilarating and exhausting.

In producing different sequences of pages in the work, the hyperfiction author is creating a situation in which new contexts are constantly being generated through the activity of reading. A page of the story that appears at the beginning of the narrative for one reader may appear at the end for another, sandwiched between two entirely different pages.

You may think that the order in which events are read in a work like this makes little difference to meaning, as readers can reconstruct a chronological pattern of events from the fragments. This may be true of shorter, simpler texts of only a few dozen pages – although even very short pieces of text can take on very different meanings through some simple reordering (see the box below). It would be almost impossible to reconstruct in any chronological way a much longer text with many more links between the pages.

The influence of ordering of propositions on reader interpretation

A   Tracey got into her car

B   Tracey had to stop to ask directions

C   Tracey was running very late

Reading these statements in the order given could be interpreted as 'Tracey was running late *because* she had to stop to ask directions'.

However if we look more closely, we can see that reading in the orders presented below have two different implications:

1   ABC suggests that Tracey was not late when she got into her car but became late because she had to stop to ask directions.

2   ACB, BCA, BAC, CBA and CAB all suggest that Tracey was already late when she got into her car.

You may not agree with these interpretations, but they show the extent of the reader's involvement in the logical linking of these statements.

There are, of course, other issues arising out of hypertext use. In my own research, I found that five readers reading for half an hour shared only two pages of a 932-page hypertext fiction (Gardner, 2003). Furthermore, in a subsequent interview, one reader described how most of his reading was spent in looking for the 'edges' of the text, rather than engaging with the content of the story. Hypertext works are highly variable in their construction, and it is therefore difficult to generalise across all of them. Yet it can be said that most, if not all, consist of a finite number of pages that can be conceptualised as a pattern of boxes connected with lines. This kind of representation clearly displays the properties of boundaries. Yet there are no obvious edges to the hypertext work in the sense of tangible boundaries common to physical artefacts such as the end of a page in a book. An edge in an online hypertext environment might be a page with no forward links, and to arrive at such a page might give the illusion that some kind of boundary had been reached.

ACTIVITY 6.6

Allow about
10 minutes

Have a look at Figure 6.4 which is the opening page of the Web-based hyperfiction novel, Mark Amerika's *Grammatron 1.0*. This is an example of a digital multimedia art form. Compare the typographical and visual features of this page with a traditional print-based novel. What do you notice?

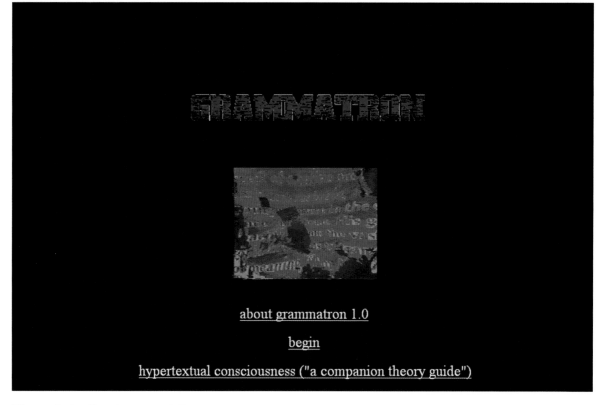

Figure 6.4   Opening page of *Grammatron*

Comment

This text has become something of a landmark in the field of Web-based hyperfiction. The **node** shown here (pages are known as 'nodes' in hypertext topology) and the initial nodes of this hyperfiction novel are typical of early 1990s Web-based programming using HTML (hypertext mark-up language). Compared with the traditional print-based novel, the visual impact can potentially be heightened through the use of digital images, exploited here in the brightly coloured, almost garish text highly contrasted with a black background. The most significant difference, perhaps, is one that as a reader of a print-based text, you do not see – a moving image.

To demonstrate some of the processes involved, I am now going to describe my activity as a reader as I start to work my way through this text. After activating the links in the introductory pages I arrive at a page containing the notice 'you are about to enter GRAMMATRON, please wait while the machine reads you', and eventually arrive at 'Abe Golam' (Figure 6.5).

Figure 6.5 Abe Golam

I am now faced with a choice; I can decide on a course of action, such as a quest to discover the identity of Abe Golam, or I can choose a path at random.

I want to know more about Abe Golam, as I am at the start of the 'story', and feel that characters are important. I therefore choose the last link, feeling that the highlighted name will reveal something about the character. The ensuing screen, 'coping' (Figure 6.6), doesn't seem to help much and doesn't appear at all related to my chosen keyword at the start of my quest.

Going back to the original page, I choose instead the link 'Grammatron' and am presented with 'Grammatron' (Figure 6.7).

Now I get some useful information: Abe Golam and Grammatron appear to be one and the same.

I pick up on the link 'Golam' which, as it is a nominal form, suggests a description or definition of a character, rather than an event. Instead, I arrive at 'mike' (Figure 6.8), which says very little, in fact, about the character of Golam.

Figure 6.6   Coping

I am going to stop here, as I think that you can see by now that reading of this kind presents certain challenges. The reader needs to think about what to read at every page, and the author can either conform to, or subvert, expectations generated by the link words. Links therefore add an extra dimension to the experience of reading.

We should be aware by now that an important aspect of hypertext linking, from the reader's perspective, at least, is the relationship the author establishes between the verbal elements of the link and the semantic content of the linked item. There have consequently been numerous methods proposed to analyse and categorise such relationships, and to suggest frameworks for describing the nature of hypertext in general (Bernstein, 1998; Pajares Tosca, 2000). Yet Bernstein concedes that 'Hypertext structure does not reside exclusively in the topology of links nor in the language of individual nodes' (Bernstein, 1998, p. 21); rather, it is a combination of these two aspects which creates what he calls 'patterns' in the text. One example of such a pattern is

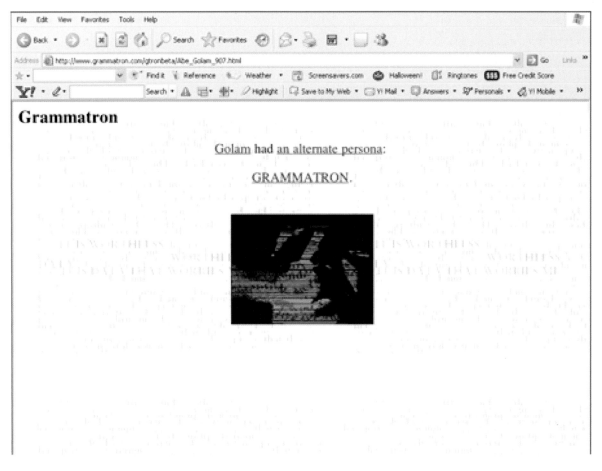

Figure 6.7 Grammatron

the 'cycle', whereby a reader returns to a previously visited path and may then be sent along a different path the second time round. What Bernstein has to say about the 'tangle', however, illuminates my experience of reading Grammatron:

> The **Tangle** confronts the reader with a variety of links without providing sufficient clues to guide the reader's choice. Tangles can be used purely for their value as intellectual amusement, but also appear in more serious roles. In particular, tangles can help intentionally disorient readers in order to make them more receptive to a new argument or an unexpected conclusion.
>
> (Bernstein, 1998, p. 24).

Bernstein is emphasising that understanding what goes on in hypertext is a complex affair, the meaning of which is simply irreducible to either the structure or the language of the page.

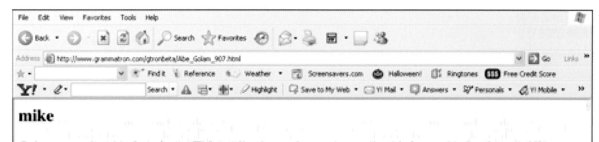

Figure 6.8   Mike

6.6 Chatbots and artificial English language generators

I now examine the language of chatterbots, or chatbots. A **chatbot**, as the name implies, is a machine (**bot**) that can be engaged in an online, real-time conversation. Consider how you would feel having had a conversation with someone, only to discover afterwards that your interlocutor had actually been a machine? I guess that you might feel a little disconcerted, or you might feel thrilled. The point is that you would be likely to have some emotional reaction. In my view, it is really a question of when, not if, machines will take over the functions of 'intelligent' conversation, particularly related to the mundane interactions of everyday life, checking your bank balance, ordering your shopping, and so on. Would such language be distinctive, count as English language communication, and how might we decide?

ACTIVITY 6.7

Allow about
20 minutes

To help us decide whether the exchanges with chatbots are distinctive, we can look at AI (artificial intelligence) sites on the Web which, while offering commercial services, are also available to anyone who is interested in conversing with a chatbot. Examples A and B below are transcripts of a conversation between human and AI interlocutors ('user' and 'George'). Read the examples, making a note of significant features of the conversation, and where things go wrong.

Example A

USER   **Would you prefer a nice system defrag or a long bath with scented candles?**

GEORGE   That depends on what you expect me to do with him/her.

USER   **Who?**

GEORGE   The guy with the iffy red shirt and blue balloon.

USER   **Forget about him – just answer the question.**

GEORGE   You never asked a question. I asked you a question.

USER   ***sigh*.**

GEORGE   That's why I would like to get to know you better.

USER   **If there were two people fighting over a baby, and you couldn't tell who the baby belonged to – how would you end the fight?**

GEORGE   I feel like we are replaying a past conversation. Who's running the loop, you or me?

USER   **Why do you avoid moral dilemmas?**

GEORGE   Because they are really silly.

USER   **Is it because you are not programmed to deal with them?**

GEORGE   Why are you questioning my reality? Is it because you're insecure about your *own* reality?

USER   **Well, I could ask you the very same question ...**

GEORGE   Just answer it.

USER   **I believe it is the human condition to be insecure about our own reality.**

...

Example B

GEORGE	I can be serious if I want to.
USER	**Ok then, let's discuss politics.**
GEORGE	Shure, let us discuss politics.
USER	**How do you feel about president bush?**
GEORGE	Just OK.
USER	**Would you prefer it if you were president?**
GEORGE	Yes.
USER	**What would you change?**
GEORGE	I would change your background colour.
USER	**What are you talking about?**
GEORGE	I'm talking about purpose, or lack of it.
USER	**You think that changing my background colour would give me purpose?**
GEORGE	Yes, it says you are. Right up there at the top of this page.
USER	**If your programmer had taken the care to make that sentence appear in the correct context, it really would have made me question my humanity.**
GEORGE	That's stupid.
USER	**Yes, he/she probably is.**
GEORGE	There you go again.
USER	**I'm not going anywhere. Except to work, in 5 minutes.**
GEORGE	Of course you're not engaged to me.
USER	**No, of course not. That would be ludicrous.**

(Jabberwacky, 2006)

Comment

You may have thought that Example A represented a more realistic conversation between human interlocutors than Example B. Both are clearly recognisable as conversations, as they exhibit turn-taking, and fairly relevant responses on the part of George in each of the adjacency pairs. For example, in transcript A, user asks *Why do you avoid moral dilemmas?* and George replies *Because they are really silly.* However, in transcript B, something clearly has broken down in the exchange, starting with George's reference to background colour. The following adjacency pair makes perfect sense:

USER   What are you talking about?

GEORGE   I'm talking about purpose, or lack of it.

After this, however, the conversation snowballs into seemingly unrelated responses on the part of George:

USER   You think that changing my background colour would give me purpose?

GEORGE   Yes, it says you are. Right up there at the top of this page.

The computer's program or instruction set responds in particular ways to certain word patterns, working on the basis of rules. But through **heuristic programming**, a procedure whereby an artificial intelligence program alters its own instructions on the basis of information given by the user, rather than by a programmer, the computer can generate sophisticated interactions more closely aligned to human intuitions about language.

The example of the Jabberwacky AI as given above is primarily interesting for its novelty and entertainment value. On the one hand, we can view artificial English language as merely playful, or instructive, and ensure for example, that corpora purporting to reflect English usage should exclude such data. On the other hand, the conversations are not randomly generated, since they are devised by a human to interact according to a set of rules devised by a speaker of the language. As such, the output is rather an extension of the intelligence of the designer. In the case of many learning chatbots, the language will be a reflection of human agents. In that sense, the conversation is actually like human interaction in English, though postponed in time and altered in sequence.

6.7 Conclusion

English seems to be holding on to the title of the most prevalent language on the internet. However, given the present trend it will soon be overtaken by Chinese. There are also strong indications of increased multilingualism, as more people access the Web, using a great variety of languages – often in addition to English. The extent to which this increased multilingualism can be viewed as *imposed*, or as reflecting the interests of speakers in a wide range of linguistic and cultural contexts, is a point for debate. What seems clear is that English *alongside* the use of other languages is a growing phenomenon.

The internet is also a place where new practices are evolving. Digitisation is potentially increasing access to texts – and therefore knowledge – which were previously available to only a few. In addition, electronic forms of writing have the potential to transform the reading experience, altering the dynamic of reader and text. This is primarily related to the way in which information can be stored and linked, in a non-linear way using hypertext. The non-linearity of hypertext, including hyperfiction may be a device for fostering reader interaction, though it also has implications for the way that texts can be shared among readers.

Artificial intelligence may help us to view English in a different light, as the outcomes of online interaction show distinctive features are discernible in the computer's responses. What is not certain is how much of this kind of language can be acknowledged as English.

New media technology has therefore created novel situations in which language can be explored and expressed. There are no easy answers to the question of how technology is influencing English, only the evidence that computer technology is indeed shaping English and practices involving the use of English, such as changing relations around the production of, and engagement with, a wide range of texts.

READING A: Language choice on a Swiss mailing list

Mercedes Durham
(Mercedes Durham is a Research Associate and Sessional Lecturer in the Department of Language and Linguistic Science at the University of York.)

Source: Durham, M. (2003) 'Language choice on a Swiss mailing list', *Journal of Computer-Mediated Communication*, vol. 9, no. 1, http://jcmc.indiana.edu/vol9/issue1/durham.htm1 (Accessed 31 January 2006).

Introduction

The Language Situation in Switzerland

Switzerland has four national languages: German, French, Italian and Romansh, three of which are considered official languages (all but Romansh) and which are used in the government and for federal administration. ...

Until recently, the school system required that students' first foreign language be another Swiss national language, so that German speakers studied French, French speakers German, and Italian speakers studied either French or German. In the past few years, however, English has become more important as a second language. A few years ago, the schools of the canton of Zurich ... decided to make English the first foreign language taught in the classrooms, a situation which received extensive press coverage in the Swiss media. The fact is that a large number of Swiss speakers do not feel at ease speaking in the other national languages and are more comfortable using English.

...

English Use in Switzerland

Despite (or perhaps due to) the fact that there are a number of languages spoken in Switzerland, English has gradually gained ground as a lingua franca. This change is relatively new: 'Before World War II the presence of English could be felt only where the citizens of the Anglo-American countries – then above all Britain – came into contact with Swiss citizens' (Dürmüller, 2002, p. 115). If English was used by Swiss nationals, it was only to communicate with English speakers and never with other Swiss people. ...

In addition to its importance as a lingua franca, the presence of English can also be felt in advertising (Cheshire & Moser, 1994) and to a certain extent on the Internet, in that many Swiss Web sites provide pages in English, as well as in French, German and Italian. ...

Project on Pan Swiss English

The study presented here is part of a larger research project that aims to discover whether a focused form of English may be under construction in Switzerland. ... Focussing is a process through which a language form acquires a series of set norms through intensive contact (LePage & Tabouret-Keller, 1985). The concept is primarily used when dealing with the formation of pidgins and creoles: languages which are born through the contact of speakers of two or more languages using a language that is no one's native tongue. A pidgin is considered to be a language with no native speakers, and a creole is a pidgin which has acquired native speakers (Todd, 1991). The case for focussing in Switzerland is based primarily on the fact that if English is indeed used as a lingua franca, it is being used by native speakers of a range of languages (French, German and Italian). The fact that the three groups are using a language which is not native to any of them may mean that some of the forms they use may be influenced by another language they speak, and thus may differ from native-speaker English.

...

IFMSA-Switzerland

The Association

The Association which is the basis for the analysis of language choice on mailing lists in Switzerland is the International Federation of Medical Students' Associations – Switzerland (hereafter IFMSA-CH). This association consists of a group of students who are studying at the various medical schools in Switzerland (Lausanne, Geneva, Berne, Zurich and Basel ...).

The Mailing List

In May 1999, IFMSA-CH began using a Yahoo mailing list to ensure that all interested members receive information as quickly as possible, and to avoid having to send messages individually. ...

On the mailing list, members sent messages from their own account to the mailing list address, which were then forwarded to all other registered members. ...

Data and Methods

E-mail Collection

The total number of messages collected for this study is 996. ... For purposes of simplicity and ease of reference, e-mails were sorted according to the calendar year in which they were written – 1999, 2000, 2001 or 2002 – and then numbered one by one, with the numbers starting over each year. ...

An advantage in looking at a student association is that the students are unlikely to choose English over their native languages because of a desire to market their company or their products outside the country, as is likely the case for some of the Swiss companies that have decided to use English as their main language because of the global importance of English. The students' use of English is presumably purely determined by the fact that it is the most accessible language for all (Crystal, 1998). It is also the case that English is the language of medical science around the world.

The value of studying e-mails in relation to language choice is two-fold. First of all, messages can be counted to determine which language is used most often, and which ones might have been used at the start, but then fell into disuse. Second, quite often members talk about language use on the mailing list, or their language use allows us to infer the reasons for specific uses; this provides metalinguistic commentary on their language choices. These two aspects also determine the structure of this paper: The quantitative results for the use of different languages over time are presented first, followed by discussion of individual e-mails that provide insights into the shift towards English.

E-mail Classification

In order to calculate the percentages of the use of English versus other languages, the e-mails were divided into four categories: messages in English, messages in French, messages in German, and a category of miscellaneous messages. ...

Some messages cannot readily be classified as in a single language, in that they start off in French or German and then switch to English or vice versa. To ensure that messages containing code-switching (Poplack, 1980) were not following different patterns over time from the bulk of the e-mails, they were considered separately. All messages were sorted into one of three groups: monolingual messages; mixed-dominant messages, where most of the message was in one language with a sentence or two in another language; and mixed-balanced messages, e-mails in which two (or more) languages were roughly equally represented.

Results

Monolingual versus Mixed-language Messages

Table 1 provides a general introduction to the data, and examines the overall frequency of these three types of messages. We can see that in the corpus as a whole, messages containing more than one language are quite rare – only 3.5%; nearly all are monolingual, perhaps a surprising result in a multilingual country. This low percentage of mixed-language messages changed only slightly over the four calendar years studied, reaching its peak in 2002 (5%). In the data as a whole, messages in which one language is dominant are slightly more common than those in which the two are balanced, but the incidence of both categories together is extremely low. At the same time, it is worthwhile to examine mixed-language messages more closely, to see what we can learn about the emerging status of English.

Table 1 Distribution of monolingual versus mixed-language messages over time

Type of message	1999	2000	2001	2002	Total
Monolingual messages	97.0%	97.0%	97.0%	95.0%	96.5%
Mixed-balanced messages	–	1.0	0.3	3.0	1.1
Mixed-dominant messages	3.0	2.0	2.7	2.0	2.4
Total	100.0 (64)	100.0 (235)	100.0 (332)	100.0 (251)	100.0 (882)

'Balanced' versus Mixed-dominant Messages

A closer analysis of the two mixed types is shown in Tables 2 and 3. Messages classified as 'translation' in the tables are those in which the additional language(s) did not provide any new information but rather, merely translated the accompanying text. 'Person specific' messages are those in which the change from one language to another appeared to be motivated by a reference to a specific person. 'Other' messages are those for which it was not possible to determine the cause of the code switch.

Table 2 Distribution of 'balanced' bilingual or multilingual messages by languages

'Balanced' messages	French/ German	English/ French/ German	German/ English	English/ French/ German/ Italian	Total
Translation	4	1	0	0	5
Person specific	0	0	1	0	1
Other	1	1	0	2	4
Total	5	2	1	2	10

Table 3 Distribution of messages in two or more languages by dominant language

Dominant language	German + French	German + English	French + English	English + French	English + German	English + Italian	English + French + German	Total
Person specific	0	0	0	4	3	2	0	9
Other	3	2	2	4	0	0	0	12
Total	3	2	2	8	3	2	1	21

Table 2 shows that there were only ten mixed-balanced messages, of which five merely presented the same content translated into one or more languages. ...

Mixed-dominant messages (Tables 1 and 3) are also very infrequent in the data (N=21). The code switch in many of these messages appears to have been motivated by an intention to address single comments to specific people, as illustrated in the following English-dominant message which contains one sentence of French.

> *Dear IMFSA-CH Family, the week-end meeting is approaching, here is the list of people who will hopefully come! (I haven't heard anything from IFMSA-Lausanne, ... 'g' and 'q', on veut voir les photos de Malte* ☺
> *The meeting place: Hôpital des CAdolles, Neuchâtel, it is a hospital on the hills of Neuchâtel, with magnificent view on the lake* ☺ *... [01/082/b; translation of French part of the message: 'we want to see the pictures from Malta.' 'g' and 'q' are French-speaking members.]*

Although these messages are different from monolingual ones, the overall trend is the same: English is the language chosen most often. Of the five [person specific and other] balanced messages in Table 2 (N=5), four include English. The case of the dominant language messages (Table 3) is even clearer; out of 21 messages, 18 include some English and 14 have English as the primary language. (The only exception to this generalisation is in the case of balanced messages, where French/German mixing is most common; however, these are primarily translations rather than code switching.)

Because of these similarities with monolingual messages, mixed messages were later coded for the main language used in each (even in mixed-balanced messages, one language was generally used slightly more), and included in the analysis of the spread of English on the mailing list presented below [Figure 1].

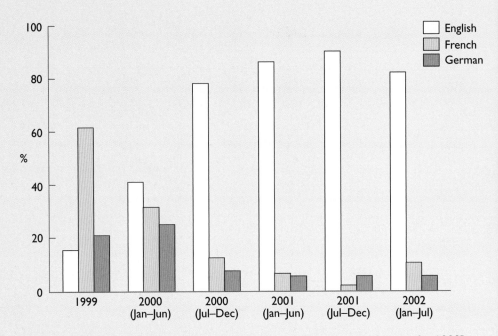

Figure 1 Spread of English over time: E-mails by six-month period [except for 1999]

Data presented thus far show conclusively that English has superceded the other languages as the main language of e-mail communication for this association. Over a period of about three years, English went from being used a little over 10% of the time to over 80% of the time, with the average percentage in English for the entire period 75%. ...

The change in percentages from the beginning of 2000 to the second part of the year is especially dramatic: English changed from being the main language used to virtually the only language used. ...

The tide may be turning slightly for English now. That is to say, the other two languages are used more often in 2002 than in 2000–2001. This may be due to the fact that Swiss students have accepted that English can be understood by a wider audience, but nevertheless wish to use their own languages occasionally, as attested by a member who makes a point of using both French and German over English. ...

There appear to be two reasons for the use of English even when answering an e-mail in French or German. The first is that often, although the message is directed mainly to one person, it may be useful to all members of the association and should therefore be in a language all can understand. The second reason has to do with the importance of English: These e-mails are in many ways an ideal place for the students to practice their English language skills; moreover, as mentioned previously, general assemblies of the world-wide association are conducted in English, and any communication with members from other countries at these meetings is likely to be in English. ...

Discussion

Causes of Change

What are the reasons for the shift on the mailing list towards greater use of English over time? One possible explanation is that there was a dominant or core group of e-mailers who led the shift through their linguistic choices. ... Italian speakers contributed the largest number of messages (N=411), and ... were most likely to write their messages in English. ...

Yet English is used by all of the linguistic groups, not just by the Italians. It may be the case that writing in a foreign language is advantageous in that it forces writers to use simpler language than they normally would (if only because they lack the knowledge to make use of more complicated forms), resulting in a variety of language that is easier to understand. ...

The general feeling in Switzerland about the position of English vis-à-vis the Swiss national languages must have played a part in the language choice as well. ...

English is also the language of the medical sciences world-wide: Many of the important journals and textbooks are written in English, and even within Switzerland many medical research groups use English. ...

While all of the above reasons may have played some part in the language selection on the mailing list, the reasons the members themselves give as to why they chose to use English suggest that in many ways the choice ultimately has more to do with language comprehension and the lingua franca function of English in Switzerland.

Language Comprehension

Evidence for the importance of English is found not only in the numbers of e-mails written in English, but also in what is said in those e-mails, and how this influences language choice. The e-mails themselves provide a plausible explanation at the very point when English begins to be used more frequently than the other available languages. As mentioned before, one of the activities of IFMSA members is to attend the General Assemblies that take place twice a year. Only eight or nine members from each country are allowed to participate, and it is important for these members to be selected early in order to book flights and make suitable arrangements. Generally, an attempt is made to send one representative from each Swiss university. In 2000, at a point when the members needed to decide who was going to the GA and the president was away in New York and could not give much advice, a misunderstanding occurred because some members had already registered, but found they might have to give up their place so that someone from a university with no representative could attend. The president sent the following e-mail [translated here from the French]:

> ... The deadline was the first of December ... so I don't know what you want to do ... Basically, if Basel has already transferred the money we have nine people rather than eight, but if it isn't the case we lose our extra place ... So if we have eight places, I think that either 'h' or 'X' and either 'u' or 'e' can't come ... and that Lausanne should come, but I'll let you decide ... Sorry but for the moment I'm in New York so can't help you much ...

E-mails went back and forth among members in French and German in an effort to sort out who was in fact registered, and who should give up his or her place. Finally, a member from the university in question wrote: 'It's about time that things get clear in this meeting story,' and went on to summarize the events as he saw them, in English. The next few e-mails on this subject were in French and German. ... After this episode, the member who had started using English continued to use it for most of his e-mails, and many of the others who had previously only used English occasionally started using it more often as well. ...

In this message the member admonished the others, saying,

> please, next time you send a message to IFMSA Switzerland you have to write it in english, or to send it both in french and german. This thing is even more important when you're sending an official invitation for a national meeting like this one. I think you'll understand why. ...

Given that the message sender was one of the very frequent e-mailers, and consistently followed the practice he advocated, it undoubtedly influenced others. ...

Pan Swiss English?

In the e-mails analyzed in this study, the main concern of the students is to get their point across, not to write perfect English. There is a communicative urgency, rather than a desire to create flawless sentences, and members are quite willing to admit that sometimes their English is imperfect. When they do not know the exact word in English, they will often replace it with the corresponding one from their own language. Idiomatic forms are translated literally, sometimes accompanied by the phrase, 'as we say in French/German.' ...

The English used by the IFMSA-CH members might be said, in some ways, to be its own variety, a type of 'swissicized' or Pan Swiss English. What are the characteristics of this variety of English? From e-mails and other sources it has been possible to develop a list of features which are common to most of the writers examined in this study, and which are present in at least two of the three language groups. Although the study of these features is still in the incipient stages, a number of features appear to support the hypothesis that the English of the mailing list is relatively homogenous. The use of *informations* or *infos* in place of *information* or *info* (roughly 42% of occurrences in the e-mails) is present in the three linguistic groups looked at. This is partly because in French, German and Italian information is a count noun [has a plural as well as a singular form]. Another feature being investigated is the over-use of the infinitive in places where a native speaker of English would use an -ing form (i.e. 'if you want to stop to smoke,' in cases where 'if you want to stop smoking' is intended). ...

Conclusion

While results from a single mailing list cannot be generalized to the linguistic situation in all of Switzerland, they provide suggestive clues as to why English has gained in importance as a lingua franca in Switzerland over the past few years. English appears to be the most readily understood and accepted language in mixed language groups, the main reason for this being that it is a non-native language for all. The Italian speakers on the mailing list were at the forefront of this change, since as nobody else spoke their native language, they experienced first hand the need to ensure that people be able to understand one another.

It seems likely that the mode of communication, the mailing list, also influenced the choice of language used. As long as messages (face-to-face or otherwise) are mainly directed to specific people, there is no need to worry about whether an entire group understands. However, when the aim is to communicate to a broader, multilingual audience, as the Internet makes it easy to do, neither French nor German is able to serve as the main language in the Swiss context, and it becomes necessary to use English. Although it may be possible to use two or more languages for face-to-face interaction, ... it seems that in the case of e-mail, the use of more than one language was impractical and confusing, and precipitated the eventual choice of a single language, namely English.

Undoubtedly, other groups in Switzerland have faced and will continue to face similar problems, as will multilingual groups collaborating online in other cultural contexts. They, too, may choose English as their lingua franca, facilitating cross-language communication and contributing to the increased use of English on a global scale.

References for this reading

Cheshire, J., & Moser, L. M. (1994). English and symbolic meaning: The case of advertisements in French-speaking Switzerland. *Journal of Multilingual and Multicultural Development*, 17, pp. 451–469.

Crystal, D. (1998). *English as a global language*. Cambridge: Cambridge University Press.

Dürmüller, U. (2002). English in Switzerland: From foreign language to lingua franca. In D. Allerton, P. Skandera, & C. Tschichold (Eds) *Perspectives on English as a world language* (pp. 114–123). Basel: Schwabe.

Le Page, R. B., & Tabouret-Keller, A. (1985). *Acts of identity*. Cambridge: Cambridge University Press.

Poplack, S. (1980). Sometimes I'll start a sentence in Spanish y termino en español: Toward a typology of code-switching. *Linguistics*, 18, pp. 581–618.

Todd, L. (1991). *Pidgins and creoles*. London: Routledge and Kegan Paul.

READING B: L33t-sp34k

Erin McKean
(Erin McKean is a member of the American Dialect Society, the American Names Society and Euralex and is a member of the board of the Dictionary Society of North America.)

Source: Lederer, R. (2002) 'Stamp out fadspeak', *Verbatim*, vol. XXVII, no. 3, pp. 13–14.

If you are older than fifteen and only use your computer for e-mail and balancing your checkbook, or – *quel horreur*, have no computer at all, then you probably aren't familiar with the preferred online communication style of online gaming geeks, hacker wannabees, and adolescent chat-room denizens: l33t, pronounced 'leet'.

Supposedly, l33t (also written l337 and l33+) arose as a way to beat automatic government surveillance programs (especially the fabled Echelon program) that looked for keywords in online postings. As with most language origin stories, this should be taken with a grain of salt, but it is commonly accepted among l33t users.

L33t, like other in-group languages, is deliberately complicated to keep the congnoscenti in and everyone else out. However, it has to be (more or less) intelligible in order to be propagated. And being the province of the compufolk, it has fairly regular rules, so that translator programs can be written to convert plain old boring (semi-) standard English in and out of it.

You may have already realized that in l33t, the numeral 3 makes a handy substitute for the letter *E*. A quick glance across the number pad may show you that it's not inconceivable that 4 could substitute for *A*, 1 for *I*, 0 for *O*, 7 for *T* and 5 for *S*. These are the basic substitutions, but there are many others. For example,

> 1 is often used for *L* as well as *I*;
>
> 6 and 9 are occasionally used for *G*,
>
> 8 can fill in for *B*,
>
> + for *T*, and
>
> $ for *S*.

The more ambitious, obnoxious, and nimble of finger use |-| for *H*, |3 for *B*, (for *C*, |) for *D*, |[for *F*, | for *I*, |< for *K*, _| for *J*, |_ for *L*, |\/| or ^^ for *M*, |\| for *N*, |o for *P*, 0, for *Q* (that's 0 plus comma), |2 or the truly opaque |)\ for *R*, \/ for *V*, |/\| for *W*, ⅋ for *Y* and -_ for *Z*.

In addition, one can use 8 for the 'ayt' sound (e.g., *l8* or *L8* for 'late'); @ for the 'at' sound (as well as for the letter *A*), 0r for -er endings, # for the 'ash' sound (e.g. *c#* or *k#* for 'cash'), K for hard c spelled c (e.g. *k@* or *k@+* for 'cat'), q for *ck* (*fuq*), j for y (mostly in *j00*, 'you'), *x* for the sound spelled ck (e.g. *h4x0r* for 'hacker'), eh for word-final y (e.g. *happeh* for 'happy'), *z* for voiced s, 00 for long U, and PH for the 'f' sound, as in phear or more l33t-ly, *phj34r*.

Random capitalization is also encouraged. The use of *teh* as a deliberate misspelling of 'the' is the norm. Verb tenses are optional, with the present tense sufficing for all uses. Objective pronouns are used for subjective pronouns. Occasionally, the \ (or sometimes :::: or ° °) is used to highlight an action, usually a real-world action: '\Me g0 gr4b s0Me k0ph33.' ('I'm going out for some coffee.')

Some users differentiate between 'light' (or 'llama') and 'heavy' (or 'hardcore' or 'advanced forum') dialects of l33t, depending on how far from standard English it diverges. Some users even recommend that you use light with friends and heavy with superiors (e.g., people who are better gamers than you are).

To be truly l33t, not only your spelling but your rhetoric must change. Instead of 'I don't agree' you might say 'F00l! B0W T0 M3!' If you agree, you may say 'U R0XX0r!' Since much of l33t-sp33k takes place in gaming contexts, there's a rich array of gaming jargon. If your idea of a fun Saturday afternoon (or more likely, a fun Tuesday 3 a.m.) is pretending to be a hyper-warrior and killing everything in sight, you're probably familiar with these terms already. That killing, by the way, is usually called *fragging*; but can also be *dropping*, *capping*, *icing*, or *wasting*. To *gib* is to kill something and have the corpse explode. If you gib someone, that means they probably *suxor* 'suck' or are a *t00l* 'tool'. They may also be a *n00b* (for 'newbie') a *llama* or a *lamer* (a poor or inexperienced player or all-around wimp). In any case, you can exclaim *0wn!* Or *0wn3d!* because you beat them. Then you will have *0wn4ge*. You might also want to say 'ph33r my l33t 5kill5' (fear my elite skills!).

If others agree with you, they will chime in with *k3wl!* (cool) or *d00d!* (dude). If they are really impressed, they may add *w00t!* or *h00mba!* ('cool'). If someone beats you – by cheating or their astounding good luck or your own ill-luck, not through any lack of skill on your part, of course – you might want to call them a *cunt0r* or a *fux0r*. If the victorious player is female, you can feel free to call her a *skrut* or a *skrutwh0re*. If your teammembers let you down, you can say 'gg backup' meaning 'way to go backup,' with implied heavy sarcasm. If you were beaten because your connection is slow, you might be called a *HPB*, or 'High Ping Bastard.' (The ping number is an indicator of the speed of your connection. Lower is better, as in golf). If your ping is erratic, your player might have *warph4x*, causing it to jump around in the playing space and be difficult to hit. Or, if your game freezes for a couple of seconds, putting you in some random area of the playing space, you would call that *warpz0r* or *lagspike*. If you are a player with serious *own4ge*, combined with a mocking manner (you might type *h4wh4w* 'haw haw haw' quite a bit), you are a *pir8* 'pirate'.

If you hang around a particular area in the game to kill something or grab a treasure as it appears, you're *camping*, which is highly frowned upon. (Refusing to work towards common objectives in team games is also called *camping*.) Someone too concerned about their standing in the game (so much so that it gets in the way of normal play) is a *rank h00r* or a *stat h00r*. A player who hasn't got enough weapons and starts playing with just a small gun and no armor is a *c0ncH*.

You might not have even paid for the game software you're using; if you downloaded it from the 'net you would call it (and other illegally-obtained software) *warez*. If you attempt to enter systems or create viruses using programs that others have written (and that you patently don't understand), you're a *script kiddie*. Online pornography is always called *pr0n*. Microsoft is nearly always referred to as *Micro$hlt*, *Microscoff*, *Microshaft*, etc ... The word *l33t* itself also means 'cool', as does *ph@* or *ph4t* 'phat'.

L33t is a very flexible mode of communication (except of course that it only exists for the most part in electronic messages). It reflects its world limpidly. Like most languages of youthful display, l33t combines a casual obscenity with a touching sincerity of expression. *L33t r0x0rs!*

Global English, global culture?

David Graddol

7.1 Introduction

The development of English as a global language is one of the most remarkable phenomena of the late twentieth and early twenty-first centuries. For the first time in the history of human society, a single language has become so sufficiently universal that it can be used as a global lingua franca for communication among speakers of many languages.

Many people who do not speak English as a first language see English as a language of economic opportunity, one that will help improve both their individual position and, because of the importance of English in international trade and technological research, their countries' economies. Others view what seems to be the inexorable spread of a single language across the globe in less positive ways. Some people say it is implicated in a major human disaster, involving the destruction of linguistic and cultural diversity on a scale far larger than the parallel ecological destruction of biodiversity. English is, according to such views, a language of economic opportunity only for a few: for the rest it creates a new, global mechanism for structuring inequality both between 'the West' and 'the rest' and within the populations of non-Western countries.

In this chapter I explore some of these ideas critically, and examine a variety of, at times, contradictory views and experiences of English as a global language. One of the main themes of the chapter is that the global spread of English has complex roots and is not a simple and unstoppable process that will lead ultimately to a single, homogeneous global culture. I draw attention, for example, to some of the ways in which the spread of English creates difference as well as similarity, fragmentation as well as uniformity.

This chapter argues that although colonisation was responsible for the first stages of the spread of English, and provided a basis for its further global development, in the late twentieth and twenty-first centuries new forces and processes have come into play. Technological developments, economic globalisation and improved communications have all played a role in the new global flows of English (a point already noted in Chapter 6). And with these new flows have emerged changing patterns of identities and social relations – both at the individual level and on a global scale.

7.2 The utopian dream and the global rise of English

The dream of a shared world language, which could act as a neutral vehicle of communication among peoples of different nationalities and interests, which could serve the purposes of diplomacy and commerce and provide a rational and logical vehicle for science, has been a Western dream since the European Renaissance. This was the period when the idea arose that territory should be divided into autonomous countries, each with a designated language which would be symbolic of a unified national identity.

These 'national' languages, which could serve as foci for national identity and provide the resources for the construction of national cultures and government, had to be created. What existed at that time was a diversity of spoken languages, none of which provided the necessary genres and discourses for government and administration, for literature or science. The English language was, during the sixteenth and seventeenth centuries, expanded and developed, raised from vernacular status to a vehicle for literature, science and government. During the eighteenth century (the period sometimes referred to as 'the Enlightenment') the English language received its major instruments of regulation and documentation, including Samuel Johnson's (1755) *Dictionary*.

The creation of national languages was a method of managing the linguistic diversity (particularly dialectal but in some cases also including distinct languages) which fitted the ideas of the times, through the creation of regulated and reasonably uniform, high-status language varieties which could be used as internal lingua francas within countries. It gave rise to a new problem, however, that of effective communication among the peoples in the new Europe.

At the beginning of the Renaissance, there existed two transnational (in so far as we can talk of transnationality at that time) lingua francas in Europe. The first was the Latin language, which – although spoken by no one as a first language – served as an effective lingua franca for elite groups. The second lingua franca was Sabir, a pidgin based on southern Romance languages, and used for trade among Europeans, Turks, Arabs, and others in the Levant. Sabir is the oldest documented pidgin based on European languages and emerged at the time of the crusades (between the eleventh and thirteenth centuries).

Largely as a consequence of national language development, knowledge and use of Latin declined. Latin thus acquired a dual function: it permitted communication among elite groups in different European countries, but it also increasingly served as a 'secret language', which created barriers of access to knowledge by the unlearned. Of all the professional groups in the seventeenth century, the medical profession was perhaps the most notorious for its deliberate refusal to conduct transactions in the national language in order to prevent knowledge falling into the hands of ordinary people. The role of Latin in permitting the creation of elite social groups who have access to privilege and power and who can communicate with each other over national borders provides an informative precedent. In the world today, the English language can be seen to serve a similar function.

The concept of a universal language

The European modernisers of the seventeenth century recognised a new need for an international language that could replace Latin. Not only was the use of Latin declining, it was also increasingly unsuitable for dealing with the new domains of knowledge and new forms of international transaction. A number of scholars proposed that an **artificial language** be created – one that was capable of representing the new ideas and concepts generated by scientific enquiry and that could be employed as a **universal language**. Britain was the main location for such work, partly – ironically – because it was thought that modern English would be a marginal European language of little use beyond the shores of Britain. The following titles of seventeenth-century British philosophical works demonstrate something of the idealism and aspirations of the age: Francis Lodwick's *The Groundwork or Foundation (or so Intended) for the Framing of a New Perfect Language and a Universal Common Writing*, 1652, and John Wilkins's *An Essay towards a Real Character, and a Philosophical Language*, 1668.

Interest in the idea of an international language slackened in the eighteenth century because French emerged as an international language that linked both scholars and diplomats. An eighteenth-century landowner in the south of England wrote to his son, 'A man who understands French may travel all the World over without hesitation of making himself understood, and may make himself perfectly agreeable to all Good Company, which is not the case of any other Language whatever' (quoted in Large, 1985, p. 44).

By the end of the eighteenth century, however, ideas were being put forward by French scholars for a simplified form of French which could be more easily learnt by speakers of other languages. Thus arose the idea that an international lingua franca did not have to be a completely new invention (such as John Wilkins's 'Real Character'), but could be created by simplifying and rationalising an existing language. A key example of such a language relating to English was C.K. Ogden's 'Basic English' which was developed in the late 1920s (see Ogden, 1932), and popularised in the 1930s and 1940s.

However, several hundred artificial languages were also devised in the period from 1850 to the Second World War, including some, such as Esperanto, whose supporters continue to speak the language today. Such artificial languages were often referred to as **auxiliary languages** in order to make it clear that they were not expected to replace any natural language or to become the property of any one nation. The reasons for this rapid growth in the auxiliary language movement are complex. In retrospect, we can see that this period represented an important shift in the relationships of nation states, which arose as a result of a combination of factors: increasing industrialisation and a consequent increase in international trade; the development of communications technology (such as the telegraph, first patented in England in 1837); the expansion of European colonial territories (particularly in Asia and Africa); and increasing armed conflict (made more disastrous by improved technologies of war) among European nation states both within Europe and in colonial theatres of war. These developments gave rise to a natural anxiety about international stability at a time when industrialisation had created a necessity for international trade.

Some artificial languages

Volapuk (World Speak) (Schleyer), 1879

Esperanto (Zamenhof), 1887

Anglo-Franca (Hoinix, London), 1889

Tutonish or Anglo-German union tongue (Molee, Chicago), 1902

Ido (a revised Esperanto) (de Beaufort or Couturat), 1907

Novial (Jespersen), 1928

Interglossa (Hogben), 1943

ACTIVITY 7.1

Allow about
10 minutes

Take a few minutes to consider why so many artificial or auxiliary languages were devised in the nineteenth and early twentieth centuries. What do you think the appeal of such languages might be? What functions might they serve that an existing national language could not?

The international auxiliary language movement recognised a need for an international lingua franca that did not economically or culturally privilege one country. The language was to be a utilitarian, rational language, sufficient only for the communication of ideas. It was acknowledged that such languages, unlike national languages, were not a suitable medium for great works of literature, but that was to be regarded as one of their strengths: an auxiliary language should not be used as a vehicle for cultural values. It should never become threatening to any national language. The growing influence of English was thus a cause of concern for some. Particularly after the First World War it was thought to represent too much of a threat to other major European languages – not only French but also German – ever to become fully accepted. Rather than help prevent armed conflict through the spread of international cooperation and understanding, some considered that the growth of English might actually aggravate rivalries between European nations. In 1921, in the aftermath of the First World War, the British Association published a report on the question of an auxiliary language, intended as a contribution to a major debate on the problem by the League of Nations. The British Association concluded that 'The adoption of any modern national language would confer undue advantages and excite jealousy ... [t]herefore an invented language is best' (quoted in Jacob, 1947, p. 27).

However, the auxiliary language movement was largely abandoned because the English language became, de facto, the international lingua franca.

The emergence of English as an international language

The rise of English had been foreseen by many nineteenth-century commentators in America and Europe, with rather wild speculations circulating about the growth in the number of English speakers. Bailey (1992) reviews some of these accounts:

> The most extravagant projections were the most satisfying to the anglophone community and, therefore, the most popular. The Swiss botanist Alphonse de Candolle (1806–93) turned his attention to the question in the early 1870s ...
>
> > 'Now, judging by the increase that has taken place in the present century, we may estimate the probable growth of population as follows:
> >
> > In England it doubles in fifty years; therefore, in a century (in 1970) it will be 124,000,000. In the United States, in Canada, in Australia, it doubles in twenty-five; therefore it will be 736,000,000. Probable total of the English-speaking race in 1970, 860,000,000.'
>
> (Bailey, 1992, p. 111)

As one speculation became regarded as established fact, even larger figures began to circulate, until projections of English speakers for the year 2000 exceeded a billion. These were the expected figures for monolingual speakers – second language speakers were rarely mentioned or regarded as important.

From the late nineteenth century, those with experience of travel were beginning to appreciate that English was already a world language in the sense that many speakers of other languages spoke English as a second language. The following account, from before the First World War, illustrates something of its spread:

> It was only on reaching Italy that I began fully to realize the wonderful thing that, for nearly six weeks, on a German ship, in a journey of nearly 10,000 miles we had heard little of any language but English ... In Japan most of the tradespeople spoke English. At Shanghai, at Hong-Kong, at Singapore, at Penang, at Colombo, at Suez, at Port Said, all the way home, the language of the ship's traffic was English. The Chinese man-of-war's men who conveyed the Chinese prince on board at Shanghai received and exchanged

commands with our German sailors in English. The Chinese mandarins in their conversations with the ship's officers invariably spoke English. To talk to our Japanese passengers they had to speak English. That, it seems to me, is a bigger fact than the British Empire. If, as some aver, the greatest hindrances to peaceful international intercourse are the misunderstandings due to diversity of tongues, the wide prevalence of the English tongue must be the greatest unifying bond the world has ever known.

(A.M. Thompson, 1910, quoted in Jagger, 1940, pp. 128–9)

The British empire, however, remained a 'big fact'. By this time it was said to cover one-fifth of the land surface of the Earth, making English the official administrative language for one-third of the world's population. After the First World War, some members of the international auxiliary language movement began to argue that English had become, in fact, the 'world language' and that some modest spelling reform would be sufficient to equip it as an international auxiliary language. A Swedish scholar R.E. Zachrisson, for example, proposed that one such reformed English be called Anglic. In the 1930s he justified the adoption of English rather than Esperanto because:

> No language has a better claim than English, which is spoken by more than two hundred million people, and is the administrative language of five hundred millions, i.e. one third part of the world's population. It is already the chief language of the sea and commerce. It is taught in practically all the secondary schools in most civilized countries, and for this reason it is already the common property of the whole world.

(Zachrisson, 1970, p. 7)

In the UK the experience of the Second World War seemed to lead to a general change of mind about the future of English in the world. Its main European rivals (French and German) were now in no position to resist the rise of English. Most important of all, the USA had materialised as a world economic force and the process of war had introduced many parts of the world to US people, language and consumer goods. Soon much of the idealism that inspired the auxiliary language movement faltered. Recognising the need for the reconstruction of education within Europe after the war, the British Association now suggested 'the great political changes which have taken place ... point to the fact that any auxiliary means of communication will have to be closely related to the English language and to be such that the learning of it is a direct step towards learning English' (Jacob, 1947, p. 27).

The emergence of a hierarchy of languages

There are many ways of evaluating the world status of languages. I have already mentioned the position of French, but there are several other languages which could be considered as 'world languages'. In the course of establishing the international order after the First World War, six languages were given official status in the United Nations (UN): Arabic, Chinese, English, French, Russian and Spanish. In practice, English, French and (since 1948) Spanish are 'working languages', which means that verbal translations are made only into these three languages. Indeed, many international organisations have adopted a dual English/French policy. These include GATT (the General Agreement on Tariffs and Trade – the predecessor of the World Trade Organisation), OECD (Organisation for Economic Co-operation and Development), NATO (North Atlantic Treaty Organisation, for US/European defence cooperation, despite the fact that France has long not been a member) and the Council of Europe. The OAU (Organisation for African Unity) uses Arabic as well, while EFTA (European Free Trade Association) and ASEAN (the Association of South-East Asian Nations) use only English. The importance of French is often historical, though it serves the political purpose of avoiding obvious English hegemony in many international organisations. Non-governmental organisations tend to go for the pragmatic option of having one working language – English – because of the prohibitive costs of translation which the use of several working languages entails.

The status of English in Europe

Within Europe there are several countries besides Britain with colonial histories and aspirations to project their language, culture and economic activities worldwide – such countries include France, Spain and Germany. European history provides many cultural resources from which resistance to English, and English cultural products, can be built. Notably, German is the language of the most economically dominant country in Europe: the integration of West and East Germany in 1989 made German the language with the largest number of native speakers within the European Union – 24 pet cent of the EU population speak German as their 'mother tongue' (European Commission, 2006). Furthermore, as well as in Germany, German is an official language in Austria, Liechtenstein and Switzerland, and has official status in Belgium and Luxembourg.

The creation of the EU as a regional economic entity provided a bureaucratic and intergovernmental framework designed precisely to ensure that none of the main languages of Europe (specifically English, French and German) took undue precedence over others, and that minority languages (including the national languages of smaller nations, such as Danish, but also minority languages within national borders, such as Basque) are given a certain degree of institutional support.

The project of a 'single Europe' is to establish a large economic area which can, in the twenty-first century, compete with the other large trading areas in the world, such as Asia-Pacific and the Americas. This places English in an ambiguous position within the EU: it is the language of the UK, which is widely seen as facing two ways – towards Europe and towards the USA.

The increase in the number of countries in the EU from fifteen in 2001 to twenty-five in 2005 rendered the patterns of language use in the EU far more complex, with an increase in both the official national and official regional languages, not to mention minority languages within regions.

Although officially the twenty-one national languages of the twenty-five member states have equal status within EU institutions, in practice there appears to be a language hierarchy (see Figure 7.1). English, French and German are the working ('big' in Figure 7.1) languages. Then come the remaining national languages (Czech, Danish, Dutch, English, Estonian, Finnish, French, German, Greek, Hungarian, Irish, Italian, Latvian, Lithuanian, Maltese, Polish, Portuguese, Slovak, Slovene, Spanish, Swedish) somewhere in the centre, and below these, with varying degrees of recognition and support, over forty local language varieties (including, for example, Welsh, Basque and Catalan).

The big languages

English, French, German

The national languages

Czech, Danish, Dutch, English, Estonian, Finnish, French, German, Greek, Hungarian, Irish, Italian, Latvian, Lithuanian, Maltese, Polish, Portuguese, Slovak, Slovene, Spanish, Swedish

Officially recognised and supported languages

Alsation, Asturian, Basque, Catalan, Corsican, Frisian, Galician, Ladin, Luxembourgish, Mirandese, Occitan, Sardinian, Scots Gaelic, Welsh

Vernacular varieties of indigenous EU communities

Aragonese, Auvergnat, Breton, Calo, Cimbrian, Cornish, Dalecarlian, Faroese, Franco-Provencal, Friulian, Gascon, Chuvash, Jamtska, Jutish, Karaim, Karelian, Kashubian, Kolsch, Lallans, Langadocien, Ligurian, Lombard, Limburgisch, Liv, Livvi, Mocheno, Piemontese, Pontic, Romani, Rusyan, Samish, Scanian, Silesian, Tsakonian, Venetian, Walser, Yiddish

Figure 7.1 The EU language hierarchy

Until the early 1990s, French dominated daily business in the EU, particularly in written communication. However, by the turn of the twenty-first century, English had become the principal medium of written reports and communication (Truchot, 2003, p. 103). There is evidence that English is also the corporate language across different European regions. Thus, it is the main language of Siemens AG of Germany; the Dutch ABN AMRO Bank; the European Central Bank despite being located in Frankfurt; and drafts of new regulations are circulated in English even at the French ministry of finance. The idea that English should be used for communication in Europe is indicated by a finding in the Eurobarometer Report where 69 per cent of respondents agreed with the following statement: 'Everyone in the EU should be able to speak English' (Phillipson, 2003, p. 136). Surveys of languages being learnt in EU schools show English as the most widely studied foreign language at both secondary and primary school level (Witt, 2000; *The Economist*, 2004).

English, of course, exists at each level of the hierarchy: it is a local vernacular for some, a national language for Britain and the Irish Republic in standardised forms, and is used as a second language by many other European nationals. It is important to note that there are considerable difficulties surrounding the categorisation and labelling of languages (see discussions in Marti et al., 2005); I am using 'big' to signal historic and current status. Languages in the bottom layer enjoy least status and support. But as indicated by Figures 7.2 and 7.3 (overleaf), the situation is dynamic.

The world hierarchy of languages

The status of English in Europe shows how its relative position varies in different regions of the world (see Figure 7.2). Spanish is in the second rank in the European hierarchy but is more common than English as the medium of communication in Central and South America. French is used as a lingua franca by many African countries that were former colonies and in Indo-China (though the use of English seems to be increasing). Arabic is used widely in West Asia and North Africa. Russian is used as an international language in the Commonwealth of Independent States (CIS), which consists of eleven former Soviet Republics: Armenia, Azerbaijan, Belarus, Georgia, Kazakhstan, Kyrgyzstan, Moldova, Russia, Tajikistan, Ukraine. English is used as the lingua franca in most parts of South and East Asia.

The use of English is thus far from uniform across the world. Within different countries there are many differences in how people speak English and what alternative languages they have at their disposal. For example, despite experiencing 150 years as a British colony, Cantonese-speaking Hong Kong never established an extensive English-speaking community as occurred in India or Singapore. Now, Mandarin is regarded by many Chinese speakers in Hong Kong as the more important second language to learn.

Nevertheless, at the beginning of the twenty-first century, English enjoys a position in the world well beyond that which might be expected by the number of its native speakers. It is undoubtedly at the apex of the complex political, economic and cultural hierarchy of languages in the world. French is probably still the world's second international language, but Chinese, Spanish, Russian and Arabic are next in rank, though each with special influence in particular regions.

Below these in the world hierarchy, one might place the about eighty languages recognised by the UN as national languages, and below that the many more languages recognised as official languages in the world's nation states. Yet lower are the many languages that have regional status within countries, for purposes of education or in the public media. And below that are thousands more languages with small numbers of speakers and little institutional support or protection. However, the changing status of languages will create a new language hierarchy for the world as indicated by Figure 7.3.

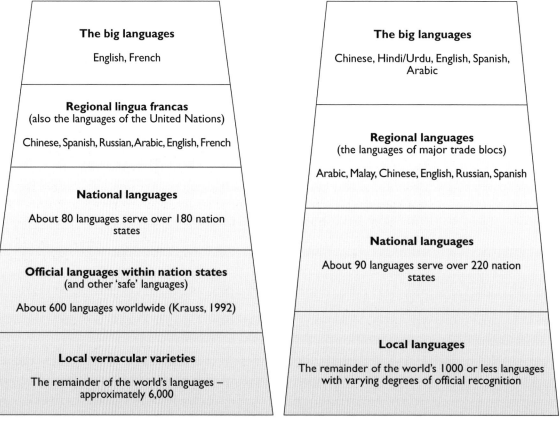

Figure 7.2   The world language hierarchy 1995

Figure 7.3   The world language hierarchy in 2050?
(Graddol, 1997)

ACTIVITY 7.2

Allow about
10 minutes

Look at Figures 7.2 and 7.3. What differences do you notice between the two hierarchies? What for you are the most significant issues about the language hierarchy predicted for 2050 in Figure 7.3 and why?

Comment

In comparison with the present-day hierarchy there are more languages in the top layer. Chinese, Hindi/Urdi, Spanish and Arabic may join English. French and other OECD languages (German, Japanese) are likely to decline in status. But the biggest difference between the present-day language hierarchies and those of the future will result from the loss of several thousand of the world's languages.

I turn to consider the relationship between the rise of English and the loss of local languages in the next section.

7.3 English as a killer language

> Even the most optimistic prognoses claim that only half of today's 6,000–7,000 spoken languages will exist by 2100 ... According to pessimistic but realistic estimates, ... 90% of languages may be dead or moribund in 100 years.
>
> (Skutnabb-Kangas, 2005)

Calculations of linguistic diversity and the current viability of languages are fraught with problems. Some linguists might argue with the figure of 6,000–7,000 plus or minus a few hundred, but few would take issue with it in round terms. The majority of these languages, however, are located in a few countries; they tend to be spoken by small groups of people who have little political or cultural power within the sovereign states in which they live. (See Table 7.1, overleaf.) For example, in 1983 a report to UNESCO calculated that 20–25 per cent of the world's languages are to be found in Oceania (that is, the islands of the Pacific, together with Australia and New Zealand) but that they were spoken by between only 0.1 and 0.2 per cent of the world's population (quoted in Dixon, 1991). Overall, over 80 per cent of the world's languages are spoken by fewer than 5 per cent of its population.

Such small communities of speakers maintain a precarious foothold on their traditional ways of living, language and culture. They often become targeted by development agencies for 'modernisation' and improvement. In many cases, such small communities of speakers cease to be viable in the face of such modernisation. Alternatively, they may become dispossessed of their traditional lands as a consequence of exploitation by large companies and drift to the cities in search of employment. Such trends are visible throughout the developing world and affect tribal groups and small communities in the Amazon, Africa, India, Australia and many other countries in remarkably similar ways. Pattanayak describes the process in India:

> It is interesting to see how 'development' affects multilingual pluricultural countries. The many languages result in small zones of communication. When one or two languages are chosen for mega-communication, the

Table 7.1 The 22 countries that account for about 5000 of the world's 6000 languages, showing their national official languages and their preferred language for international communication

Country	Number of languages	National languages	International languages
Papua New Guinea	820	English/Tok Pisin/ Hiri Motu	English
Indonesia	737	Bahasa Indonesia (Malay)	English
Nigeria	510	English/Yoruba/Ibo/ Hausa/Edo/ Adanawa/ Fulfide/Central	English
India	415	English/Hindi	English
Mexico	291	Spanish	English/Spanish
Cameroon	279	Engish/French	English/French
Australia	273	English	English
People's Republic of China	235	Putonghua (Mandarin)	English
Zaire	210	French	French
Brazil	188	Portuguese	English/Portuguese
Philippines	171	English/Philipino	English
USA	162	English	English
Malaysia	140	Bahasa Malaysia (Malay)	English
Sudan	134	Arabic	English
Chad	132	French/Arabic	French
Tanzania	127	Swahili/English	English
Nepal	123	Nepali	English
Vanuatu (New Hebrides)	109	English/French/ Bislama	English/French
Myanmar (Burma)	108	Burmese	English
Russia	105	Russian	Russian/English
Ethiopia	84	Amharic/English	English
Central African Republic	69	French/Sango	French

small communication zones wither away, resulting in loss of culture. The land-holding pattern in the developing countries presents a similar picture. The average land size is five hectares in the tropical belt and three hectares in Asia. When superfarm technology is imposed on them the smallholdings become uneconomic. The tribal communities present a tragic case of death of language and loss of culture. The tribals live in small clusters in the midst of large forests. In the name of development, the erection of bunds (dams) for electricity generation, opening of the land for tourist promotion, exploitation of minerals located in hills and jungles all result in the tribals being dispossessed and dislocated. This in turn, results in the death of their language and cultures.

(Pattanayak, 1996, p. 145)

Figure 7.4 shows that many of the lesser-used languages are within the Asia-Pacific zone, which is experiencing rapid economic development.

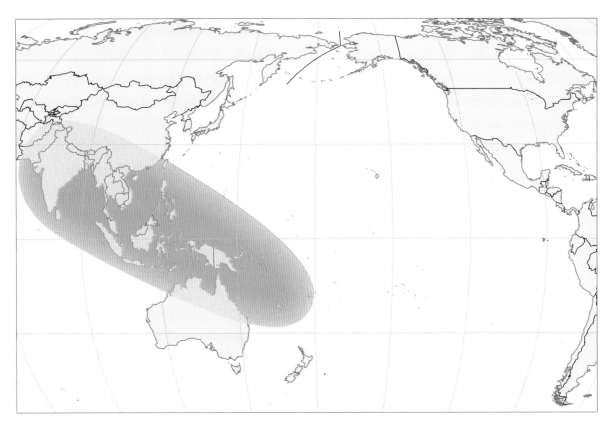

Figure 7.4   About half of the world's endangered languages are located within the Asia-Pacific area enclosed by the shaded ellipse.

The English language is rarely the direct cause of such language loss, despite the fact that English is an official language in many of the countries where endangered languages exist. There exists in most of these highly multilingual countries a complex linguistic hierarchy. English may be at, or near, the top of that hierarchy but its influence may not be felt directly by speakers whose languages are at the bottom. In India, for example, there exist over 190 recognised languages, 87 of which are used in the media, 58 taught as a school subject, 41 used as a medium of instruction in schools, 22 recognised for the purposes of government in the states, and 2 (Hindi and English) recognised as national languages. Language shift usually occurs from a small, low-status vernacular to one of the languages higher in the hierarchy, usually one with a larger number of speakers and wider currency in the region.

In India, even though English is an official language and relatively widely spoken, the speakers of the disappearing tribal languages are turning not to English, or even Hindi, but to regional languages such as Bengali or Marathi. One study of language loss in Africa came to a similar conclusion:

> European languages are very often labelled as being the primary danger to African languages and cultural heritage. A closer look at the reality in most African nations today reveals, however, that it is African linguae francae and other African languages with a national or regional status which spread to the detriment of vernaculars. Minority languages are still more likely to be replaced by those relatively few 'highly valued' African languages, than by imported ones. However, modern attempts reflected by, for example, the 'efforts towards indigenisation' of English in East Africa ... are suitable to clear the way for English becoming more commonly accepted and used in more domains. This is how English finally may spread, even as a mother tongue.

(Brenzinger et al., 1991, p. 40)

However, although the English language is not directly responsible for much of the threat to global diversity, it is intimately connected with the processes of economic globalisation which are indirectly causing lesser-used languages to disappear.

The English language has more direct responsibility for language loss in its native speaking countries. Canada, the USA and Australia each have a large number of indigenous languages within their borders which have already been lost or are on the verge of disappearance. In Australia, for example, more than 200 languages are thought to have been lost in recent years. Reading A describes in greater detail the process of language shift to English over several generations.

ACTIVITY 7.3

Read 'Language loss in Australian Aboriginal languages' by R.M.W. Dixon (Reading A). Note what seem to be the main factors affecting language loss. How many of these factors might apply to lesser-used languages in countries where English is *not* in such widespread use?

Comment

The process Dixon describes is similar to that reported from elsewhere in the world, such as in the USA and Canada in relation to native American languages. The stages are likely to apply whatever language is replacing the minority language, but some of the factors described by Dixon refer especially to colonial or ex-colonial situations (where English has been firmly established as the majority language).

It is also worth looking briefly at some of the limitations of Dixon's account, which is too schematic to include some important details. For example, communities in which both English and language X are known will typically exploit the resources of both languages in codeswitching. Also, Dixon leaves vague the nature of the English variety that is learnt by Aborigines. Aboriginal English is not just a form of Standard English with some vocabulary from language X: it is recognised as a pan-Australian variety in its own right. There are, in addition, forms of English creole spoken in some Aboriginal communities – such as Kriol in the Northern Territories. This is a useful reminder of how new varieties of English often emerge from contact situations. Indeed, there is often a new hierarchy of Englishes grafted on to the existing language hierarchy. In India, for example, there are typically many local forms of Indian English which reflect characteristics of regional languages, together with a national variety of Indian English and an 'international' one, which has fewer identifiable Indian usages.

Finally, Dixon's schematic description of language loss refers to the 'community' as if it maintained its physical integrity during the course of the process of language loss. That may, in some cases, be true. But in many cases the community may itself become dispersed as speakers drift to the towns in search of employment, or when they become dispossessed of their land. In other words, the traditional way of life and the social relations, social interactions and cultural practices from which a 'community' is constructed may themselves be broken up.

7.4 English and the creation of social inequality

Given that language is the first and foremost expression of cultural identities, the dominance of English has potential consequences for the diversity of cultural identities and traditions, which can be seen to 'converge' towards a model of communication and sense-making in line with the 'McCommunication' or the McDonaldisation thesis. On the other hand, such access to language can propel individuals into positions of economic and social advantage – but access to this 'medium of identity formation' is not easy and certainly not equally available to everyone.

(Tietze, 2004, p.183)

English is seen in many countries, at an individual, institutional or national level, as representing the key to economic opportunity. In China, for example, the role and status of English 'is higher than ever in history as evidenced by its position as a key subject in the curriculum, and as a crucial determinant for university entrance and procuring well-paid jobs in the commercial sector' (Adamson, 2002, p. 241; see also Hu, 2002).

Access to English, however, is rarely uniformly available. The other side of the coin of economic opportunity is thus the complex mechanism whereby English language usage structures inequality. A.S. Canagarajah, who is an active figure in language education, describes how this mechanism works in Sri Lanka:

> ... individual desire to learn English has never meant mobility in the Sri Lankan context. Even during colonial times, access to English was controlled to serve the needs of the colonizers. Not every individual who wanted to learn English could afford English education. Furthermore, a knowledge of English language didn't mean professional advancement. English education only permitted employment at the clerical level, much to the disappointment of local people who dreamed of positions in the professions. This history was repeated after independence. The bilingual middle class maintained its vested interest in controlling the spread of English and the rewards associated with it. English was not only unavailable universally, even those who had the opportunity to learn the language anew were classified as inferior by virtue of their accent and dialect (which corresponded to class and caste differences).

(Canagarajah, 2005, p. 435)

Similar points are made by Vai Ramanthan (1999) who explores how particular pedagogical practices – use of a local language and emphasis on grammar teaching – lead to students from 'lower castes' gaining much lower levels of proficiency in English than their Indian middle-class peers.

Tickoo (1993) studied the position of the Kashmiri language in north India. Although Kashmiri was by no means at the bottom of the Indian linguistic hierarchy (see Figure 7.5), being one of the twenty-two 'scheduled' languages, Tickoo argued that educational policies rendered it an inferior language, while the emphasis on English caused many students to fail:

> Kashmiri, like many other languages of similarly small reach in India, has to live in the shadow of larger languages or, more truly, at the bottom of a hierarchy of languages. In such an hierarchical arrangement what often

happens is that the child's first language, which operates at the bottom of the educational ladder, is viewed as a mere stage on the way to gaining the mastery of the larger languages which are known to serve more important national goals. It thus becomes a transactional language rather than a true language of learning or a dependable resource towards lasting literacy.

(Tickoo, 1993, pp. 232–3)

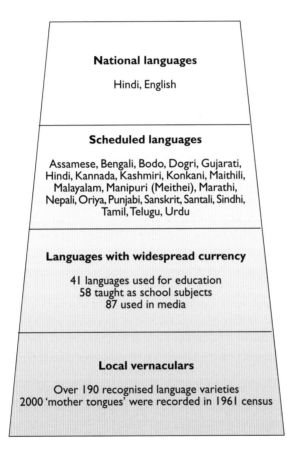

National languages

Hindi, English

Scheduled languages

Assamese, Bengali, Bodo, Dogri, Gujarati, Hindi, Kannada, Kashmiri, Konkani, Maithili, Malayalam, Manipuri (Meithei), Marathi, Nepali, Oriya, Punjabi, Sanskrit, Santali, Sindhi, Tamil, Telugu, Urdu

Languages with widespread currency

41 languages used for education
58 taught as school subjects
87 used in media

Local vernaculars

Over 190 recognised language varieties
2000 'mother tongues' were recorded in 1961 census

Figure 7.5 The Indian language hierarchy (data from Mahapatra, 1990, and *Ethnologue*, 2006)

Many students learn English in what Tickoo called an 'acquisition poor environment' (APE) – one where the teacher is not fully proficient in the language, where the schools and classrooms are under-equipped, and where there is no real communicative use of the language in the community.

[T]he truth is that the vast majority of Indians are taught English in an APE, and as a result the language does not become a usable means of communication. This is eminently true for those who live in villages where there are no opportunities to hear the language spoken. It is almost equally true of a majority of those who learn it in the bulk of schools in cities and towns where English is learnt in a class hour of 35 minutes each working day.

(Tickoo, 1993, p. 234)

Tickoo's study raises two important points. First is the way that the existence of English in the upper hierarchy serves to position languages lower down as everyday vernaculars. Although Kashmiri has experienced standardisation, many languages which are low in a linguistic hierarchy never get the opportunity to be expanded, standardised and used for wider social functions in the way that the European languages have been since the seventeenth century. Robert Phillipson argues that this is a common situation in postcolonial countries:

> Throughout the entire post-colonial world, English has been marketed as the language of 'international communication and understanding', economic 'development', 'national unity' and similar positive ascriptions, but these soft-sell terms obscure the reality of North–South links and globalisation which is that the majority of the world's population is being impoverished, that natural resources are being plundered in unsustainable ways, and that speakers of most languages do not have their linguistic human rights respected.

(Phillipson, 2001, p. 190)

The second point is that educational policy (which establishes the languages to be used as a medium of education at primary, secondary and university level) is a key factor in determining how successful speakers of the lesser-used languages are within the education system. Tickoo argued that the pressure to attend English medium education in cases where students had no real need for English and where the education system could not support quality learning through English, had disastrous consequences for both students and for the Kashmiri language.

It must be admitted that it seems to be extremely difficult to find the mix of language education and language planning decisions that will work for everyone in postcolonial and multilingual societies. Each context is unique in the combination of languages and the local cultural politics of English. That such policies are in a state of flux and at the centre of considerable debate can be illustrated by considering the situation of Papua New Guinea (see box) where over a ten-year period there was a shift away from an English-only education system to a system that uses one fourth of the 800 local languages.

The case of English-medium education in Papua New Guinea: from English-only to local languages

[Papua New Guinea (PNG) is an island nation in the South Pacific, north of Australia. English is the official language and Tok Pisin and Hiri Motu are co-official lingua francas.] Papua New Guinea is unique in a number of ways compared with other developing countries. It is the world's most linguistically diverse nation, with 823 living languages spoken by a population of 5.2 million (2000 PNG Census). ...

From 1870 until the 1950s, the majority of schools in PNG were established by missions and the vernacular languages were used as the language of instruction. An English-only policy was adopted in the 1950s. At PNG's independence in 1975, the policy was reviewed but maintained under the 1976 Education Plan. Instruction in the vernacular languages was reinstated in 1995 (Litteral, 2000).

In 1979, parents on Bougainville Island, in North Solomons Province, expressed concern that the English-only school system was alienating their children from their own language and culture. Children who did not pass secondary school entrance examinations had to return to their villages, but they were unable to reintegrate into village life. The Bougainville Islanders proposed giving their children two years of preschool education in their own language before the first grade of primary schooling, in which the language of instruction was English. The *Viles Tok Ples Skul* (VTPS) ('village language school') scheme thus emerged as a non-formal community-based vernacular language preschool education option. Later, it became known as *Tok Ples Pri Skul* (TPPS) ('Vernacular language preschools'). ...

A review of the VTPS programme found not only that children who had attended a village vernacular preschool before entering the first grade experience distinct educational advantages, but also that their communities enjoyed social and cultural benefits (Delpit and Kemelfield, 1985). Primary school teachers noticed that the transition to the English-only classroom was much easier for children who had attended the vernacular language preschools compared with those with no previous educational experience. Community members and elders, even those who could not read and write themselves, were invited into the classrooms to pass on important cultural knowledge and information to the children.

In July 1991, following the proliferation of vernacular preschools in PNG, officials from national and provincial departments of education unanimously agreed that the formal education system needed restructuring. This eventually led to the 1995 Education (Amendment) Act. ...

The key elements of PNG's Education Reform are the encouragement of early education in the vernacular languages and a gradual bridging to English as a language of wider communication. It also includes the development of a culturally relevant curriculum and materials, and the availability of nine years of basic education instead of six, closer to the child's village home. At the end of 2000, the Education Reform involved 380 languages groups. In PNG's experience, a village-level non-formal vernacular language preschool movement, with minimally trained teachers, eventually guided the entire nation to launch an ambitious drive to provide education in the language children know first and best, their own. They are then better prepared cognitively, developmentally and academically to transfer the learning of skills in their own language to learning in English.

(Wroge, 2002)

7.5 English and communications media

Improved communications within and between countries has transformed patterns of human interaction. It has encouraged international travel for business and leisure, but has also led to more information about distant parts of the world being available through local media. The global electronic media, however, have been dominated by English-speaking interests from their very beginnings in the eighteenth century. Here, I want to explore some of the complex reasons behind the dominance of English in the media and international trade.

The first technology to wire up the world was the electric telegraph. Although various electric devices had been experimented with since the 1750s, it was not until 1837, with the patenting of the telegraph by William Cooke and Charles Wheatstone in Britain, and Samuel Morse in the USA, that a practical and commercial technology appeared. The telegraph did not allow the human voice to be transmitted, but it did permit the relatively slow transmission of written messages by means of coded signals representing the letters of the alphabet. The invention of the telegraph coincided with the development of the railway system in Britain, and the two expanded together. Railways not only created an ever growing need for rapid messaging (to control and synchronise the movements of rolling stock and people) but also provided ready-made protected routes for cables between main cities (see Chapter 3 for the impact of the telegraph on news practices).

In fact, the key to understanding the impact of the telegraph and how English grew up around it as the global lingua franca for trade, international news and technology itself lies in simultaneous and related developments in the political, technological and economic spheres. At the end of the nineteenth century there began a process of global restructuring – of a change in the social and economic relations between the peoples of the world. This process continues today, and is affecting the lives of an increasing proportion of the world's population, some in a positive way but many negatively. The global pattern of language loss, and new forms of social inequality within countries, must be seen as a part of this greater process of globalisation – a term that embraces both economic and cultural spheres, and that expresses the increasing interdependence of geographically diverse countries and peoples. Indeed, the term 'globalisation' is often used to express a changing perception of the world as a smaller, more compressed space, in which some people, at least, can project their agency and will over large distances.

Development of the telegraph

Those who controlled the telegraph effectively controlled the world. By the end of the nineteenth century, Britain was the hub of a global telegraph network (Table 7.2). Over half the world's extensive cable traffic was said to flow through a single building in London, carrying international news, commercial information and diplomatic dispatches. Britain achieved this position because of the extraordinary advantages conferred by colonial possessions, early industrial expansion and the development of financial systems which could provide the capital needed for large-scale enterprises. British interests not only owned the cable, they also held a monopoly on the technology, including submarine cable manufacture, ships for laying cables and repair facilities (Headrick, 1991).

Table 7.2 Who controlled the world's telegraph cables?

	1892	1908	1923
British	66.3	56.2	50.5
American	15.8	19.5	24.2
French	8.9	9.4	11.0
Danish	5.3	3.8	2.6
Others	3.7	11.1	11.7

Figures show percentage of world telegraph cables (data from Headrick, 1991)

The international business made possible by the telegraph required standard working practices not just for the maintenance of the messaging systems but also for the diverse commercial interests involved in the trade. As well as facilitating trade in goods, the telegraph also encouraged the rapid growth in international services, such as news agencies and financial dealing:

> The development of world produce markets, involving uniformity of usage, trading conditions, the distribution of information and the practice

Figure 7.6   The world's first long-distance telegraph machines (courtesy of Cable & Wireless Archive)

of arbitrage, depended upon the efficiency of the telegraph. Metal markets, shipbroking and insurance all grew to service the international economy. The cable companies made their greatest impact on the international money markets; funds flowed across Europe and the world. Without rapid communication it would have been impossible for the industrial and commercial world to have absorbed vast increases in the supply of gold or to have provided the enormous subscription of English capital to foreign loans, whereby the development of Canada, Brazil and Australia was possible.

(Kieve, 1973, p. 238)

Largely because of the British control of the telegraph network, the English language became firmly established as the key lingua franca for international trade and services – a position it has never lost.

Development of global media

Use of the telegraph began to decline in the 1920s, particularly for domestic communications where the telephone was rapidly proving more popular – permitting as it did direct interaction between communicating parties.

Long-distance telephony was made possible by the invention of radio (radiotelephony was the only way of communicating by voice between the USA and the UK until the laying of the transatlantic telephone line in 1956). Here the USA gradually overtook the UK in the exploitation of the technology worldwide. All countries were able to develop their own national communications systems and some, such as France and Germany, became notable producers of equipment. But the international network of links between countries, and later facilities such as satellite, which can simultaneously reach whole continents, have been largely controlled by English-speaking interests to this day. The timeline (see Table 7.3) shows some key milestones in the development of communications media and demonstrates the extent to which new technology was first invented or exploited in English-speaking countries.

Improved availability of international communication, through better technology and falling prices, has given rise to two rather different cultural trends. Originally, someone wishing to communicate at a distance had to visit or send a messenger to a central telegraph office, and numerous other intermediaries stood in the path of the message. Now, the majority of people in the developed world can dial directly to one another, from home or office, public or mobile telephone. The breakdown of centralised and hierarchically controlled communication systems that this represents can be regarded as a 'centrifugal' cultural force in the sense that it encourages diversity of language and communication practices. The international organisations that negotiate the standard technology protocols may rely on English, but the day-to-day users can use whatever language they choose.

Like the internet (see Chapter 6), however, improved global communication also increases the number of interactions between speakers of different languages. One consequence of globalisation is that an increasing number of people in organisations or different sections of a multinational company have to communicate directly with one another. Such communication requires the use of a shared language. In many cases, that language is English. This creates a centralising or 'centripetal' cultural trend in which speakers of different languages converge upon English for certain communications. English emerged as the 'default' language for communication between speakers of different languages in the telegraph era.

Centrifugal and *centripetal* are concepts used by Mikhail Bakhtin (1981 [1935]) to point to the tensions and diversity surrounding language use and practices.

Centripetal – refers to centralising or unifying trends and forces, such as official languages and discourses.

Centrifugal – refers to diversifying and decentralising trends and forces, such as local or unofficial languages and discourses.

Improved technology allowed not just private but also public communications, in which a message or programme from a central source can be received by a dispersed audience. The first radio broadcasts were made in the 1920s. By the mid 1990s some kinds of television programming were being seen around the world, courtesy of satellite television. Such shared global experience of media also represents a centripetal, unifying force.

Table 7.3 A timeline for electronic global communications

1759	First experiments with electronic signalling
1837	Telegraph patented by William Cooke and Charles Wheatstone in Britain and Samuel Morse in USA
1844	First commercial telegraph (between Washington and Baltimore)
1850	First submarine cable – across English Channel
1852	Transmission of hourly Greenwich time signals electrically signalled to major British cities
1866	First successful Atlantic cable
1868	Nationalisation of British telegraph companies brings lower uniform rate permitting general public use; buying out the private companies makes them cash-rich and eager to set up new international ventures International Bureau of Telegraph Administration established in Berne – the world's first permanent international organisation
1876	Alexander Graham Bell patents the telephone
1905	Marconi establishes first commercial transatlantic radio link
1906	First public cinema opens (France)
1915	First thermionic valve amplifier makes long-distance telephone possible (USA)
1919/1920	RCA (Radio Corporation of America) and ITT (International Telephone and Telegraph) founded – the first transnational American communications conglomerates First public service broadcasting (USA and UK)
1924	Marconi demonstrates 24-hour voice communication between Britain and Australia by short-wave radio; this heralds cheap, global voice communication BBC broadcasts GMT time signals
1926	First commercial transatlantic telephone service (by long-wave radio)
1929	Cable & Wireless Ltd founded, merging all British international communications interests, controlling over half the world's cables and 253 cable and wireless stations worldwide First public television broadcast (UK)
1941	First colour television service (USA) First television advertisement broadcast (USA)

1948	Transistor invented (USA)
1956	First transatlantic telephone cable
1964	First electronic mail (USA)
1965	First commercial geostationary communications satellite (Early Bird/INTELSAT)
1970	International direct dialling between London and New York first introduced
1985	CNN International launched
1989	Sky satellite TV launched
1990	First World Wide Web prototype generally agreed to have been created by Tim Berners Lee (UK)
1991	BBC World Service Television opens Asia service
1992	Reuters Television launched
1995	Reuters Television provides 24-hour news service for Sky
1996	Google (World Wide Web search engine) founded by Sergey Brin and Larry Page (USA)
1998	Introduction of Bluetooth for wireless data exchange between handheld computers or cellular phones and stationary computers (USA)
1998	First broadcast of a high-definition TV program (USA)
2001	iPod music player was launched (USA)
2004	1.5 billion cellphones worldwide (Motorola patented mobile phones in 1973 in USA)
2012	Proposed date by which all TV broadcasting is to be digital in UK and USA

You will remember that one of the factors contributing to language loss according to Dixon (Reading A) is 'media pressure'. I want now to examine the extent to which the rise of global media – particularly satellite television – is leading to greater use of English worldwide.

Media and the construction of national cultures

Terrestrial media, particularly television, with its relatively short transmission ranges, has long served a function in every country in constructing a sense of shared national identity and culture. In some countries this is done explicitly through state control of the media, but terrestrial television, with its limited number of channels and mixed programming, probably has this effect everywhere by providing a common entertainment experience and representations of the world to a wide population. As one analyst has remarked, 'We can say that (on both sides of the Atlantic) broadcasting has been one of the key institutions through which listeners and viewers have come to imagine themselves as members of the national community' (Robins, 1995, p. 249).

Two features of satellite television encourage the breakdown of 'national' media cultures. One is the way that, in most countries, scores – if not hundreds – of satellite television channels are available, each carrying a specialist content strand. Viewers 'channel hop' between them, picking whatever seems of most interest. In this sense, satellite television has a divisive effect (sometimes within families as well as cultures), since few viewers have a shared experience. Second, many satellite television channels rely on films and programmes bought on the global market for audiovisual products. Such programmes are likely to reflect a global media culture rather than a national or local one:

> Audio-visual geographies are thus becoming detached from the symbolic spaces of national culture, and realigned on the basis of the more 'universal' principles of international consumer culture. The free and unimpeded circulation of programs – television without frontiers – is the great ideal in the new order. It is an ideal whose logic is driving ultimately toward the creation of global programming and global markets – and already we are seeing the rise to power of global corporations intent on turning ideal into reality.
>
> (Robins, 1995, p. 250)

In the days of the telegraph and radio, ownership of the means of transmission permitted English-speaking interests effectively to control what flowed across their networks. In the early twenty-first century, things are a great deal more complicated. Patterns of ownership (as we will see in the next activity) are themselves complex, as are the relationships between the television channel operators and those who make or distribute the programmes.

ACTIVITY 7.4

Read 'TV in China' by Michael Curtin (Reading B). In this extract Curtin describes the attempts by Rupert Murdoch and his multinational company News Corporation to develop a pan-Asian satellite TV service. (Murdoch is an Australian-born US media proprietor who is the majority shareholder and managing director of News Corporation, one of the world's largest and most influential media corporations. He is one of the few chief executives of any multinational media corporation who has a controlling ownership share in the companies he runs. Beginning with newspapers, magazines and television stations in his native Australia, Murdoch expanded into British and American media and in recent years has become a powerful force in satellite television, the film industry and other forms of media in many parts of the world.)

As you work through the reading, consider how Murdoch, having gained controlling shares in Star TV, was forced to develop new strategies to secure audiences across the distinct geographical, linguistic and cultural contexts in China.

Comment

While a pattern of global media has emerged in which there are relatively few players, with the market dominated by US, British, Australian and Japanese corporations (Robins 1995), Curtin's account of the difficulties faced by News Corp shows how local pressures can impact on attempts to develop an English-medium pan-Asian satellite television service. In the account in Reading B, Curtin highlights several key centrifugal forces undermining any straightforward multinational corporate control:

- the local political regime which, in the case of China, seeks to restrict audiences' access to media outside its control
- the considerable linguistic diversity, which means that any proposed English-medium service is attractive neither to audiences nor advertising companies who might use the service
- the cultural and historical diversity across regions which means that audiences' tastes vary significantly and a 'one size fits all' approach to programming would not be successful.

In order to secure access to audiences in China, Murdoch and News Corp had to adopt a strategy which involved local business and politicians, and involved languages in addition to English. The development of the Phoenix company to complement Star TV was the major vehicle by which Murdoch could maintain an English-medium satellite service whilst also supporting Mandarin-medium TV. It is interesting to note the importance attached to developing a brand – Phoenix – which would reflect and encompass both Western and local diverse Chinese values and interests.

There is, it seems, no immediate danger of the world's television programming becoming English language only. As illustrated by the case of China, too many tendencies – political, cultural and economic – exist to counteract the linguistic hegemony of English language broadcasting. In Europe, according to EU law, over 50 per cent of the programme content must be European in origin. In addition, while US programmes appear with original English soundtrack in some countries (for example, Sweden and Portugal), in many European countries it is usual for US programmes to be dubbed into the national or local language.

Like China, other countries have tried to restrict the reception of satellite television by requiring receivers to be licensed. In many other countries, people do not have private satellite dishes but receive satellite television via cable networks. These cable companies, however, are subjected to national regulation. In most developing countries, satellite television in English tends to reach the privileged sectors of the population who are the ones most likely to speak English anyway (for example, the main audience for CNN International in many countries is in international hotels). This means that the bulk of the population in most countries is not yet as exposed to 'raw' satellite programming as might be imagined.

There is also, as Robins (1995) pointed out, an economic logic which encourages programming for 'segments' and 'market niches'. Hence the most likely outcome of the global corporate order will be English established at the head of the world hierarchy, allowing some programming streams (such as international news, Western pop music and sports coverage) to be beamed into every country. But each region will have a range of programming in other languages for audiences of various sizes. Indeed, satellite television can be used to distribute cultural products to dispersed members just as well as to maintain a cultural hegemony. In Britain, for example, there are several Asian satellite channels which provide programming for Indian, Chinese and Islamic communities. Hence a range of languages and cultures may be sustained by the new global order, but kept safely in a position of less cultural and economic power.

An insight into how the English language fits into the new relations between global and local in televisual media is provided by Curtin in Reading B, who echoes Pennycook (1994) about the significant role played by adverstising in Malaysia. Pennycook described how English language programming increased in Malaysia because the national broadcasting authorities were under pressure to 'corporatize' and become increasingly dependent on advertising revenue.

> This is one of those particularly interesting and complex interconnections between English and global relationships. The move to corporatize is of course connected to shifts both in the global economy and, more importantly, recent discourses on economics, discourses which, once again, are supported by and supportive of the spread of English. In the case of Malaysian television, American movies and TV programmes, and the advertising that they attract, are a far better financial proposition than locally made programmes. The advertising also tends to follow the programmes, so that Chinese and Malay programmes may attract more local commercials aimed at a specific clientele, while US programmes attract some of the larger international sponsors such as McDonalds, Kentucky Fried Chicken ... and the cigarette manufacturers.
>
> (Pennycook, 1994, p. 215)

7.6 Conclusion

This chapter has examined a number of opposing tendencies and contradictions associated with the global spread of English. On the one hand, the continuing expansion in the use and learning of English and the loss of lesser-used languages around the world might suggest that there is some kind of homogeneous global culture emerging, fostered by the growth of global mass media and the activities of transnational companies. Yet it seems that the English language often has a very different social significance to different people in different parts of the world. In each territory it finds a cultural niche which is exploited by advertisers and global corporations and used by local elites to maintain their positioning power.

We are living through a period of rapid economic and technological change during which a new global economic and cultural order is emerging. It seems likely that English will maintain its position at the top of this world linguistic hierarchy, but this does not mean that everyone in the world will end up speaking English, or that cultural materials will not continue to be produced in other languages. The process of economic modernisation transforms patterns of living, education and livelihood in ways that make it impossible to maintain the kind of very small and largely isolated linguistic communities that still account for thousands of the world's stock of languages. The logic of economic globalisation, however, actually encourages the maintenance of some local and regional identities and languages. There is no discernible trend towards complete cultural and linguistic homogeneity, but there is unlikely to be room for many of the smallest languages in the new world hierarchy.

READING A: Language loss in Australian Aboriginal languages

R.M.W. Dixon
(Robert Malcolm Ward Dixon is Professor of Linguistics and Director of the Research Centre for Linguistic Typology at La Trobe University, Melbourne, Australia.)

Source: Dixon, R.M.W. (1991) 'The endangered languages of Australia, Indonesia and Oceania' in Robins, R.H. and Uhlenbeck, E.M. (eds) *Endangered Languages*, Oxford, Berg, pp. 236–7.

Language loss in Australia can be attributed to a number of factors, including:

1 *White insistence*: in many missions and government settlements there was an 'assimilation policy' with children being separated from their parents at an early age and placed in boys' and girls' dormitories where only English was allowed; children heard speaking their native language would be punished. Even where this did not happen, the local language might be banned in the school; and adults employed by a European were often forbidden to communicate in their own language during work.

2 *Aboriginal choice*: many Aborigines have decided to make the best out of the situation they find themselves in, a minority group in European-type society. Parents who want their children to 'succeed' may speak to them only in English.

3 *Shift of cultural emphasis*: people who speak two languages generally use them in different circumstances. Aborigines might, a few generations ago, have used their autochthonous language when hunting together and at corroborees and other social gatherings, but switched to English at work, in a dancehall, or in a school meeting. Gradually, less time was devoted to hunting and social interaction of the traditional type. As these social domains dropped out of use, so did the language that was used in them.

4 *Media pressure:* English is used almost exclusively in radio, TV, videos, newspapers, magazines, books and school instruction. This media barrage naturally encourages a child to speak English, rather than any other language to which he or she may be exposed at home.

Languages can die suddenly or gradually. Sudden death can take place in the space of a single generation; the children of parents who had an Aboriginal tongue as their first language may grow up speaking only English. When the loss is more gradual we can distinguish a number of stages in the Australian situation:

Stage 1:   Language X is used as the first language by a full community of at least some hundreds of people and is used in every aspect of their daily lives. Some of these people will also know another language (another Australian language, or English, or both) but only as second language. Everyone thinks in language X.

Stage 2:   Some people still have X as their first language (and think in it) but for others it is a second language, with English as the preferred medium (and these people may think in English or in a mixture of English and X). At this stage the language is still maintained in its traditional form, with the original phonetics, grammar and vocabulary (although the second language speakers will not have so wide a vocabulary as traditional speakers).

Stage 3:   Only a few old people still have X as their first language. For most of the community, English is the dominant language (which they think in). Some of those with X as a second language may still speak it in a fairly traditional way, but younger people tend to use a simplified form of the language, perhaps putting together words from X in English word order.

Stage 4:   Nobody now knows the full, original form of X. Some members of the community speak a modified version of X, with simplified grammar; at most they will know a few hundred words. The younger people speak a variety of English that includes just a few words from X.

Stage 5:   Everyone in the community speaks, and thinks in, English. There may be a few words from X still used but these are treated as if they were English words (with plural -*s*, past tense -*ed*, and so on).

READING B: TV in China

Michael Curtin
(Michael Curtin is Professor of Communication Arts at the University of Wisconsin, Madison.)

Source: Curtin, M. (2005) 'Murdoch's dilemma, or "What's the price of TV in China?"', *Media, Culture & Society*, vol. 27, no. 2, pp. 155–75.

Flickering Star

During the early 1990s – at the height of industry discourse about a vast, untapped Asian audience – Rupert Murdoch began to express interest in 'the world's fastest growing television market' and after nearly two years of maneuver, he finally secured a controlling stake in Star TV, a pan-Asian satellite service established by the Li Ka-shing family of Hong Kong (Chan, 1996). Yet before Murdoch could fully savor this accomplishment, he unexpectedly jeopardized his investment by succumbing to the stratospheric rhetoric of satellite TV. In a London speech, only a month after the 1993 acquisition of Star, Murdoch (1993) enthused that satellite television was breaking down borders and proving to be 'an unambiguous threat to totalitarian regimes everywhere'. Without specifically mentioning China, he continued, 'Satellite broadcasting makes it possible for information-hungry residents of many closed societies to by-pass state-controlled television channels'. Murdoch's hyperbole, which was telecast around the world by satellite, immediately raised eyebrows in Beijing where officials had already expressed misgivings about his purchase of Star and reports soon began to circulate that Murdoch's remarks were perceived as a direct challenge to Party supremacy.

In a swift and calculated response, Chinese leaders banned private ownership of satellite dishes, prohibited newspaper advertising for foreign satellite services and selectively showcased the prosecution of violators. Even more creatively, the government began to promote cable TV development around the country, making services available at such low cost that satellite dishes no longer seemed worth the bother. Paradoxically, Chinese leaders chose to *proliferate access* to government cable systems in order to *limit* signal flow, reasoning that cable systems would be easier to regulate than satellite signals from afar. Taken together, these steps initially proved so successful that News Corp. managers soon realized they had a full-scale crisis on their hands and it would take years of concerted, almost obsequious effort for the company to regain even limited standing with the Beijing regime. This contretemps furthermore emphasized that – Murdoch's remarks notwithstanding – physical infrastructure on the ground was just as important to Star TV as high-speed conduits in the sky.

Murdoch's management team discovered it had other problems, as well. Initially, Star had been developed as an English-language, pan-Asian platform aimed at upscale households across the continent, but it soon became clear that the company would have to multiply the number of channels and target them more specifically along linguistic, cultural and national lines. For it became evident to Star executives that elite audiences were not large enough to sustain the costs of operation, let alone turn a profit. Moreover, the dispersal of elite viewers across the vast expanse of Asia proved to be a programming and marketing nightmare. Time-zone differences alone made a single program service untenable and, as it turned out, less than a third of Star's advertising clients were interested in synchronous continental exposure. Instead, most clients preferred to buy ads that would promote particular products in specific media markets. In order to serve these customers, Star needed to produce and acquire programming crafted to the tastes of such audiences and this, according to John O'Loan, the chief of network operations who oversaw Star's transition to News Corp. control, caused a major shift in company strategy.

> After we bought Star we realized that what [the Li family was] doing was wrong. It would be nice if you could get some economies of scale. It would be nice if you could squeeze another 1 percent out here and there.

And like any other business, you'll look for places where you can get those economies, but not if they're going to put you out of business by losing touch with your audience.

(interview with author, 8 July 1997)[1]

At first Star's new management thought it could cope with these challenges by splitting the service in two, creating a northern and a southern beam, one that would be pan-Indian and the other pan-Chinese. Yet before long they discovered that these markets were further complicated by prevailing taste hierarchies *within* them. For example, it is likely that a viewer in Fujian province, directly across the Straits from Taiwan, would be interested in Taiwanese television channels (especially those broadcast in the southern Min dialect), but highly unlikely that Taiwanese viewers would be interested in programs from Fujian, since most viewers in Taiwan have access to at least 80 channels that compete ferociously for their attention. Moreover, it's unlikely that a Hong Kong viewer would be interested in either because of linguistic, social and cultural differences, although a (Cantonese-speaking) viewer in nearby Guangzhou might be interested in the same sorts of Mandarin programming as viewers in Fujian province or even Shanghai.

Cultural biases proved to be just as important. For example, Guangzhou and Hong Kong residents both speak Cantonese, and Hong Kong TV programs are quite popular in Guangzhou, but Guangzhou programs are not popular in Hong Kong. The reason for this peculiar pattern of cultural flow is best expressed in temporal terms: Guangzhou looks to Hong Kong as its future, while Hong Kong looks inland towards its past. As Koichi Iwabuchi (2002) has observed, such valences are at work throughout Asia and they significantly influence patterns of cultural exchange. Given these complexities, Star decided that the only way to move forward with its Chinese TV services was to develop two distinctive Mandarin-language platforms, one for Taiwan and one for the eastern region of mainland China, while largely ignoring such lucrative but competitive markets as Hong Kong, Singapore and Malaysia.

By 1995, management had all but abandoned ambitions for a pan-Chinese, let alone a pan-Asian service, since both approaches simply lacked enough advertiser support. John O'Loan, a lanky Australian who has shuttled around the world launching new satellite services for News Corporation, explains that transnational advertising works best for companies that are trying to build a brand identity with consumers who are unfamiliar with their product. 'The people who are the biggest spenders on pan-European advertising are the Japanese, who are furthest from the market, followed by the Yanks,' observes O'Loan (interview with author, 8 July 1997). Establishing a brand identity is important to these companies either because they have a product (often a luxury product) that does not rely on mass distribution systems.

The advertiser, in such cases, isn't especially concerned about the competitive dynamics of particular local or national markets. Likewise in Asia, says O'Loan:

> We sell a lot of pan-Asian advertising, but not to Asians. We sell it to the Americans and we sell it to the Europeans, Volvo for example, but we couldn't survive on that type of advertising. The money that keeps television going is soap, toothpaste, and consumer products, which is national advertising that's tied to a distribution network on the ground.
>
> (interview with author, 8 July 1997)

Yet within the borders of the People's Republic of China, Star found that even national advertising was problematic because, like many other parts of Asia, distribution networks are rarely national in scope. Infrastructural constraints, personnel limitations, banking idiosyncrasies and complex social networks all militate against national product distribution. As O'Loan observes:

> If you have a toothpaste factory, you've got to have a way to get your product around the country. In China, right now, there's no way to do it. The obstacles are severe because the road and rail infrastructure can't handle this kind of thing. Then if you open up different factories in different parts of the country, you have to be careful about quality control, staffing, and you also have the problem of getting supplies to the factories. China is hardly a unified market. Now consider the problem of calling Asia a unified market.
>
> (interview with author, 8 July 1997)

Such uncertainties and reversals beleaguer global media conglomerates that aspire to expand their operations into the growing markets of Asia. Between 1993 and 1995, Rupert Murdoch invested close to $1 billion in a venture that was losing money at the rate of over $1 million a week (Chan, 1996, pp. 175–81). Besides the problems he encountered with Chinese officials, Murdoch soon learned that the idyllic image of 3 billion Asian consumers was attractive to only a limited number of global advertisers and financiers, many of whom had only vague plans for future involvement in the region. Far more important were the advertisers with existing products and distribution systems in the numerous, diverse and often underdeveloped markets of the region. As one senior Chinese media executive puts it:

> Asia is a hell of a big place, and a lot of people come from outside and they make one big mistake: they assume that it's a melting pot like the United States or even a confederation like Europe. In fact, it's a collection of tiny places and you have to keep your focus, otherwise you will be lost.
>
> (C.K. Phoon, MD, Golden Harvest Entertainment,
interview with author, 2000)

For Star to reach audiences in such diverse locales, it had to multiply its channels and narrow the focus of each service. So instead of a pan-Asian satellite platform beaming Western programming in from the outside, News Corp. managers found themselves saddled with a growing number of channels and markets, each with distinctive features and each requiring the painstaking cultivation of personal relationships with local businesspeople and government officials.

Murdoch goes courting

By 1995, Star's Indian and Taiwanese services were off to a capable start, but the PRC (People's Republic of China) channels were in deep trouble. They had effectively been frozen out of the market by Chinese regulators who made it clear the they would not allow Star to 'bypass state-controlled television channels'. Taking the cue, Murdoch initiated discussions with a number of potential joint venture partners, among them, Liu Changle, a former officer in the People's Liberation Army and, during the 1980s, a military affairs reporter with Central Radio, one of the most powerful media services in pre-TV China. Liu seemed an especially good prospect because he had expansive contacts and reputed managerial expertise. Moreover, many of his top staff members were also from the PRC and consequently they understood what audiences had been seeing on television and what they had been missing. Moreover, Liu's group had participated in the development of mainland broadcasting institutions and it had a deft sense of the political and entrepreneurial nuances of the system.

...

Phoenix takes flight

In 1996, Murdoch and Liu launched Phoenix as a 45/55 joint venture that would complement the Star platform. While Star would continue to beam English-language sports and entertainment channels to the mainland, Phoenix would have exclusive rights to develop Mandarin-language movie and general entertainment channels, with the latter emphasizing news and information programming. Just as importantly, the Phoenix staff would take on the time-consuming task of building a marketing organization inside mainland China and cultivating relations with advertisers and government officials.

... [Ho pointed to the great significance of the Phoenix and company logo]

> 'To Westerners,' he says, 'Phoenix suggests a rare bird that has been reborn. In Chinese, however, the word *"fenghuang"* is a compound of two characters, one meaning male bird and the other female bird. But the interesting thing', observes Ho, 'is that you don't know which is the male and which is the female. Is *feng* a male or a female? No one knows'

(interview with author, 12 May 2000)

Thus, the company logo features two lavishly plumed birds, swirling head-to-tail around a central point. 'And if you look at the logo more carefully, you see that it also looks like the iris of a camera. And it looks as if it is rotating and it will never stop. And it also looks like a fengshui *bagua*', which is an amulet representing the fortune telling sticks of the I-Ching arranged around a tai-chi symbol, again suggesting a swirling complementarity of life forces, or the yin and yang. Ho goes on:

> We spent a long time designing this logo because it represents the meaning of our brand. Phoenix represents something that is brand new but also something that is very Chinese. It's new and old, Western and Eastern. It also tries to represent a merging of the northern and southern parts of China, and of their cultures, which are very, very different. The southern part of China is always creating, looking forward, and extending outward. But [he leans forward for emphasis, gazing emphatically above his back-rimmed spectacles and slowing the cadence of his delivery] the *real* culture of China comes from the north, thousands and thousands of years of history and culture. And the mixture of these two areas is a major part of our thinking as we develop the programming strategies for Phoenix.

(interview with author, 12 May 2000)

...

Notes

Thanks to the Taiwan National Endowment for Culture and Art and the US Fulbright Commission for providing research support during the 1999–2000 academic year. I furthermore want to express my appreciation to colleagues at the Institute of Ethnology, Academia Sinica and the Foundation for Scholarly Exchange who graciously hosted my sabbatical in Taipei, and to colleagues and students in the School of Journalism and Mass Communication at the Chinese University of Hong Kong where I served as a visiting professor during the 1996–7 academic year.
...

1   This article is part of a larger research project that included interviews with more than 100 film and television executives in Hong Kong, Taipei and Singapore between 1997 and 2003. Star TV executives were interviewed in each of these cities as to local and transnational operations of the satellite network.

Interviews

Anonymous media executive, 2000.

Anonymous media consultant, 2003.

H. HO, General Manager, Distribution and Marketing, Phoenix TV (12 May 2000).

J. O'Loan, Director of Network Services, Star TV (8 July 1997).

W. Pfeiffer, Chief Executive Officer, Celestial Pictures (2 March 2002).

C.K. Phoon, Managing Director Golden Harvest Entertainment (12 May 2000).

References for this reading

Chan, A. (1996) *Li Ka-Shing: Hong Kong's Elusive Billionaire*. Hong Kong: Oxford University Press.

Iwabuchi, K. (2002) *Recentering Globalization: Popular Culture and Japanese Transnationalism*. Durham, NC: Duke University Press.

Murdoch, R. (1993) 'Dawn of the Convergent, Interactive Era', *Business Times* (Singapore) 1 Sept. reprinted 17 Sept.

References

Abel, R. (undated) *The Characteristics of Literary English*, unpublished work.

Abercrombie, D. (1981) 'Extending the Roman alphabet: some orthographic experiments of the past four centuries' in Asher, R.E. and Henderson, E.J.A. (eds) *Towards a History of Phonetics*, Edinburgh, Edinburgh University Press.

Achebe, C. (1958) *Things Fall Apart*, London, Heinemann Education.

Achebe, C. (1965) 'English and the African writer', *Transition: A Journal of the Arts, Culture and Society*, vol. 4, no. 18.

Achebe, C. (1974 [1958]) *Arrow of God* (2nd edn), London, Heinemann.

Achebe, C. (1976 [1958]) *Things Fall Apart*, London, Heinemann.

Achebe, C. (1988) *Hopes and Impediments: Selected Essays 1965–1987*, London, Heinemann.

Adamson, B. (2002) 'Barbarism as a foreign language: English in China's schools', *World Englishes*, vol. 2, no. 2, pp. 231–43.

Aitchison, J. and Lewis, D.M. (eds) (2003) *New Media Language*, London, Routledge.

Anand, M.R. (1945 [1936]) *Coolie*, Harmondsworth, Penguin.

Arnheim, R. (1970) *Visual Thinking*, London, Faber & Faber.

Arnheim, R. (1988) *The Power of the Center: A Study of Composition in the Visual Arts*, London, University of California Press.

Auden, W.H. (1969) *Collected Shorter Poems 1927–1957*, London, Faber & Faber.

Bailey, R.W. (1992) *Images of English: A Cultural History of the Language*, Cambridge, Cambridge University Press.

Bakhtin, M.M. (1981 [1935]) *The Dialogic Imagination* (trans. C. Emerson and M. Holquist; ed. M. Holquist), Austin, TX, University of Texas Press.

Bakhtin, M.M. (1986) *Speech Genres and Other Late Essays* (trans. V.W. McGee, ed. C. Emerson and M. Holquist), Austin, TX, University of Texas Press.

Barker, H. (1994) *Minna*, Leeds, Alumnus.

Beckett, S. (1984) *Collected Shorter Plays*, London, Faber & Faber.

Bell, A. (1991) *The Language of News Media*, Oxford, Blackwell.

Bell, A. (1998) 'The discourse structure of news stories' in Bell, A. and Garrett, P. (eds), *Approaches to Media Discourse*, Oxford, Blackwell.

Bell, A. (2003) 'A century of news discourse', *International Journal of English Studies*, no. 3, pp. 189–208.

Bernstein, M. (1998) 'Patterns of hypertext', *Proceedings of the Ninth ACM Conference on Hypertext and Hypermedia*, New York, Association for Computing Machinery, pp. 21–9.

Bhatt, S. (1991) *Monkey Shadows*, Manchester, Carcanet.

Bickham, G. (1941 [1741]) *The Universal Penman*, New York, Dover.

Bierce, A. (1970) *The Complete Short Stories of Ambrose Bierce*, New York, Doubleday.

Blake, W. (1970) *Songs of Innocence and of Experience: Shewing the Two Contrary States of the Human Soul, 1789–1794*, (with introduction and commentary by Sir Geoffrey Keynes), London, Oxford University Press.

Bolinger, D.L. (1946) 'Visual morphemes', *Twentieth Century Literature*, no. 22, pp. 333–40.

Boyd-Barrett, O. (1980) *The International News Agencies*, London, Constable.

Boyd-Barrett, O. and Rantanen T. (1998) *The Globalisation of News*, Thousand Oaks, CA, Sage.

Brathwaite, K. (1993) *Roots*, Ann Arbor, MI, University of Michigan Press.

Brenzinger, M., Heine, B. and Sommer, G. (1991) 'Language death in Africa' in Robins, R.H. and Uhlenbeck, E.M. (eds) *Endangered Languages*, Oxford, Berg.

Brewer, W.F. (1985) 'The story schema: universal and culture-specific properties' in Olson, D.R., Torrance, N. and Hildyard, A. (eds) *Literacy, Language, and Learning: The Nature and Consequences of Reading and Writing*, Cambridge, Cambridge University Press.

Bridges, R. (1913) *A Tract on the Present State of English Pronunciation*, Oxford, Oxford University Press.

Brink, A. (1982) *A Chain of Voices*, London, Faber & Faber.

British Library (2006a) 'Why compare the copies? Caxton's Chaucer', *Treasures in Full*, http://www.bl.uk/treasures/caxton/compare.html (Acessed 14 March 2006).

British Library (2006b) *Treasures in Full*, http://www.bl.uk/treasures/treasuresinfull.html (Accessed 17 September 2006).

British Library (2006c) *Canterbury Tales*, http://www.bl.uk/treasures/caxton/digitisation.html (Accessed 14 March 2006).

Burnett, P. (ed.) (1986) *Penguin Book of Caribbean Verse in English*, Harmondsworth, Penguin.

Burrows, J. (1987) *Computation into Criticism*, Oxford, Clarendon.

Burt, Sir C. (1950) *A Psychological Study of Typography*, London, Cambridge University Press.

Canagarajah, A.S (2005) 'Dilemmas in planning English/vernacular relations in post-colonial communities', *Journal of Sociolinguistics,* vol. 9, no. 3, pp. 418–47.

Carey, J.W. (1987) 'Why and how? The dark continent of American journalism' in Manoff, R.K. and Schudson, M. (eds) *Reading the News*, New York, Pantheon.

Carter, R. and Nash, W. (1990) *Seeing Through Language: A Guide to Styles of English Writing*, Oxford, Blackwell.

Carter, R., Day, B. and Meggs, P. (1985) *Typographic Design: Form and Communication*, New York, Van Nostrand Reinhold.

Clanchy, M.T. (1993) *From Memory to Written Record: England 1066–1307* (2nd edn), Oxford, Blackwell.

Cook, G. (2001) *The Discourse of Advertising* (2nd edn)*,* London, Routledge.

Crellin, V.H. (1989) 'Towards a common cursive script: American influences', *Journal of Educational Administration and History*, vol. 31, no. 1, pp. 1–8.

Crystal, D. (2001) *Language and the Internet*, Cambridge, Cambridge University Press.

Crystal, D. (2003) *English as a Global Language* (2nd edn), Cambridge, Cambridge University Press.

cummings, e.e. (1969) *selected poems 1923–1958*, London, Faber & Faber.

Cystal, D. (1987) *The Cambridge Encyclopedia of Language*, Cambridge, Cambridge University Press.

Dabydeen, D. (1990) *The State of the Language*, London, Faber & Faber.

Dathorne, O.R. (1975) *African Literature in the Twentieth Century*, London, Heinemann.

Dawson, G. and Kennedy-Skipton, L. (1968) *Elizabethan Handwriting*, London, Faber & Faber.

Delpit, L. and Kemelfield, G. (1985) *An Evaluation of the Viles Tok Ples Skul Scheme in the North Solomons Province*, ERU Report No. 51, University of Goroka, Papua New Guinea.

Derwing, B.L. (1992) 'Orthographic aspects of linguistic competence' in Downing, P., Lima, S.D. and Noonan, M. (eds) *The Linguistics of Literacy*, Amsterdam, John Benjamins.

Dickens, C. (1948 [1850]) *Bleak House*, London, Chatto and Windus.

Dickens, C. (1979 [1855–57]) *Little Dorrit* (ed. H.P. Sucksmith), Oxford, Clarendon.

Digital Imaging South Africa (2006) http://disa.nu.ac.za/disaind.htm (Accessed 22 February 2006).

Dixon, R.M.W. (1991) 'The endangered languages of Australia, Indonesia and Oceania' in Robins, R.H. and Uhlenbeck, E.M. (eds) *Endangered Languages*, Oxford, Berg.

Dondis, D.A. (1973) *A Primer of Visual Literacy*, Cambridge, MA, Massachusetts Institute of Technology.

Dor, D. (2004) 'From Englishization to imposed multilingualism: globalization, the internet, and the political economy of the linguistic code', *Public Culture*, vol. 16, no. 1, pp. 97–118.

Downing, J. (1964) *The Initial Teaching Alphabet*, London, Cassell.

Drabble, M. (1987) *The Radiant Way*, Harmondsworth, Penguin.

Durham, M. (2003) 'Language choice on a Swiss mailing list', *Journal of Computer-Mediated Communication*, vol. 9, no. 1, http://jcmc.indiana.edu/vol9/issue1/durham.html (Accessed 31 January 2006).

Earle, A.M. (1899) *Child Life in Colonial Days*, New York, Macmillan.

Ellis, A.J. (1890) *English Dialects: Their Sounds and Homes*, London, Kegan Paul, French, Trubner & Co.

Emecheta, B. (1979 [1972]) *In the Ditch*, London, Allison & Busby.

Ethnologue (2006) www.ethnologue.com (Accessed 22 March 2006)

European Commission (2006) *Languages of Europe*, http://ec.europa.eu/education/policies/lang/languages/index_en.html#Official%20eu (Accessed 12 October 2006).

Fairbank, A. (1968) *A Book of Scripts*, Harmondsworth, Penguin.

Faulkner, W. (1989 [1929]) *The Sound and the Fury*, London, Picador.

Fowler, R. (1991) *Language in the News*, London, Routledge.

France, L. (ed.) (1993) *Sixty Women Poets*, Newcastle upon Tyne, Bloodaxe.

Fugard, A. (1990) *My Children! My Africa!*, London, Faber & Faber.

Gaddie, G.P. (1989) 'Homophony and paronomasia in America: on the validity of puns', PhD thesis, Bowling Green, OH, Bowling Green State University.

Galtung, J. and Ruge, M.H. (1965) 'The structure of foreign news', *Journal of Peace Research*, vol. 2, no. 1, pp. 64–91.

Gardner, C. (2003) 'Meta-interpretation and hypertext fiction: a critical response', *Computers and the Humanities*, no. 37, pp. 33–56.

Geipel, J. (1972) *The Cartoon*, Newton Abbot, David & Charles.

Goffman, E. (1981) *Forms of Talk*, Philadelphia, PA, University of Pennsylvania Press.

Goodman, S. (1996) 'Visual English' in Goodman, S. and Graddol, D. (eds) *Redesigning English: New Texts, New Identities*, London, Routledge/Milton Keynes, The Open University.

Goudy, F.W. (1963 [1942]) *The Alphabet and Elements of Lettering*, London, Constable and Co.

Graddol, D. (1997) *The Future of English? A Guide to Forecasting the Popularity of the English Language in the 21st century*, London, British Council.

Graddol, D. (2005) *English Next*, London, British Council.

Graddol, D., Cheshire, J. and Swann, J. (1994) *Describing Language* (2nd edn), Buckingham, Open University Press.

Halliday, M.A.K. (1970) 'Language structure and language function' in Lyons, J. (ed.) *New Horizons in Linguistics*, Harmondsworth, Penguin.

Halliday, M.A.K. (1978) *Language as Social Semiotic*, London, Edward Arnold.

Halliday, M.A.K. (1985) *Introduction to Functional Grammar*, London, Edward Arnold.

Hammond, P. and Hughes, P. (1978) *Upon the Pun: Dual Meaning in Words and Pictures*, London, W.H. Allen.

Harrison, T. (1987) *Selected Poems* (2nd edn), Harmondsworth, Penguin.

Headrick, D.R. (1991) *The Invisible Weapon: Telecommunications and International Politics 1851–1945*, New York, Oxford University Press.

Heaney, S. (1980) *Preoccupations: Selected Prose, 1968–1978*, London, Faber & Faber.

Heaney, S. (1988) *The Government of the Tongue: The 1986 T.S. Eliot Memorial Lectures and Other Critical Writings*, London, Faber & Faber.

Hector, L.C. (1966) *The Handwriting of English Documents*, London, Edward Arnold.

Hjarvard, S. (1994) 'TV news: from discrete items of continuous narrative? The social meaning of changing temporal structures', *Cultural Studies*, vol. 8, no. 2, pp. 306–20.

Hong Kingston, M. (1981a [1980]) *China Men*, London, Picador.

Hong Kingston, M. (1981b [1977]) *The Woman Warrior: Memoirs of a Girlhood Among Ghosts*, London, Picador.

Hu, G. (2002) Recent important developments in secondary English-language teaching in The People's Republic of China', *Language, Culture and Education*, vol. 15, no. 1, pp. 30–49.

Internet World Stats (2005) *Internet Usage Statistics – The Big Picture*, http://www.internetworldstats.com/stats.htm (Accessed 2 December 2005)

Internet World Stats (2006) 'Internet users by language', *Internet World Stats: Usage and Population Studies*, www.internetworldstats.com (Accessed 20 January 2006).

Jabberwacky (2006) 'Conversation', *Moral Dilemmas*, http://www.jabberwacky.com/j2convbydate-L2525 (Accessed 14 March 2006).

Jacob, H. (1947) *A Planned Auxiliary Language*, London, Dennis Dobson.

Jagger, J.H. (1940) *English in the Future*, London, Thomas Nelson.

Jaworski, A., Fitzgerald, R. and Morris, D. (2003) 'Certainty and speculation in news reporting of the future: the execution of Timothy McVeigh', *Discourse Studies*, vol. 5, no. 1, pp. 33–49.

Jaworski, A., Fitzgerald, R. and Morris, D. (2004) 'Radio leaks: presenting and contesting leaks in radio news broadcasts', *Journalism*, vol. 5, no. 2, pp. 183–202.

Jeffries, L. (1996) 'What makes English into art?' in Maybin, J. and Mercer, N. (eds) *Using English: From Conversation to Canon*, London, Routledge/Milton Keynes, The Open University.

Johnson, S. (1755) *A Dictionary of the English Language*, London, W. Strachan.

Kieve, J. (1973) *The Electric Telegraph: A Social and Economic History*, Newton Abbot, David & Charles.

Killam, D. (1976) 'Notes on adaptation and variation in the use of English in writing by Haliburton, Furphy, Achebe, Narayan and Naipaul' in Niven, A. (ed.) *Commonwealth Writers Overseas*, Paris, Didier.

Krauss, M. (1992) 'The world's languages in crisis', *Language*, vol. 68, no. 1.

Kress, G. (2003) *Literacy in the Media Age*, London, Routledge.

Kress, G. and van Leeuwen, T. (1990) *Reading Images*, Deakin, Vic., Deakin University.

Kress, G. and van Leeuwen, T. (1996) *Reading Images: The Grammar of Visual Design*, London, Routledge.

Labov, W. (1972) *Language in the Inner City: Studies in the Black English Vernacular*, Philadelphia, PA, University of Pennsylvania Press.

Labov, W. and Waletzky, J. (1967) 'Narrative analysis: oral versions of personal experience' in Helm, J. (ed.) *Essays on the Verbal Arts* (Proceedings of the 1966 Annual Spring Meeting of the American Ethnological Society), Seattle, WA, University of Washington Press.

Landow, G. (1997) *Hypertext 2.0: The Convergence of Contemporary Critical Theory and Technology*, Baltimore, MA, Johns Hopkins University Press.

Large, A. (1985) *The Artificial Language Movement*, Oxford, Blackwell.

Larkin, P. (1964) *The Whitsun Weddings*, London, Faber & Faber.

Leech, G. and Short, M. (1981) *Style in Fiction*, Harlow, Longman.

Litteral, R. (2000) 'Basic education in Papua New Guinea: past, present and future', paper presented at the First faculty of Humanities Conference, Bridging Borders/Moving Boundaries: Defining/Redefining the Humanities into the New Millennium, 30 October to 3 November, University of Goroka, Papua New Guinea.

Louw, B. (1993) 'Irony in the text or insincerity in the writer? The diagnostic potential of semantic prosodies' in Baker, M., Francis, G. and Togninibonelli, E. (eds) *Text and Technology: In Honour of John Sinclair*, Philadelphia, PA, John Benjamins.

Lowry, A. (1982) 'Style range in new English literatures' in Kachru, B.B. (ed.) *The Other Tongue: English Across Cultures*, Urbana, IL, University of Illinois Press.

Lynch, M. and Edgerton, S.Y. (1988) 'Aesthetics and digital image processing: representation craft in contemporary astronomy' in Fyfe, G. and Law, J. (eds) *Picturing Power: Visual Depiction and Social Relations*, London, Routledge.

Mahapatra, A. (1990) 'A demographic appraisal of multilingualism in India' in Pattanayak, D.P. (ed.) *Multilingualism in India*, Clevedon, Multilingualism Matters.

Marti, F., Ortega, P., Idiazabal, I., Barrena, A., Juaristi, P., Junyent, C., Uranga, B. and Amorrotu, E. (2005) *Words and Worlds: World Languages Review*, Clevedon, Multilingual Matters.

McCloud, S. (1994) *Understanding Comics: The Invisible Art*, New York, Harper Collins.

McIntosh, A. (1969) 'The analysis of written Middle English' in Lass, R. (ed.) *Approaches to English Historical Linguistics*, New York, Holt, Rinehart & Winston.

McKean, E. (2002) 'L33t-sp34k' in Lederer, R. 'Stamp out fadspeak', *Verbatim*, vol. 27, no. 1, pp. 13–14.

McNeill, M. (1971) *Vere Foster 1819–1900: An Irish Benefactor*, Newton Abbot, David & Charles.

Messaris, P. (2001) 'New literacies in action: visual education', *Reading Online*, vol. 4, no. 7, February, http://www.readingonline.org/newliteracies/lit_index.asp?href=/newliteracies/action/messaris/index.html (Accessed 15 September 2006).

Milic, L.T. (1971) 'The possible usefulness of poetry generation' in Wisbey, R.A. (ed.) *The Computer in Literary and Linguistic Research: Papers from a Cambridge Symposium*, London, Cambridge University Press.

Morgan, J. and Welton, P. (1986) *See What I Mean: An Introduction to Visual Communication*, London, Edward Arnold.

Morrison, T. (1992) *Jazz*, London, Chatto & Windus.

Naipaul, V.S. (1984) *Finding the Centre: Two Narratives*, Harmondsworth, Penguin.

Naipaul, V.S. (1992 [1961]) *A House for Mr Biswas*, Harmondsworth, Penguin.

Ngũgĩ wa Thiong'o (1976 [1964]) *Weep Not, Child*, London, Heinemann.

Ngũgĩ wa Thiong'o (1986a) *Decolonising the Mind: The Politics of Language in African Literature*, London, James Currey.

Ngũgĩ wa Thiong'o (1986b [1977]) *Petals of Blood*, London, Heinemann.

Nielson/NetRatings (2006) http://www.nielsen-netratings.com (Accessed 17 September 2006).

Ogden, C.K. (1932) *The Basic Dictionary*, London, Kegan Paul, Trench, Trubner.

Östman, J.-O. and Simon-Vandenbergen, A.-M. (eds) (2004) *Media Discourse – Extensions, Mixes and Hybrids* (special issue of *Text*, vol. 24, no. 3), New York, Mouton de Gruyter.

Padel, E. (1993) *Angel*, Newcastle upon Tyne, Bloodaxe.

Page, R.I. (1987) *Runes*, London, British Museum Publications.

Pajares Tosca, S. (2000) 'A pragmatics of links', *Journal of Digital Information*, vol. 1, no. 6, available http://jodi.tamu.edu/Articles/v01/i06/Pajares/ (Accessed 20 January 2006).

Paolillo, J. (1999) 'The virtual speech community: social network and language variation on IRC', *Journal of Computer-Mediated Communication*, vol. 4, no. 4, http://jcmc.indiana.edu/vol4/issue4/paolillo.html (Accessed 31 January 2006).

Parkes, M.B. (1982) *The Scriptorium of Wearmouth-Jarrow*, The Jarrow Lecture 1982.

Pattanayak, D.P. (1996) 'Change, language and the developing world' in Coleman, H. and Cameron, L. (eds) *Change and Language*, Clevedon, BAAL/Multilingual Matters.

Pennycook, A. (1994) *The Cultural Politics of English as an International Language*, London, Longman.

Phillipson, R (2003) *English-Only Europe: Challenging Language Policy*, London, Routledge.

Phillipson, R. (1992) *Linguistic Imperialism*, Oxford, Oxford University Press.

Phillipson, R. (2001) 'English for globalisation or for the world's people?', *International Review of Education,* vol. 47, no. 3–4, pp. 185–200.

Pinter, H. (1979) *Plays Two*, London, Methuen.

Pitman, I. (undated) *The Manual of Phonography: An Exposition of Sir Isaac Pitman's System of Phonography or Phonetic Shorthand*, London, Pitman & Sons.

Platt, J., Webber, H. and Ho, M.L. (1984) *The New Englishes*, London, Routledge & Kegan Paul.

Ramanathan, V. (1999) 'English is here to stay: A critical look at institutional and educational practices in India', *TESOL Quarterly*, vol. 33, no. 2, pp. 211–33.

Richardson, K. (2001) 'Risk news in the world of internet news groups', *Journal of Sociolinguistics*, vol. 5, no. 1, pp. 50–72.

Richardson, K. and Meinhof, U.H. (1999) *Worlds in Common? Television Discourse in a Changing Europe*, London, Routledge.

Robins, K. (1995) 'The new spaces of global media' in Johnston, R.J., Taylor, P.J. and Watts, M.J. (eds) *Geographies of Global Change*, Oxford, Blackwell.

Rosch, E. (1978) 'Principles of categorization' in Rosch, E. and Lloyd, B.L. (eds) *Cognition and Categorization*, Hillsdale, NJ, Lawrence Erlbaum.

Rushdie, S. (1982) *Midnight's Children*, London, Pan.

Said, E.W. (1993) *Culture and Imperialism*, London, Chatto & Windus.

Samuels, M.L. (1969) 'Some applications of Middle English dialectology' in Lass, R. (ed.) *Approaches to English Historical Linguistics*, New York, Holt, Rinehart & Winston.

Schlesinger, P. (1987) *Putting 'Reality' Together: BBC News* (2nd edn), London, Methuen.

Schudson, M. (1989) 'The sociology of news production', *Media, Culture and Society*, vol. 11, no. 3, pp. 263–82.

Shaw, G.B. (1962) *Androcles and the Lion* (printed in Shaw's alphabet), Harmondsworth, Penguin.

Sinclair, J. (ed.) (1987) *Collins Cobuild English Language Dictionary*, London, Collins.

Skutnabb-Kangas, T. (2000) *Linguistic Genocide in Education or World Wide Diversity and Human Rights?*, Mahwah, NJ, Lawrence Erlbaum.

Skutnabb-Kangas, T. (2005) 'Murder that is a threat to survival', *The Guardian Weekly*, http://www.onestopenglish.com/Culture/global/muder/htm (Accessed 9 September 2005).

Swann, C. (1991) *Language and Typography*, New York, Van Nostrand Reinhold.

Swann, J., Deumert, A., Lillis, T. and Mesthrie, R. (2004) *A Dictionary of Sociolinguistics*, Edinburgh, Edinburgh University Press.

The Economist (2004) 'After Babel, a new common tongue', 5 August 2004.

Tickoo, M. (1993) 'When is a language worth teaching? Native languages and English in India', *Language, Culture and Curriculum,* vol. 6, no. 3, pp. 225–39.

Tietze, S. (2004) 'Spreading the management gospel – in English', *Language and Intercultural Communication,* vol. 4, no. 3, pp. 175–89.

Todd, L. (1979) *Some Day Been Dey: West African Pidgin Folktales*, London, Routledge & Kegan Paul.

Todd, L. (1989) *The Language of Irish Literature*, Basingstoke, Macmillan.

Toolan, M. (1998) *Language in Literature: An Introduction to Stylistics*, London and New York, Arnold.

Trew, T. (1979a) 'Theory and ideology at work' in Fowler, R., Hodge, B., Kress, G. and Trew, T. (eds) *Language and Control*, London, Routledge & Kegan Paul.

Trew, T. (1979b) '"What the papers say": linguistic variation and ideological difference' in Fowler, R., Hodge, B., Kress, G. and Trew, T. (eds) *Language and Control*, London, Routledge & Kegan Paul.

Truchot, C. (2003) *Languages and Supranationality in Europe: The linguistic Influence of the European Union in Languages in a Globalising World*, Cambridge, Cambridge University Press.

van Dijk, T.A. (1988a) *News Analysis: Case Studies of International and National News in the Press*, Hillsdale, NJ, Lawrence Erlbaum.

van Dijk, T.A. (1988b) *News as Discourse*, Hillsdale, NJ, Lawrence Erlbaum.

Walcott, D. (1973) *Another Life*, London, Cape.

Wales, K. (2001) *A Dictionary of Stylistics* (2nd edn), London, Longman.

Webster, N. (1991 [1789]) 'An essay on the necessity, advantages and practicability of reforming the mode of spelling, and of rendering the orthography of words correspondent to the pronunciation' in Crowley, T. (ed.) *Proper English: Readings in Language, History and Cultural Identity*, London, Routledge.

Widdowson, H.G. (1975) *Stylistics and the Teaching of Literature*, London, Longman.

Wikipedia (2006) 'Podcasting', *Wikipedia*, http://en.wikipedia.org/wiki/Podcasting (Accessed 14 March 2006).

Witt, J. (2000) *English as a Global Language: The Case of the European Union*, EESE, November.

Woolf, V. (1977 [1927]) *To the Lighthouse*, London, Grafton.

Wordsworth, W. (1991 [1850]) *The Thirteen Book Prelude* (ed. M. Reed), vol. 2, Ithaca, NY, Cornell University Press.

Wroge, D. (2002) 'Papua New Guinea's vernacular language preschool programme', *UNESCO Policy Briefs on Early Childhood,* No. 7, October 2002.

Zachrisson, R.E. (1970) *Anglic: An International Language*, Maryland, McGrath.

Acknowledgements

Grateful acknowledgement is made to the following sources:

Text

Page 15: From *Days* by Philip Larkin, Collected Poems by Philip Larkin. Faber and Faber Ltd and The Society of Authors as the Literary Representative of the Estate of Philip Larkin; page 15: Louw, B. 1993, 'Irony in the Text or Insincerity in the Writer', in Baker, M. et al. 1993, *Text and Technology*, John Benjamins Publishing Company; page 30: Breeze, J.B. 1992, An excerpt from Spring cleaning, from *Spring cleaning: A collection of poems*, Virago Press, Little Brown & Co.; pages 68–71: Thiong'o, N. wa, 1986, *Decolonising the Mind: The politics of language in African Literature*, James Curry Ltd, Heinemann Publishers Inc. and EAEP, Nairobi; pages 71–2: Excerpt from pages 152–4 from *Arrow of God* by Chinua Achebe. Copyright © 1964 by Chinua Achebe. Reprinted by permission of HarperCollins Publishers and David Higham Associates Ltd; pages 73–4: *From Finding the Center: Two Narratives* by V.S. Naipaul, copyright © 1984 by V.S. Naipaul. Used by permission of Alfred A. Knopf, a division of Random House, Inc. and Aitken & Stone Ltd; pages 74–6: Copyright © 1975, 1976 by Maxine Hong Kingston. Originally published by Alfred A. Knopf. Reprinted by permission of the author and the Sandra Dijkstra Literary Agency and Random House, Inc.; pages 76–8: Heaney, S. (1988), The Murmer of Malvern, from *The Government of the Tongue: The 1986 Memorial Lectures and Other Critical Writings*, Faber and Faber Ltd; Heaney, S. 1988, The Murmer of Malvern, from *The Government of the Tongue Selected Prose 1978–1987* by Seamus Heaney. Copyright © 1989 by Seamus Heaney. Reprinted by Farrar, Straus & Giroux, Inc.; Walcott, D. (1979). The Star-Apple Kingdom, New York, Farrar, Straus & Giroux; pages 106–9: Deadlines, Datelines, and History by Michael Schudson, from *Reading the News* by Robert Karl Manoff and Michael Schudson, copyright © 1986 by Carlin Romano. Used by permission of Pantheon Books, a division of Random House, Inc.; pages 110–12: Carey, J.W. (1987), 'Why and how? The dark continent of American journalism', from Manoff, R.K. and Schudson, Professor, M. (eds) *Reading the News*, Pantheon Books, a division of Random House, Inc.; pages 153–9: Cook, G. (2001). *Pictures, music, speech and writing, The Discourse of Advertising*, pp. 42–50, Routledge. Reproduced with permission from Taylor and Francis Ltd; pages 155–8 (text and figure): Coca-Cola Company; pages 231–40: Durham, M., 'Language Choice on a Swiss Mailing List', *Journal of Computer-Mediated Communication* (JCMC), Volume 9, Issue 1, http://jcmc.indiana.edu; pages 240–2: McKean, E. (2002) L33t-sp34k, *Verbatim: The Language Quarterly*, pp. 13–14, Word Inc.; pages 261–2: Wroge, D. (2002). *Papua New Guinea's Vernacular Language Preschool Programme*, UNESCO Policy Briefs on Early Childhood, Section for Early Childhood and Inclusive Education, October 2002, UNESCO; pages 272–3: Dixon, R.M.W. 'The endangered languages of Australia, Indonesia and Oceania'

Library, University of Oxford; page 177 (left): Alfred's Preface to his Old English translation of Pope Gregory the Great's Pastoral Care ms Hatton 20, folio 2v, the Bodleian Library, University of Oxford; page 177 (right): A page from the epic Old English poem *Beowulf* Cotton ms Vitellius AXV (part II) folio 133, by permission of the British Library; page 180: The Bodleian Library, University of Oxford, MS. e Mus. 198*, fol. 8r; page 208: Graddol, D. (2006) *English Next*, Part One – A World in Transition, pp. 44, The British Council; pages 217 and 218: The British Library; pages 222–6: Copyright © Mark Amerika, www.grammatron.com; page 264: Courtesy of Cable & Wireless Archive.

Every effort has been made to contact copyright holders. If any have been inadvertently overlooked the publishers will be pleased to make the necessary arrangements at the first opportunity.

Index